MORE PRAISE FOR
A Complaint Is a Gift

"Barlow and Møller rev... ing cus... ...pany's most valuab... ...set... ...how to get ... customer back, win a... more bu... and garner positive test... ...s. If succe... busi... ...rt... to you, you want to read this book."

Ron Kaufman, author and Founder of UP Your Service! College

"For businesses spending an ever-increasing amount of money researching customers' expectations, this book is a breath of fresh air. This book could have been aptly titled 'Converting Common Sense into Business Cents.'"

Paul Clark, General Manager, Customer Services, Country Energy, Australia

"*A Complaint Is a Gift* provides a great means for explaining how a company can provide service excellence and handle complaints through improved customer relationships, which ultimately will increase revenue and satisfaction."

Thom Ray, General Manager, British Telecom

"Everything seems so complex these days. But Barlow and Møller have taken a tough issue and made it accessible, not only in the world of business, but also in our personal lives. I will never experience a complaint as destructive again."

Russ Volckmann, PhD, Publisher and Editor, *Integral Leadership Review*

"In the convenience store business, after speed of delivery, service is everything. *A Complaint Is a Gift* drills down to the conditions necessary to make service recovery happen on a consistent basis."

Lee Barnes, President, Family Fare Convenience Stores

"This book provides an inspirational attitude shift for service employees, a how-to formula for service recovery when faced with tough complaints, and a managerial makeover."

Rick Brandon, coauthor of *Survival of the Savvy*

"This book treats service recovery as an art. The true test of a great brand is to leverage the opportunity to forge a new customer relationship. Through a careful blend of analytics, business creativity, and examples, these pages will convince you that complaints truly are gifts!

Mike English, Vice President, Customer Contact
Centers, Starwood Hotels & Resorts Worldwide, Inc.

"This book's concept is a mind-set that we at Royal Plaza on Scotts, Singapore have adopted to complement our brand promise. We have ingrained its importance among all our staff to be genuinely grateful for our guests' feedback, whether favorable or not."

Patrick Garcia Fiat, General Manager, Royal Plaza on Scotts, Singapore

"This book is spot on. It gets back to the fundamentals that drive our industry. The authors take you through the process of addressing a negative guest experience and turning that same guest into a Guest for Life. The title of this book could not be truer."

Rich Hicks, President, Tin Star Restaurants

"We have one of the most spectacular sites in the world: the Sky Walk at Grand Canyon West. And we still get complaints! This book can help any organization achieve its customer experience goals. This concept works extremely well across many different cultures. This is very important today towards creating a truly international flavor regarding the customer experience."

Waylon Honga, CEO, Grand Canyon West

"This book is for any executive who understands that truly satisfied clients breed the best opportunities for more clients, *A Complaint Is a Gift* is a powerful tool to be shared company-wide."

Andy Jorishie, Senior Vice President, Ideas and Innovation, The Zimmerman Agency

"This book is a piece of art. I recommend it to anyone seeking excellence and learning about customer care in general and complaints in particular!"

Omran Al Shansi, Senior Complaint Manager,
Emirates Telecommunications Corporation

"*A Complaint Is a Gift* is a marvelous book of practical tools and techniques for ensuring positive customer experiences and resolving even the most challenging customer complaints. It is packed full of tips to provide legendary customer service in even the most trying situations. These tools just work, hands down!"

Michael Krumpak, former Director of Learning and
Development, United States House of Representatives

"The Complaint Is a Gift concept provides lasting differentiation. We believe that, as a network of banks, we can correct a large number of mistakes from our customers' feedback. It will help us become more unique in the way we serve them. Complaint management is a critical element of our business strategy."

Andrey Litvinov, Senior Vice President, Life Financial Group, Russia

"How exciting that 'complaints' have finally been addressed and embraced. Our business, based upon relationship building, has benefited greatly from the insights provided in *A Complaint Is a Gift*."

Cliff Miller, Owner, M. J. Christensen Diamonds

"The Complaint Is a Gift philosophy has empowered our frontline associates to enhance and strengthen our guess and client relations. This unique communication approach to service breakdowns has enriched our organization, resulting in stronger teams and performance."

Patricia LaMont, Director, Training and OD, Business Services, and Sheila
Morehead, Senior Director, Training and OD, Business & Industry Group, ARAMARK

"*A Complaint Is a Gift* will challenge you to rethink complaints. This is a must-read book for anyone in business who wants to learn the secret of meeting customer expectations by redefining complaints as gifts. This powerful eight-step formula really works and empowers people to deal effectively with difficult situations."

Peta Peter, Education and Training Manager, Amway of Australia and New Zealand

"This book is an invaluable part of our tool kit to create a compelling and differentiated customer service culture. It focuses on embracing customer complaints to refine services and re-engage customers, rather than viewing complaints as a necessary evil."

Muriel Roake, Manager, Brand and Organizational Development, Air New Zealand

"I have been a disciple of Janelle's and Claus's work in this field for a number of years. The channels and the transparency in which complaints can now be made, through blogs and chat rooms, have necessitated an even more essential need to handle complaints efficiently and promptly."

Nigel Roberts, Senior Vice President, Operations,
The Langham Hotels & Resorts

"Customer service is a paradox: the more customer interactions a business has, the more it learns about the 'negatives' but also the more opportunities it has to create new 'positives.' Many of the elements in *A Complaint Is a Gift* have been used by Boyd Gaming and have been helpful as we continue to build our on-brand customer service delivery, monitoring, and proactive response programs."

Brian Shultz, Vice President of Marketing, Midwest and
South Region, Boyd Gaming Corporation

"This is a book about psychology—the psychology of customers who still care enough to complain, the psychology of organizations that are confident enough to still solicit complaints and act on them, and most importantly, the psychology of individual men and women in organizations and their varying degrees of confidence in entertaining complaints."

Sanjay Tiwari, Director, Sales and Customer Services, KLM Cargo USA

"If you want to know what really works in complaint management, then study this book! It's packed with powerful examples and the latest thinking on the topic. It is rare to find a book that packs a wallop for people involved in the practicalities of handling complaining customers and yet draws heavily on solid academic research."

Jochen Wirtz, Professor, National University of Singapore, and
coauthor of *Services Marketing: People, Technology, Strategy*

"This refreshing approach to service recovery and customer loyalty has become part of the Butterfield Bank corporate lexicon. Janelle and Claus provide food for thought, examples that teach and entertain, and easy-to-use guidelines for putting their strategy into practice."

Lori Baker-Lloyd, Vice President, Organizational Development and Human
Resources, The Bank of N. T. Butterfield & Son Limited, Bermuda

A
Complaint
Is a
Gift

A Complaint Is a Gift

Recovering Customer Loyalty When Things Go Wrong

Janelle Barlow

Claus Møller

Berrett–Koehler Publishers, Inc.
San Francisco
a BK Business book

Berrett-Koehler Publishers, Inc.
235 Montgomery Street, Suite 650
San Francisco, CA 94104-2916
Tel: (415) 288-0260   Fax: (415) 362-2512   www.bkconnection.com

Ordering Information
Quantity sales. Special discounts are available on quantity purchases by corporations, associations, and others. For details, contact the "Special Sales Department" at the Berrett-Koehler address above.
Individual sales. Berrett-Koehler publications are available through most bookstores. They can also be ordered directly from Berrett-Koehler: Tel: (800) 929-2929; Fax: (802) 864-7626; www.bkconnection.com
Orders for college textbook/course adoption use. Please contact Berrett-Koehler: Tel: (800) 929-2929; Fax: (802) 864-7626.
Orders by U.S. trade bookstores and wholesalers. Please contact Ingram Publisher Services, Tel: (800) 509-4887; Fax: (800) 838-1149; E-mail: customer.service@ingrampublisherservices.com; or visit www.ingrampublisherservices.com/Ordering for details about electronic ordering.

Berrett-Koehler and the BK logo are registered trademarks of Berrett-Koehler Publishers, Inc.

Printed in the United States of America

Berrett-Koehler books are printed on long-lasting acid-free paper. When it is available, we choose paper that has been manufactured by environmentally responsible processes. These may include using trees grown in sustainable forests, incorporating recycled paper, minimizing chlorine in bleaching, or recycling the energy produced at the paper mill.

Library of Congress Cataloging-in-Publication Data
Barlow, Janelle, 1943-
    A complaint is a gift : recovering customer loyalty when things go wrong / Janelle Barlow and Claus Møller.
        p. cm.
    Includes bibliographical references and index.
    ISBN 978-1-57675-582-2 (pbk. : alk. paper)
    1. Consumer complaints. 2. Customer services. I. Møller, Claus, 1942-
II. Title.
    HF5415.52.B37   2008
    658.8'343—dc22   2008017877

Cover design by Richard Adelson.
Copyediting and proofreading by PeopleSpeak.
Book design and composition by Beverly Butterfield, Girl of the West Productions.
Indexing by Rachel Rice.

SECOND EDITION
13 12 11 10 09 08   10 9 8 7 6 5 4 3 2 1

This book is dedicated to Confucius,
who wisely pointed out,

"A person who commits a mistake
and doesn't correct it
is committing another mistake."

Confucius probably didn't know it,
but he handily summed up
why complaining customers
give us a gift.

CONTENTS

FOREWORD

The title of this book can be a little misleading because ostensibly this is just a book about how to deal with complaints. And while complaints are talked about on just about every single page, this book is really about a much more important and broader topic: delivering great service.

Everyone knows that great service is important, yet very few companies deliver it well. Why is that? The concept of great service is a simple enough concept, but in practice it's actually a very hard thing to do right. We work at our service delivery every single day at Zappos. This book serves as a how-to guide for taking the first step to building a customer-service-oriented organization.

Think about the last time that you complained to a company about a bad experience. Now think about how your loyalty to that company was affected by the way someone responded or didn't respond. Millions of complaints are made every day to companies all around the world, and while most companies try to hide from complaints, this book will show you how each complaint is actually a huge opportunity to increase the value of your company.

At Zappos.com, our goal is for the Zappos brand to be about great customer service. We believe that the best way to achieve that goal is by making a service-focused culture our number one priority. We believe that if we get the culture right, most of the other things necessary for delivering great service will fall into place on their own.

If you can turn your organization into a complaint-friendly organization by following the steps outlined in this book, then you will be well on your way to being one of those rare companies that deliver great service. It's not an easy path, and it won't happen overnight. It happens one step at a time, and reading this book is probably one of the best first steps you can take.

TONY HSIEH
CEO, ZAPPOS.COM

INTRODUCTION

The Customer Speaks

I t has been over ten years since the first edition of *A Complaint Is a Gift* was published. It's embarrassing to admit that we naively believed poorly handled complaints would be a thing of the past as a result of the widespread distribution the original edition enjoyed. We heard a number of "wow" examples, such as a medical supply company in Kiev, Ukraine, that completely reorganized its approach to complaint handling based solely on the contents of the Russian-translated version. With examples like this from around the world, we assumed we'd soon be able to stop talking about complaints—even though we would miss that. Complaints are a fun topic for speeches. Stories about poorly handled complaints arouse a great deal of eye rolling and tongue clucking. We thought everyone would have understood that complaints are gifts.

It didn't happen. In a 2006 survey of 3,200 U.S. and European consumers, 86 percent of respondents said their "trust in corporations has declined in the past five years."[1] In 2007, RightNow Technologies reported that after suffering a negative service experience,

- 80 percent of U.S. adults decided to never go back to that company
- 74 percent registered a complaint or told others
- 47 percent swore or shouted
- 29 percent reported they got a headache, felt their chest tighten, or cried
- 13 percent fought back by posting a negative online review or blog comment[2]

1

Finally, a Gallup poll commissioned by the Better Business Bureau, conducted between August 22 and September 8, 2007, found that 18 percent of adult Americans said their trust in business had dropped in the last year. Yet 93 percent of those surveyed said a company's reputation for honesty and fairness is extremely important to them. The report concludes that if companies don't deliver what they promise (the source of most complaints), customers will go somewhere else.[3] It's not a pretty picture.

While the ideas from this book have influenced a great many people, companies still get things wrong, and customers continue to complain— if we're lucky. Service providers too often either blame customers for the mistakes they complain about or make them prove their positions. In many cases, they take so long to respond that customers forget what they complained about when they finally hear back from organizations. Customers frequently are forced to talk with robotic electronic voice systems that feebly attempt to replicate real conversations, and unfortunately, in some cases, these exchanges are better than live human interactions. And we won't even cite the statistics for how long customers wait on telephones to talk with someone. When they finally are connected with a live person, it's often someone living halfway around the world who reads from a script. Many customers become so frustrated with this type of communication that by the time they get to talk with someone, they start out angry and are automatically labeled problem customers—even though they may have been trying to buy something or have a simple question answered.

The deck is stacked against businesses trying to satisfy their customers. Customers expect satisfactory service. As a result, unsatisfactory service stands out. Because it stands out, it is more likely to be remembered and weighed more heavily compared to everything that went right. Ten transactions can go right, but that one mistake is what grabs consumer attention. This reality demands that we focus on what we can learn from customers who aren't happy.[4]

Organizations, however, don't seem to learn from their customers, as witnessed by the fact that most consumers face repeats of the very problems they already complained about. Most importantly, many service providers still see complaints as something to be avoided, as indicated by the fact that many organizations continue to pay bonuses to their managers based on reductions in complaints. Yet surveys conducted around the world demonstrate over and over again that companies with the best-rated service in their industry are the most profitable. It's really that simple. And complaint handling is an integral part of that service rating.

It is true that many people and organizations have learned how to handle complaints better. Several large companies have instituted sophisticated technological approaches to more efficiently respond to complaints. And many companies educate their staff in the best ways to respond to upset customers. But every year, a new group of service providers show up to work in organizations around the world—fresh representatives who haven't had the advantage of the training offered by their employers. (Given the high rate at which call-center staff leave their jobs, they probably wouldn't have much use for that knowledge in any case.) Every year, new types of complaints are presented by consumers. Eager and desperate managers somehow continue to delude themselves into thinking that the best tactic is to eliminate all the problems that create complaints, as if zero defects is actually attainable. And today, twelve years since *A Complaint Is a Gift* hit the bookshelves, more and more complaints are made public on the Internet, posted in vitriolic tones by dissatisfied customers.

Because of what customers are forced to endure, many call-center staff regularly have to serve unpleasant, upset customers whom they personally did nothing to create. Yet to be good service providers, they must be able to calm these customers down and deal with them in a way that makes them want to return to do business again at some time in the future. Unfortunately, many staff take customer bad behavior just as personally as customers take the bad service they have been offered, and staff defensive reactions leak out onto customers.

Is it any wonder that most call centers have such a difficult time holding on to staff unless they offer the best-paying jobs in the area? This rapid and regular loss of staff requires constant hiring of new, untrained staff. As a result, many call centers do not have staff who know how to effectively handle complaints, let alone understand that a complaint is being delivered unless it is spelled out with the precise words "I have a complaint."

Academic research on complaint handling hasn't revealed earth-shaking new information since we surveyed studies for the original book. Greater and greater refinement, however, of what happens in the complaint process has been achieved over the past ten years. For example, more research has been conducted on differences of complaining styles between different national groups.[5] This more detailed knowledge about consumer behavior has opened up additional areas to be researched. Here's our conclusion after reading hundreds of research studies:

- The more we know about service recovery, the more complex our understanding becomes.
- The more we know, the more we need to know to get the results we want with service recovery.
- The more we know, the more we need to experiment to see what works in specific situations.

While specific data may have changed, the research conducted in the 1960s through the 1990s has, more or less, held into the 2000s. No complaints there! In fact, it would be scary to think that a completely new understanding about complaints has popped up, necessitating an entirely new approach to complaint handling. Bottom line: the concept that a complaint is a gift holds true today as much as it did over ten years ago. Complaints are never going to go away, and organizations and their staffs need to adopt a strategy that enables them to recover customer loyalty when things go wrong.

What's Changed

What has changed is that many organizations, led in this direction by very convincing research,[6] have gained a deeper understanding about how important effective complaint handling—service recovery, as it has been referred to since the early 1980s—is in retaining loyal customers. These organizations understand the cost they pay in loss of both customers and staff when upset and dissatisfied customers are not handled well.

Several organizations have also come to recognize that effective service recovery is an important part of creating powerful brands. In 2004, *Branded Customer Service* (by authors Janelle Barlow and Paul Stewart) examined the importance to brands of effective complaint handling.[7] The conclusion: customers are remarkably forgiving of brands with promises that are not initially delivered as long as brand representatives respond to customers effectively, make good on original promises, and demonstrate that matters are improving. It also helps if the brand has a strong market image. One big key here is to rein in the marketing department so it does not make promises that the rest of the organization can't deliver.[8]

Janelle Barlow also coauthored *Emotional Value* during this period.[9] *Emotional Value* went into depth on how broken promises, mistakes, and inappropriate treatment affect customers emotionally. Some customers will accept outrageous mistakes as long as service providers are sincere, helpful, and concerned. At least they'll accept mistakes if they don't regularly recur. If staff maintain an attitude that feedback is one of the best types of communication they can have with customers, strategically they start off on the right foot to build emotional value with customers.

Saying "thank you" for negative feedback is just as powerful today as it was a dozen years ago. More importantly, the strategy behind thanking for feedback is even more important today than it was in 1996. Our mind-sets really do influence how we respond to our customers, and "complaints as gifts" is a powerful business mind-set for delivering service when our best efforts have collapsed and we don't give customers what they expect.

Before we tell you how this new edition is organized, let us start this tale with an extraordinary "feel-good" example of complaint handling that is going to be talked about for a long time at Family Fare, a North Carolina convenience store chain. It's a "remember the time," epochal example for showing Family Fare store operators that they must never dismiss even the smallest customer disappointment that at first glance is due to just an honest mistake.

We'll set the foundation first. Family Fare aspires to offer the best customer service of any U.S. convenience store—period. It invests a substantial sum of money in educating its store owners and managers about the brand of service it wants delivered and how to handle complaints. The company has created a simple brand promise and works like crazy to deliver it perfectly.

Family Fare is a classic example—of the type covered by Patrick Barwise in *Simply Better*—of building a brand by getting the fundamentals right most of the time.[10] Family Fare wants to be a midweek grocery store; it knows it can't compete for the weekend supermarket shopping excursion. But it also doesn't have to be a bottom feeder, gouging customers with high prices when they have nowhere else to shop. Family Fare stores are clean and well lighted, and staples are often priced the same as at supermarkets. Most Family Fare customers know the store operators (among the nicest and most sincere people you'll ever meet) personally and love them. They are community for a bunch of people.

Lee Barnes, president, lives and breathes customer service. Complaints sent by e-mail to the Family Fare Web site come directly to him, and he responds personally. The following complaint was, in his words, a "real heart stopper." Sitting in his car (hopefully not driving!), Barnes read a complaint (on his BlackBerry) from a customer who said she was refused entry into an Xbox sweepstakes because her home address was not close enough to a Family Fare store. She wrote that she owned rental property near one of the stores and that her military husband purchased gas there. She was so incensed, she would never shop again at a Family Fare, and other military families that she knew would follow suit. "What a pity that you overlook customers who WORK near your locations even if they don't RESIDE by them. There are simply too many other places for us to buy our gas and sodas. Good Bye. Next time maybe you should hire someone with promotional experience to execute future giveaways." Ouch. Her words stung—and from a military family.

Barnes sent a quick response from his BlackBerry thanking her for contacting him and assuring her that he would make it possible for her to enter the sweepstakes. It turned out that there was no problem with her address. Back-end Web commands unfortunately kicked people in her situation out of the contest. She wasn't the only one, but she was the only one who complained. Once back at his office, Barnes sent the customer a longer message, again thanking her for bringing the situation to his attention so that he could help her and improve Family Fare's customer experience. In an engaging letter, he told her that he would never have otherwise known and that he would personally sign her up for the contest.

Her response to this second letter was considerably toned down. She said that two of her friends had had the same problem. More valuable information was given to Family Fare when she also indicated that the first e-mail she sent to complain didn't go through because, according to an error message, she was more than ten miles away from a Family Fare store. In a third communication, this "complaining customer" wrote about her life and her children. "Okay well now you're just being too darned nice so I won't boycott your stores. I really do love Family Fare." In a two-page e-mail, the woman revealed that her husband's company commander had been killed the morning she had sent the original complaint. She had an adopted son and recently had taken in two additional foster children, one born addicted to drugs. The older son's birthday was coming up and he wanted an Xbox, but they simply couldn't afford one on their military budget. As she said, "Sooooooooooo I see your contest and I'm thinking, 'hey I will WIN Jess an Xbox,' but alas, I was unable to enter. It was just sort of the last straw at that moment."

By this time, Barnes and his customer were on a first-name basis. He was touched and decided to give Jessie an Xbox, whether he won or not. The company's Web designer, who was also thoroughly involved, offered a video game to go along with the Xbox. The customer's next letter carefully explained that she wasn't after sympathy or charity. In fact, she was embarrassed by what she had originally written. As she said, "I don't expect you to send us a game system. I just find it refreshing that a business truly cares, listens AND responds to a customer's complaint." Barnes responded that he hadn't heard a request for sympathy; the company had an extra Xbox, and he felt that sending it to Jessie and his younger brother was a way to thank her for taking the time to explain her Web site problems so they could be fixed. Two weeks later, Jessie had his Xbox. The thank-you letters from mother and sons are difficult to read without tearing up.

This example is about much more than just retaining a customer, though you can be sure that will happen. The story line is emotional and human. This mother's grief and complaint gave Barnes and Family Fare a chance to behave as humanitarians. At a nitty-gritty customer service level, however, Barnes created a classic teaching example that shows all his store owners what can happen when a complaint is received from someone who simply buys gasoline and soda pop at a convenience store.

Most complaints don't create such opportunities to show how good you really are. Most complaint examples don't let you in on a person's personal life in a way you never would have experienced without the complaint. Most complaint examples, however, all have a little piece of what happened in this remarkable situation. When they come along as complete as in this case, treasure them. Everyone benefits.

And don't worry that the next time you offer an Xbox competition, everyone will write complaint letters with made-up sob stories to get a free one. You'll recognize the believable when it happens.

The Complaint Is a Gift Metaphor

Without customers, businesses simply do not exist. Yet it seems as if customers have only recently been discovered. It is in the last twenty-five years or so that customers have begun to be talked about in a meaningful way. Today, phrases such as *total customer service, customer centricity, customer-driven marketplace, customer satisfaction indexes, customer-oriented culture, customer-centered selling, customer care, core and peripheral customer services, customer sensitivity, internal and external customers, customer focus,* and even *soft and hard customer relationships* regularly roll off the tongues of businesspeople—especially consultants.

Service recovery courses (on how to turn dissatisfied customers into loyal ones) have been among the most popular seminars around the world for quite some time. In the service industry today, the concepts of service and quality have become inexorably linked. For the first edition, we conducted a Dialog computer search of articles written since 1981 mentioning customer complaints in academic journals and uncovered a dramatic increase in articles, reflecting an explosion of interest in the topic. Since that time, the academic interest in complaints and service recovery has steadily increased, as the graph below indicates. And to take full advantage of the Web, we decided to see how many entries about customer complaints were listed by Google for each year within the same time period.[11] The results are presented below.

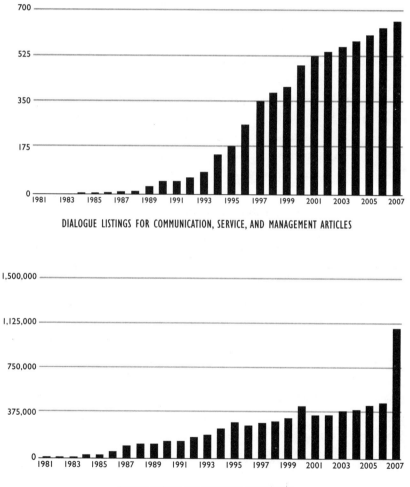

DIALOGUE LISTINGS FOR COMMUNICATION, SERVICE, AND MANAGEMENT ARTICLES

GOOGLE LISTINGS FOR "CUSTOMER COMPLAINTS"

Obviously, there are repeats in the Google listings, and without going through each year's listings in detail, it is impossible to know how many earlier entries are relisted. But as the years advance, the numbers continue to steadily increase, except for the period following 2000. It is difficult to say for certain what caused that decline in listings, but many will recall that it seemed almost impolite to complain after the events of September 11, 2001. In 2007, there was a dramatic increase, probably caused in part by all the cross-linking done by bloggers. The steady increase over the years (except for the post-2000 drop) demonstrates that there has been a great deal more information and interest about complaints as each year has passed.

The concept of *customer* has expanded over the past twenty-five years. *Customer* means not just the paying customer but anyone who receives the benefit of goods and services, including patients in hospitals, students in schools, and public-transit riders. It has also come to mean internal organizational customers, such as work colleagues and bosses. Though some may not like calling their friends and family members customers, many customer ideas apply equally well to personal relationships. We will discuss some of them in this book.

The message is clear: customers have moved to the center of the discussion. Or you might say, customers have gone to the top of the organizational hierarchy. And every single management book on service and quality will echo Peter Drucker's original 1951 refrain: customers are the reason we get to stay in business.

Yet all too often we forget this. Many companies have their "we live for our customers" talk down to a fine art but believe that issuing orders about this topic is all they need to do. As service consultants, we have met far too many executives who just don't comprehend that it's not enough to tell staff to behave a certain way. "We told them that already," they lament, as if simply telling people to change will ever be enough. Dozens of customer surveys suggest that there is enormous room for improvement in how customers are treated once they have bought and, at times, before they buy. Employees, and the systems they are forced to operate in, persistently get in the way of customers' having a positive experience. This is particularly meaningful because of the ever-growing shift from a goods economy to a service economy. In the United States in 1920, the service sector was responsible for 53 percent of the nonfarm workers; by 1960 that percentage had jumped to 62 percent; in 2000 the number increased to 81 percent. This pattern is consistent in every developed economy in the world.[12]

If businesses are truly interested in developing a customer-centric culture, heightening customer care, or providing total customer service, then customer dissatisfaction should be of central interest. One of the most direct and meaningful ways customers can express their dissatisfaction to companies is through what we have come to call a complaint.

In fact, most businesses view complaints as either proof of failure on their part that they would rather not admit or as confirmation of their suspicion that customers are out to get something for nothing. However a company is inclined to perceive or experience complaints, most companies desire to eliminate them. Yet complaints are one of the most direct and effective ways for customers to tell businesses that there is room for improvement. And if in a competitive market economy this improvement does not occur, customers will take their business elsewhere. It is very likely that they will eventually receive equally dissatisfying service from another company and will return to the first company after a period of time. But customer churn is very costly to businesses and has a strong negative effect on brand equity.

The metaphor we use in this book is that of complaints as gifts. Complaints are a feedback mechanism that can help organizations rapidly and inexpensively shift products, service style, or market focus to meet the needs of their customers—who, after all, pay the bills. It is time for all organizations to think of complaint handling as a strategic tool—an opportunity to learn something about products or services that maybe they did not already know—and as a marketing asset, rather than a nuisance, a cost, and a royal pain.

Customer complaints provide one of the primary and most direct means to communicate with customers. After all, how many consumers pick up the phone to just chat with organizations if they have no problems? Customers practically have to be bribed to get them to fill out survey forms. But when a complaint situation occurs, there's at least a small chance that customers will talk with us directly. We'd better be prepared to listen.

This book speaks to those who deal with customers, those who would like to benefit from customer feedback, and those who have the responsibility of retaining dissatisfied customers as loyal ones. We suggest that a fundamental change in attitude is required if businesses are going to retain complaining customers. If companies get better at complaint management and complaint handling and begin to see complaints as gifts, they will open clearer lines of communication with customers. Our goal is to show you how a strategic shift in how you view customer complaints can be the first step to improve and, indeed, grow your business.

How This Book Is Organized

A Complaint Is a Gift is divided into three parts. The first part, "Complaints: Lifeline to the Customer," examines the strategy that will help us maintain a positive mind-set toward complaining customers. This part establishes the value of listening to customers. The role of complaint handling as a strategic tool for cultivating more business is presented. We will also consider why most dissatisfied customers rarely complain. (The overwhelming majority of them never do, though the Internet may be impacting that.) We look at what is in the mind of complaining customers in terms of what they say, do, and want when they are not satisfied.

The second part, "Putting the Complaint Is a Gift Strategy into Practice," focuses on how to handle the complaints you do receive. We review our eight-step Gift Formula for keeping our language, interactions, and actions consistent with the belief that a complaint is a gift. We've learned a lot about how that formula can be used even more effectively. We also address specific suggestions for turning angry customers into partners. (We stopped calling them terrorist customers after September 11, 2001.) Complaint letters are discussed as a special category of complaints. When this book was first published, the Web was a forum just beginning to be available for upset customers. Remember, it wasn't until 1995 that large numbers of people even began to use the Internet. In the last ten years, what used to be a whisper can now easily become a global shout. The good news is that we are far from defenseless to complaints posted on the Web. We therefore consider how organizations can use the Web to their own advantage.

The first edition of this book had a part titled "How to Make Your Organization Complaint Friendly." Because this book has been expanded by over fifty pages, we have decided to put the discussion of this topic on the TMI US Web page (www.tmius.com). There you will find papers you can download and comment on. We'll keep updating (1) how to align your service recovery with your brand position, (2) how to evaluate your policies and systems so they are complaint friendly, and (3) how to develop and sustain a complaint-friendly culture. On our Web page you'll also find an implementation process for making your organization more customer focused by concentrating on managing complaints.

Because of the considerable feedback we received from readers of the first edition of *A Complaint Is a Gift*, we decided to add an additional part: "Dishing It Out and Taking It In: The Personal Side of Complaints." People have told us that applying the Gift Formula within their marriages has actually saved them! One of the best ways to find out what customers want is to listen to their complaints. And one of the best ways to improve a personal relationship is to notice when someone is upset and to respond in a way that leads to resolving the conflict. Quick dialogue, with open lines for feedback from friends, colleagues, and family members, that moves toward resolution of others' irritations—complaint management, so to speak—can keep relationships harmonious and make them even stronger. If we hint to our partners that we do not want to hear any nagging, our partners may not say anything about what is bothering them, but it does not mean that they are not bothered. Like customers, they may leave without saying much. Or perhaps they'll bash us on MySpace. Gordon Bethune, CEO of Continental Airlines until 2004, says, "You can't take your girlfriend for granted, and you can't take your customer for granted. Every time, it always works out the same way. Somebody else gets them."[13]

At the conclusion of each chapter is a set of discussion questions about complaints and what you or your organization can do about them. These questions can be used at staff meetings to stimulate discussion and understanding of customer complaints or as part of training efforts to improve complaint handling.

Actual cases of successful organizations managing and handling customer complaints are presented. We have expanded our examples and replaced most of the ones used in the original edition. We did receive feedback that our examples were too focused on the airline industry, the industry that so many love to hate. We listened to our readers, and as a result, we have broadened our array of industry examples, even though some of the best examples of bad service and poorly handled complaints are still coming from the airlines. (We, and most of our professional colleagues, happen to spend quite a bit of time sitting in airplane seats, so we hear about or notice a lot of bad service and associated complaints or a lack of them.) We recommend borrowing good ideas from other companies, even other industries, so just because you are not running an airline does not mean you cannot learn from airlines and their disastrous satisfaction records. In fact, many industries eventually go through some type of crisis, just as the airline industry is currently experiencing. September 11 and intense competition from "no frills" airlines shook up an entire industry, and airlines have had to learn how to adjust.[14] Wally Bock, blogger par excellence, says, "Ideas that are almost sure to work are the best practices of other companies in your industry. But the breakthrough ideas often come from outside, from an industry that routinely solves a problem that's new to you."[15] We agree.

All of our examples are very real. If we got some details wrong, we apologize in advance. In most cases, when the experience was negative, we removed the company name unless the company is no longer in existence or the complaint is part of the public record. This was a careful decision. It is tempting to conclude that a company provides poor service or offers poor products after hearing just one example. In fact, some customers will leave a business, never to return, because of one slipup. Every company makes mistakes from time to time. We would not want our readers to decide that a particular company is bad because someone had a reason to complain.

Finally, this book contains a lot of summarized research data. Readers will quickly learn that there is a great deal of variation in the literature on complaints, but all the research points in the same direction: customers who are dissatisfied generally do not complain, and when they do, their feedback is all too often poorly handled and inadequately managed. If we are to treat complaints as gifts, we have to make major shifts in both our behavior and our thinking. The good news is that opportunity exists for almost all organizations to make dramatic improvements in how they handle complaints.

≈

PART ONE

Complaints
Lifeline to the Customer

When customers feel dissatisfied with products and services, they have two options: they can say something or they can walk away. If they walk away, they give organizations virtually no opportunity to fix their dissatisfaction. Complaining customers are still talking with us, giving us an opportunity to recapture their interest so they will be more likely to buy from us again. In the world of the modern Internet, word of mouth has grown from simple dinner-table conversation to a global shout at a banquet with thousands of diners. So as much as we might not like to receive negative feedback, customers who complain directly to us are giving us a gift.

If we shift our mind-set to see complaints as gifts, we can more readily learn from difficult situations. Customer complaints continue to be one of the most available and yet underutilized sources of consumer and market information; as such, they can become the foundation for a company's quality and service recovery programs. This is no small gift!

In order to better understand complaining customers, part I of this book explores the mind of the complaining customer. With understanding comes acceptance. We must welcome these complaining and admittedly difficult customers at times and make them want to come to us with their feedback instead of trashing us behind our backs.

A Complaint Is a Gift Strategy

 It's not easy to listen to complaining customers all day long. The following tirade by a service representative venting on the Internet is not all that different from many we have heard in person. You can almost hear the conflict this service provider is experiencing about her job, especially when she confronts an upset customer.

Customer complaints suck. Customers complain 90 percent of the time because they have had a bad day and need someone to take it out on. I work for a wireless company and I get so many complaints that it is sickening . . . My job is to help the customer, but there is a limit that any employee of any company can tolerate. I am sick of customer complaints. No matter how hard I try, customers are not satisfied within the limit of what we as employees can do by company policy . . . but when a customer comes into an establishment with an attitude from the start, it is hard to keep a level head when they are screaming at you and accusing you of being rude.

Anonymous

How About a Slightly Different Scenario?

Imagine that a friend comes to visit on your birthday with a lovely present in hand. The first thing you would say after greeting him or her would, most likely, be an expression of gratitude. "Thank you. Thank you for coming and thank you for the lovely present." Your entire verbal and nonverbal language would signal your pleasure at seeing your friend and receiving the gift.

What if you then opened this gift and found a CD purchased just for you? What would you say? "Wow! I'm so pleased. I've wanted this CD for some time. How thoughtful of you to get it for me. How did you know this is my favorite artist? I'll think of you every time I listen to it." Okay, maybe not that profuse but something along those lines.

Now imagine that a customer has called you with a complaint. "My name is Chris Cooper, and your wireless service never works. I keep getting disconnected, and your advertising goes on and on about how you can be heard anywhere in the country. And that's not all. My first bill had charges for calls I know I didn't make. But that doesn't surprise me. If you can't get the connections right, you probably can't get your billing right!" Would you say, "Thank you for calling and telling us about this. How thoughtful of you. We really appreciate it"? Probably not.

But when we receive a birthday present, we do not hesitate. We say, "Thank you." Why do we do this? Because a friend took time to get us something special—in most cases. What about complaining customers? Are they friends? Or do they look like enemies? What are they trying to do? What are they giving us?

Complaining customers are giving us an opportunity to find out what their problems are so we can help them and they will be encouraged to come back, use our services, and buy our products. It's as if they have gifted us with a blog written just for us: "A Chance to Survive: Listen to Me and You'll Stay in Business." So don't say, "Go away. I've already got one CD by this artist, and I don't want to listen to another. I'm too busy."

When encountering the customer who complains about phone calls that are continually dropped and repetitive billing errors, many company representatives will start by asking a barrage of identification questions: "What is your name? How do you spell that? What is your phone number? What is your address? When did you start your service? What is the product number of your telephone? (By the way, if you don't have it handy, it's on the bottom of your phone in such tiny digits that you'll need a magnifying glass to read it.) Do you have your monthly bill in front of you? What is our order number? What is your Web order number? What is your PO number?[1] When did you send in your last payment?" They may blame billing by sighing and saying, "We hear a lot of complaints about incorrect billing." They may attack their own company by saying, "Those dropped calls happen a lot. It's rather unbelievable that our advertising says we're the best in the business. If that's true, it makes you wonder about all the other wireless companies." If customers are very lucky, they will get an apology.

But very few customer service people will say "Thank you" right off the bat. They may thank you at the end of the conversation, by which time you may be so annoyed, it's a meaningless phrase.

What if someone gave you a CD for your birthday and you responded with a barrage of questions: "Where did you buy it? Did you pay cash or charge it? Did you pay full price for it or get it at a discount store—or on eBay? Come on. Fess up. How many songs does it have on it? Have you already listened to it and downloaded it onto your iPod? Why did you give it to me if you haven't heard it yourself? Based on some silly best-seller iTunes list, you want me to spend my time listening to this thing?" You would never be so ungracious about a gift unless you have genuine social problems, in which case no one would be likely to give you a gift in the first place. You would say, "Thank you," and you would mean it—even if you already had a copy of this CD or didn't like most of the songs on it.

The mind-set of customer-facing staff has a huge influence on what is going to happen in any service encounter, particularly when complaints are being made or help is requested. In a study relevant to the impact of mind-set on complaint handling, researchers at the University of Alabama questioned how service employees themselves impact the use of self-service technologies (SSTs).[2] Employees whose mind-set was that SSTs helped them do their own jobs better took time to educate customers facing problems on how to operate the SST devices. When faced with customers who couldn't get the devices to do what they wanted, employees who held the mind-set that SSTs are a burden and not a convenience for anyone would simply step in and operate the devices themselves. Their customers didn't have a chance to learn themselves, ensuring that when they returned they would face the same difficulty. Mind-set definitely matters, even though the service employees had no awareness of how their attitudes were impacting their behavior.

A survey of European retail banks revealed a direct connection between the way that leaders at financial institutions think about complaints and the way that customers behave when they have a complaint and ultimately how they are treated.[3] Customers, in other words, can sense that an organization sees complaints as a gift or as a necessary evil. An in-depth study of two Swedish banks also supports the idea that the way branch managers think about complaints impacts how customers are treated and how they respond. The researchers found that successful managers used complaint handling as their *primary* tool for creating long-term customer satisfaction with small-business customers.[4]

So, how can we begin to internalize the strategic idea that a complaint is a gift? It starts by understanding what a complaint is.

What Is a Complaint?

In simplest terms, complaints are statements about expectations that have not been met. They are also, and perhaps more importantly, opportunities for an organization to reconnect with customers by fixing a service or product breakdown. In this way, complaints are gifts customers give to businesses. Everyone will benefit from carefully opening these packages and seeing what is inside.

On the surface, customers may complain that their newly purchased blue jeans shrank or the color ran and ruined a load of white clothing. At a deeper level, customers are giving the store where they bought the item an opportunity to respond so they will continue buying more clothing from that business.

On the surface, customers may complain that the vacuum cleaner they just purchased doesn't suit their needs. At a deeper level, they are testing the retailer to see how it takes back the vacuum cleaner.

On the surface, customers may complain that they waited on hold for three and a half hours to get help setting up their expensive new computer. At a deeper level, they are speaking about their fears that they made a stupid purchasing decision, a fear that will periodically rear up to impact how they think about their computer during the years it remains functional.

On the surface, customers may complain to the grocer that the turkey they purchased did not contain any giblets, which they discovered only on Thanksgiving day itself, when the store was closed. At a deeper level, customers are wondering whether the grocer will take their word for it and how the store will compensate them for this disappointment.

On the surface, customers let their insurance agents know in no uncertain terms that when they call the insurance company to ask a simple question, their calls are not returned for days. At a deeper level, customers are warning their agents that they may look at a competitor when their policy comes up for renewal.

What do you suppose most service representatives hear—the surface complaint or the deeper message? We contend that, unfortunately, all too many hear only the direct, surface message. ("You won't believe what I heard today from a customer! Their turkey didn't have any giblets. I say, 'Get a life.' People are starving, and they are complaining because their twenty-five-pound turkey didn't have any giblets!") And the end results are mismanaged complaints, lack of empathy, and loss of customers.

When organizations listen to customers with open minds and more flexible points of view, they can experience complaints as gifts. Unfortunately, most of us don't like to hear complaints and we erect enormous psychological blocks to hearing them. Even more fundamentally, as we will discuss later, most customers simply don't grace us with their complaints. They just take their business elsewhere.

Why We Don't Like Complaints

On the surface, it seems apparent why complaints have a bad reputation. Customers are saying that they do not like something about us. Who likes to hear that? It means there's something wrong with us. Complaints are about blame, or what psychologists call negative attribution.

When something positive happens, people have a tendency to attribute it to themselves or to take credit for their own behavior. For example, a customer buying a dress will likely think herself rather clever for finding it if she receives compliments on it, even if a shopkeeper clearly found the dress, brought it to the buyer, and urged her to purchase it.

Something different happens, however, when a failure occurs. Most of us like to blame other individuals or systems when things aren't working out. In fact, according to Saint Louis University research, customers tend to blame specific firms or specific individuals. For customers, this usually means that employees, specifically those we are eye-to-eye or ear-to-ear with, are to blame when there is a product or service failure. Employees do the same thing in reverse. When they hear complaints, they tend to blame the customers, and when customers engage in socially unacceptable behavior (such as shouting or swearing), employees almost always develop a negative attitude toward them. When employees hold this negative judgment, they tend not to make product exchanges for customers, or at a minimum, they do not make product exchanges easy.[5] Many employees understand, however, that blaming customers is not a behavior likely to get them high marks from customers or promoted by their managers, so they mask their feelings and try to come up with more acceptable theories as to why things went wrong. A common explanation is that the organization, its policies, or management is to blame. Employees may say to customers, "I'd really like to help you, but there's nothing I can do. Our policy . . ." or "My hands are tied. I'll get in trouble if I do that for you. Sorry."

Unfortunately, blaming policies has little impact on customers because it does nothing to resolve their problems. Nor does it stop customers from blaming the employees. Even if employees indicate that they do not agree with the policies that are stopping them from satisfying customers, most customers don't separate employee behavior from company policies. The father of modem attribution theory, Fritz Heider, notes that most of us attribute blame to individuals rather than the circumstances surrounding a product or service failure.[6] For example, if a service provider says, "I know this sounds ridiculous, but I need . . . ," customers will likely think, "If it's ridiculous, then why are you asking for this information?"

Most service delivery today is complex, and a number of firms or individuals may have been involved in the service failure.[7] This means that service providers need to carefully explain what happened without sounding as if they are attempting to pass blame onto someone else. They can probably accomplish this by saying, "I'm going to take responsibility for this, even though several people were involved. We need to find out what happened so I can solve this problem for you."

Wegmans Food Market, a popular chain in the upper northeastern United States, operates under the promise "Every day you get our best," and that means "[we] will listen to your complaints so [we] can get better." Wegmans, founded in 1916, has won more than thirty significant awards for its uniqueness and customer service and for "changing the way we shop." It won the 2007 Food Network Award for the Best Grocery Store.[8] And Wegmans has been named one of the one hundred best places to work in America by *Fortune* magazine every year since the list started in 1988. It was number one in 2005, number two in 2006, and number three in 2007.[9]

Wegmans honors the implicit contract that customers assume has been made: if they do not like what they purchased, if it does not meet their needs, if it is substandard, or if they have changed their minds, they are buying the right to say something about this. It asks for complaints on its Web site; feedback forms are easy to fill out, and it is obvious someone reads them. The site states clearly that a live person will address the complaint and get back to the customer within a few days. We tried it, and it works. The vice president of consumer affairs, Mary Ellen Burris, incorporates information about complaints into her weekly columns, letting consumers know what Wegmans is doing about the feedback it receives. In one column posted on the Wegmans Web site, for example, she noted that customers complained about not being able to clearly see measurement lines on one of its detergent caps. Wegmans listened and changed the cap color.

Complaining Customers Are Still Customers

In order for us to treat complaints as gifts, we need to achieve a complete shift in perception and attitude about the role of complaints in modern business relationships. This requires separating the message of the complaint from the emotion of being blamed, which, in turn, means understanding the dynamics of disappointed people and rethinking how complaints can help us achieve our business goals. Consider these examples from the homebuilding industry, and imagine what these companies would say if they were asked if complaints are gifts.

- Marvin Windows and Doors learned that the wood frames on its windows and doors were rotting. It turns out that the complaints came in after the one-year warranty period was up. The cause of the problem was actually wood preservative provided by Pittsburgh Paint and Glass (PPG). PPG refused to take responsibility for the rotting, but Marvin Windows did. It replaced the damaged products, ditched PPG as a supplier, and sourced a better preservative so it could extend its product warranty from one year to ten. In 2007, after also winning the award in 2006, Marvin Windows received the highest numerical score in the J. D. Powers and Associates Award for Builders and Remodelers.
- Dryvit produces exterior insulate and finish systems. Moisture was rotting its siding products basically because of builder installation mistakes. Dryvit took responsibility and created a moisture drain to keep its product dry. Dryvit also increased its warranty to ten years. Following this change, Oak Ridge National Laboratory, the most respected testing facility of the U.S. Department of Energy, ranked Dryvit's product 84 percent higher than the next-best-performing system.[10]

- In the late 1980s, Louisiana-Pacific Building Products began hearing complaints about rotting of its InnerSeal siding, especially in the wet Pacific Northwest. Eight hundred thousand homes had used the product, and a major class-action lawsuit was filed. Louisiana-Pacific decided to take responsibility, even though the rotting was an installation problem, not a product problem, and replaced the damaged siding. The company completely redesigned the siding so it would work in humid climates, called it SmartSide, and announced a fifty-year warranty. After taking a major hit in the press, six years later the company more than regained market share. It, too, has been recognized with numerous awards.[11]
- Dudley Webre purchased a lumberyard in Luling, Louisiana, when that area wasn't an up-and-coming business sector in the region. Webre went directly to his contractors to find out what was bothering them. It turned out that they had a serious problem that Webre could help them with. Lumberyards typically shipped only full truckloads, which meant that the contractors had to safeguard their inventory against theft. Webre sent out smaller loads, which eliminated the theft problem and resulted in a savings to his customers from reduced pilferage, even though they ended up paying more for the lumber. Between 1982 and 1994, Landry Lumber and Building Supply increased its business by 300 percent.[12]

Customers who take time to complain have at least a little confidence in the organization. After all, if they're complaining, they are still customers somewhat. Former president Bill Clinton, campaigning for his wife in the tightly fought Democratic Party 2008 nomination process, told a story intended to inspire all the campaign workers to keep contacting undecided voters. He said that when he was governor of Arkansas, he never gave up on getting someone's vote. Clinton was campaigning at an oil company where, because of government action, three hundred jobs had been saved. Clinton met an employee who obviously didn't like him and told him, "I'm never voting for you. If you were the last person on earth, I wouldn't vote for you." Clinton told the man, "Hey, I saved your job." The man responded, "Yeah. But you only did it so you'd have one more person to tax." Clinton said, "I marked him as undecided."[13]

All those customers who come to you with their complaints are also undecided. They're still talking with you. Don't give up.

Treating Customers as Honest Is Part of the Complaint Is a Gift Strategy

See complaints through the eyes of your customer and you have a better chance of viewing complaints as a gift. Imagine that whatever the customer is complaining about has just happened to you. What would you be thinking and feeling? How would you react? What would you expect? What would it take to make you happy? What response would be necessary for you to walk away from this encounter and feel good about your complaint and better about the company? Being treated as if you are honest would be a beginning point.

Are there customers who try to rip your business off? No doubt there are. But companies cannot treat all customers as if they were thieves in order to protect themselves against the few who are. Guy Kawasaki, author of the best-selling book *Selling the Dream*, writes on his blog, "The point is: Don't assume that the worst case is going to be the common case . . . If you put in a policy to take care of the worst case, bad people, it will antagonize and insult the bulk of your customers."[14]

It is estimated that 1 to 4 percent of customers will systematically try to cheat.[15] Most companies factor in this kind of behavior as part of the cost of doing business, though obviously it would be better to minimize that type of loss. No doubt the Internet has spawned a number of scams. Fraudulent activities of all types have exploded on the Web. The key is to keep your fraud antennae on alert without offending customers who would never cheat you.

George Sarris, owner of The Fish Market Restaurant in Birmingham, Alabama,[16] received a demand for $6.89 from a disgruntled customer who supposedly had dined in his restaurant. Sarris gets close to his customers, so when he couldn't remember this particular customer, he became suspicious and decided to put on his detective cap. He made a few telephone calls and learned that this disgruntled diner had been busy eating all over town, demanding $6.89 from everyone! Most of the other restaurants simply paid up because the amount was so small.[17] This type of scam even has a name: Phony Customer Con. In such an instance, it's best to write a very pleasant, courteous response (follow the Gift Formula in chapter 6) and indicate that you will be more than happy to return the sum in question. Don't in any way question the integrity of the "customer," but ask for a copy of the receipt or for more details for your own records. If you want, include a self-addressed stamped envelope to make it easy for this person to respond—in case the complaint is legitimate.

Always be aware that if someone does try to take advantage of your organization through exaggerated claims, chances are that other customers who witness your interaction will be impressed that you treated the customer with respect and considered the feedback a gift. Onlookers will be more reasonable when expressing their own complaints.

Tom Weir, executive editor of *Grocery Headquarters*, describes watching a swearing, ballistic customer return a carton of milk that had supposedly been purchased earlier in the day but was way past its sell-by date and was spoiled. The manager of this supermarket remained seated in a booth overlooking the checkout lanes and yelled back that customers should always check expiration dates before buying anything. This is a good example of advice that blames. After all, how many of us check sell-by dates every time we shop? Since when have customers become responsible for inventory control?

It's not a pretty story, but Weir poses some interesting questions about the message sent to the customers who watched this scene. What was being said to them? Weir asks. Were they taught a lesson as to what would happen to them if they had a complaint? What was the impact on this supermarket brand? Did the customers conclude that this is the chain's policy? And then Weir asks about the message the store staff received. Do they not have to take any guff from angry customers? If this is the case, then where is the line drawn after which staff get to attack customers?[18] Obviously, the other customers saw an out-of-control

customer, but as Weir points out, they probably also noted that this customer had a legitimate complaint and was treated rudely. The customers who were watching may have questioned whether the company was
genuinely interested in taking care of its customers.

The moment individuals or companies give any hint that they view
complainers with suspicion or rudeness, customers will take a defensive
position or fight back. Or even worse, they may go away angry and not
say anything to the company headquarters but tell everyone they know,
and the company will have no chance to defend itself.

Some individuals lack gracious social skills and may appear inappropriate when they complain. They get nervous and may seem harsh, angry,
or even stupid. They may not have experience with what is reasonable.
The service provider must learn to focus on the content of the complaint
and the emotions presented and not whether the complaint is delivered
in a socially acceptable way. This is asking a lot of service providers, but
if they adopt the mind-set that complaints are gifts, they start from the
best foundation to handle one of the most difficult aspects of customer
relations.

DISCUSSION QUESTIONS

- What is your organization's mind-set about complaints? What are the varied opinions about complaints within your organization? How do you talk about your complaining customers? Do you talk about them as if they are giving you gifts?

- What are the differences between how customer-facing staff see complaints and how managers see complaints? How strong is the view that complaints are opportunities to satisfy dissatisfied customers?

- What do your customer-facing staff say when they can't solve a customer's problem? Do they tend to blame policies? What kinds of excuses do they give? What kinds of reactions do these cause in your customers?

- What specific lessons have you learned from your complaining customers?

- What approaches does your organization have in place to encourage and then learn from complaints?

- Do you have any idea how effective you are at complaint handling compared to other businesses in your industry sector? If so, where do you stand?

- Do you set targets to reduce complaints? How does that affect your approach to complaint handling?

~ 2 ~

Complaints

Necessary Evil or Opportunities?

 If you are a parent, you may have sternly said to your children, "I'm really angry at you because you're better than that." Or when punishing them, you may have said, "Believe me, this hurts me more than it does you." Children typically don't believe this for a second, but once they have their own children, they have a different take on the negative feedback they received as children. At times, children drive their parents crazy because they don't do what is expected of them. Children say one thing and do another. They forget to do what they promised. They speak out of turn. And as parents, we will not tolerate this behavior if we want our children to grow up to have good lives and be people we can be proud of. Sound familiar?

Fred Wiersema, business strategist and author, makes an interesting point about losing customers, saying that organizations have to be doing some pretty stupid things to lose them: "I disagree with the broad statement that says loyalty is dead . . . most customers are incredibly sticky . . . if you lose a customer, you have really messed up. Is there something wrong with your values? Is there something wrong with the day-to-day interaction of your people and their people? What's wrong? Because you really have to mess up something to lose a customer."[1]

Considering the frequency at which organizations lose customers, it must be easy to be stupid. Jeffrey Pfeffer, in his book *What Were They Thinking?* says that when companies do stupid things, like driving customers away, it's primarily because they aren't looking at feedback. They just take a position and act without considering the impact of their decisions.[2] The Horizon Group found that retailers lose between 25 and 40 percent of their core customers every year. This means that most have to replace up to 40 percent of their business with new customers just to stay even.[3]

There are many ways to get customers to hang up on you or steam out of your doors, and some companies have tried them all. Two of the most common methods are to ignore negative feedback and to handle complaints poorly. Yet well-handled complaints can create strong bonds between customers and organizations. Sometimes, it's a simple matter of letting customers know you value them.

Nurse Next Door, operating in Vancouver, British Columbia, uses the "humble pie" approach (acknowledging that it needs to learn something) to keep its customers. When it flubs, it sends a fresh-baked apple pie to the customer with a note that says, in effect, "We messed up and we are humbled." This company estimates that it has kept $90,000 worth of customers with an expenditure of $1,300 on pies.[4] The experience of Nurse Next Door is not unusual. Researchers some time ago demonstrated that effective complaint management can lower total marketing expenditures by substantially reducing the need for advertising. This savings in advertising can, in fact, offset the cost of compensating customers for their complaints. According to these researchers, you shouldn't calculate just the profit margin on a single item of contention with a customer. Look at the whole picture—your total budget—they advise.[5]

In 2004, we received an excited e-mail from a gentleman who had attended one of our Complaint Is a Gift seminars. He told us about a telephone call that he answered as a favor to the Logistics team, who all went out together for a team lunch.[6]

The customer was furious and wanted service immediately. Unfortunately, there was no way she could get it over this particular lunch hour since the entire department was away for lunch. She ranted and raved about never buying another product from this major computer company. The representative listened carefully. In his assessment, the customer had been given "the royal runaround." When she finally wound down, he hesitated a moment and then said, "My gosh! Thank you for calling and letting us know. This is a huge help to us. I'm so sorry you've had to experience this. We're definitely a lot better than this. I'm going to do everything I can to fix this for you." A long silence followed. He said that by the time the Logistics team came back and resolved her problem, the customer thought he was the greatest. He wrote, "If I hadn't been exposed to the Gift Formula, I don't know what would have happened. I probably would've said something that made her angrier. I also would've probably felt shell-shocked."

Other times, a difficult situation provides an opportunity to wow the customer. Zappos, an online shoe company, learned that a customer purchased seven pairs of shoes for her mother, who was terminally ill. But because her mother had lost a lot of weight, the daughter wasn't sure of the right shoe size. The mother passed away not long after the shoes arrived. Under the circumstances, returning shoes to an online retailer was at the bottom of the daughter's immediate to-do list, even though the Zappos free return period expired after fifteen days. In the meantime, since Zappos knew that the size of these shoes had been a guess, a representative contacted the customer and asked whether she wanted to return any of them. The woman told the Zappos representative about her mother's death and said she would send the shoes back as soon as she could.

Not exactly a complaint initiated by the grieving woman, but most customers hope that organizations will cut them a little slack when they face personal circumstances that make it difficult to comply with company policy. Zappos stepped up to the plate. It arranged for UPS to go to the woman's house and pick up the shoes so the grieving daughter wouldn't have to go to a UPS store herself. The next day, a big flower arrangement was delivered to her home—from Zappos. As the woman wrote online, "I burst into tears. I'm a sucker for kindness, and if that isn't one of the nicest things I've ever had happen to me, I don't know what is. So . . . IF YOU BUY SHOES ONLINE, GET THEM FROM ZAPPOS. With hearts like theirs, you know they're good to do business with."

A "wow" story if there ever was one. This comment was posted on July 7, 2007.[7] Over the next four months, 181 responses were posted. The comment has been linked with literally thousands of other Web sites by people referring to Zappos' heart; it's been discussed in hundreds of blogs, and now you are reading it here.

Complaints Define What Customers Want

Customer complaints tell organizations how to improve services and products and thereby help them maintain market share. Leslie Byrne said that when she was the director of the U.S. Office of Consumer Affairs (OCA), she could tell which companies were doing a good job of pleasing customers and which ones were not by simply listening to the OCA helpline, where complaints come in about all sorts of companies. She cites a landmark study on complaint handling from which the OCA concluded, "far from being a pain in the neck as too many managers regard customer complaints, they are a marvelous source of crucial management information." She advises, "Put a CEO on the company hotline. He will find out what customers think and he will find it out fast."[8] John Davis, former IBM representative, puts it in terms of competition: "The selling edge trick is to establish a continuously flowing pipeline from the customer's mind to the salesperson's ear. When you keep track of what customers want and do not want, what pleases and gripes them, you can adjust your sights accordingly and stay a step ahead of competitors."[9]

Eileen McDargh, author and speaker, wanted to order an inflatable water bag that sits in a bathtub and can hold gallons of fresh water. It's a great product idea for anyone living in hurricane-plagued Florida. McDargh, who lives in California, saw the product advertised in the *Fort Lauderdale News* and called to order one for her mother, who lives in Florida. The number in the ad was invalid, but McDargh thought the product was so great, she persisted, going online to try to order there. Unfortunately, she couldn't order online because the product would be shipped to an address different from the one for her credit card. She found the company's phone number and called directly. The operator reiterated that the company would not accept her order—period—if the product was for an address different from the credit card billing address!

This company missed valuable information as McDargh hung up in frustration. First, the incorrect toll-free line in its paid advertising isn't going to get it any customers. Second, as McDargh pointed out, there are a lot of part-time residents in Florida. They are just as likely to be out of state when they see the ad but would want such a product for their Florida homes. McDargh pointed out, "With service like this, why would anyone even trust their product."[10] Fred Wiersema says that customers like McDargh may drive you nuts, but ultimately they are leading you to your future. He explains that these "lead" customers—if you listen to them—will take you places that in the future will seem perfectly normal.[11]

If businesses are able to identify and meet customer wants and needs, customers will typically pay more for their products, even if they say they shop strictly on price. The companies, in turn, will spend money on developing products that they know their customers want. Repeat customers and their repeat business lower per-unit sales costs.

Customer complaints also provide an opportunity to form incredibly tight relationships with customers. A lack of them can result in the loss of customers. In simple language, one commenter on Matt Woodward's blog stated the obvious: "Don't you love companies that just get it? Companies that reach out and make an effort to be available and accountable to all of their customers inspire a real sense of trust and loyalty."[12]

Peek in on Jim Norton, who blogs for Small Business Boomers, lamenting about the cost of not getting complaints.[13] He describes a business-to-business situation that still bothers him after many years. A major error caused by his former company ended up making the client look very bad. No complaint was expressed, but as a result of the error, the client's senior vice president decided to replace Norton's company when the contract expired. The vice president swore his staff to secrecy. A year later, Norton's company received a letter from the client's lawyer indicating that the contract would not be renewed. Norton came to believe, "Those who say something about the short comings of your product or service want you to do better. The others want you to fail." He says that that client was a dream to deal with in that final year, but as a consequence, he didn't learn a thing about how to keep its business. He didn't have a clue that the client was about to ditch his company.

A research group surveyed 1,179 department-store shoppers. It found that those satisfied with the department stores were more likely to complain than others. It also found, adding to a wide body of research literature that confirms these findings, that the complainers were more likely to remain loyal customers after they complained. This research group also compared so-called secure customers—those who were very satisfied with their shopping experience—with complainers. It found that the two groups had similar profiles in terms of age and frequency of shopping: forty-five years old and at least once-a-month shoppers.[14] In other words, loyal customers and complaining customers look alike, even though they may not be the same people. If this is the case, then when you talk with a complaining customer, it would not hurt to assume that this is one of your loyal customers. That might impact how you deal with the customer under trying circumstances.

Time and time again, when companies listen to customers, they learn how to fashion products and services to meet customer needs, how to revamp internal processes for greater speed and accuracy, and how to lay the groundwork to better serve customers. Think about how many more inflatable water bags (there's got to be a better name for this product!) the Fort Lauderdale company might sell if it could enable people to purchase from one part of the United States and have the product delivered to another. Amazon.com does it every day. This simple switch could mean the difference between death or survival of the business.

In many instances, the information a company obtains through customer complaints is impossible to get through any other means. Even if complaints are several levels away from a company executive who might act on a good idea (as in the case of the inflatable water bags where the complaint was made to the operator), companies can set up communication channels to learn about specific service gaps and product failures. Such an approach also enables the service provider to be able to say, "What a good idea. I'll be sure to pass this along to our executive committee." It is one of the easiest ways to make customers feel that they're part of your business. Remember, your organization is being presented with an opportunity to prove its commitment to customers by addressing their concerns, even when a complaint seems minor. If your company wants to further engage customers, someone should contact them and tell them that their ideas were implemented.

Complaints: One of the Least Expensive Marketing Tools

Complaints brought directly to businesses are the most efficient and least costly way of getting information and an understanding of customer expectations about products and services. Other, more costly and less direct, methods include reviewing customer expectations in parallel industries; conducting transaction-based studies, such as using mystery shoppers or external auditors; and conducting comprehensive customer-expectation research, such as focus groups. And none of these methods will bring customers closer to you while the studies are being conducted. Further, while large companies can afford to conduct or commission market research of the type noted above, medium and small companies must rely on their customers to tell them what they think about their products and services.

Customers, in most cases, aren't going to generate groundbreaking ideas for companies. They won't come up with the idea for the Toyota Prius hybrid; they won't think up the iPhone or the iPod, the Bose noise-reduction headset, or the Segway. Innovation is the purview of any company's research and development department. But customer feedback can help fine-tune product concepts for particular groups of people. (Here's a good example: call the product identified as an inflatable water bag a hurricane rescue pouch.) Richard Branson with Virgin

Atlantic says that he gets a lot of implementable ideas by listening to Virgin passengers. For example, the idea for onboard massages came from his wife's masseur, who flew with them.[15]

Furthermore, businesses may never understand customer needs until there is some kind of product or service failure. Complaining customers tell a company what does not work once its product has been invented and is being sold or serviced. But organizations must be willing to listen and have internal systems capable of integrating this type of feedback. Computer technology, for example, has been developed almost as much by users as by its owners.

For businesses that need to be responsive to quickly changing market conditions, listening and rapidly responding to complaints helps them stay in touch with customer expectations. Convenience stores, for instance, sell items that may remain in high demand for just a few months. Customer complaints ("Why aren't you carrying . . . ?") rapidly communicate changing marketplace interests. Other, less trendy businesses have learned this lesson as well. Market research can be static compared to the complaining, dynamic, talking marketplace. Notice how many times your own complaints actually contain a good idea for the organization. And when this happens, ask yourself whether you think there's any chance that this idea will be presented to someone else and acted on inside the company. Chances are, it won't.

The following is an example that we used in the first edition of this book, but it is a classic example of how important it is to listen to customers. In 1985, Coca-Cola was blasted with complaints on its 1-800-Get-Coke lines and protests at its Atlanta headquarters when it substituted its New Coke for what is today known as Coke Classic. Coca-Cola responded immediately to the outraged public, mollified shaken customers, and averted a potentially huge financial loss. When a company pays attention to its marketing research, it may hear only part of the story. After all, Coca-Cola had thoroughly researched the New Coke concept.

One of the most commonly talked about bad service experiences around dinner tables is the outsourcing of call centers. The trend to outsource this critical part of customer service seems to have turned a corner in 2007. Many American companies are beginning to realize that they lost customers because they outsourced call centers. Dell Computers, for one, brought back technical support to the United States for its corporate customers after hearing a numbing number of complaints about the quality.[16]

Alan Angelo with Afni, a call-center operation in Tucson, Arizona, points out, "We saw a lot of companies chase the low dollar overseas. But they weren't seeing the level of customer service that Americans have come to expect. Now top companies are looking to bring things back to the U.S."[17] Most people know the comfort that comes from communicating with someone who shares their accent and cultural background. It is difficult for customers to understand how they can talk with someone in India to solve a billing question and then be transferred to someone in the Philippines to get a clarification on the question that the Indian call center couldn't answer. Customer care is not a phrase that comes to mind when this happens. Albert Einstein summed it up nicely: "It has become appallingly obvious that our technology has exceeded our humanity."

Some companies have been aware of the language barriers for some time and simply refused to outsource their call centers, among them Toyota Financial Services and Zappos. Because these companies resisted the urge to reduce costs in this way, they've had to make up for it on the service side. Both Zappos and Toyota Financial Services run top-notch call centers.

Marketing experts measure what they think is important when gathering customer feedback on a ratings feedback form. Hotels, for example, ask about cleanliness of rooms and friendliness of staff. Guests expect these things. What draws them in close, however, may be quiet rooms that have bright lightbulbs in the lamps next to the beds and alarm clocks that are easy to set so people can read themselves to sleep and know they'll be awakened on time the next morning. Unfortunately, hotels almost never ask questions about lightbulb wattage or how easy their alarm clocks are to use or even quiet rooms. They don't ask whether the point size in their room-service menus or the direct line of the hotel listed on the phone is large enough to read. But if hotels listen to complaints, and even encourage them from guests, they may learn about an entire array of good ideas.

Market research can reveal these kinds of issues if carefully conducted, but complaints cut to the quick.

Hotels, in fact, create high numbers of problems for customers. One survey of people who have experienced service failures in hotels indicates that almost half of frequent-stay guests find it "common or frequent" to experience problems.[18] The researchers, however, found that even with frequent problems, hotel guests can be won back. If guests believe that the hotel is not at fault or if an employee makes a mistake through carelessness, they are more willing to forgive. Nonetheless, speed of response to correct the problem is important—even in forgivable types of situations. Yet the researchers report that in 15 percent of the cases, the hotels studied did nothing when customers pointed out a problem. That's not an option, according to customers. Guests are less likely to forgive when employee attitudes are inappropriate, when hotel policies are not clear (even if the customer misread them), and if service is slow or unavailable. Lack of cleanliness is the most difficult service failure to recover from. The researchers conclude, "The clear message here is that hotels need to review their policies and procedures with regard to service recovery and to ensure they are not falling into the traps identified."[19]

In addition to calling attention to product defects, service shortcomings, and poorly designed systems, complaining customers can also alert managers to front-line personnel problems. Customers are usually the first to know when the company is being poorly represented by staff. In fact, managers may *never* learn about poor treatment of customers through simple observation of staff because employees generally behave better when their managers are around or when they know their telephone calls are being taped.

The Value of a Customer over a Lifetime of Buying

Loyal customers are not easily produced, though disloyal ones are. The multitude of statistics generated in this area suggest that if customers believe their complaints are welcomed and responded to, they will more likely repurchase.[20] In addition, long-term customers are not only easier to sell to but also easier to serve because they know how to get their needs met; they know your products, your people, and your systems for conducting business.

You might say that customers buying inexpensive services or buying where the margins are low are not worth significant sums of money. Besides which, the argument goes, if they have a complaint, there are always more customers where they came from. Here is where a long view is critical. If a customer purchases one $20 book on Amazon each month on average, the total payment to Amazon will be $240 each year and possibly $10,000 over that person's lifetime. Each dry-cleaning exchange may only be $10 or $15. Over a lifetime, however, a customer can easily spend $30,000 on dry cleaning. And this says nothing about the number of friends or relatives a satisfied customer might send to a responsive dry-cleaning establishment. A household that spends $25 each weekend for pizza and sodas equals about $5,000 in just four years to the pizza company lucky enough to keep that household as a regular customer.[21] It might not be a bad idea to imagine customers with Post-It notes on their foreheads with an estimated lifetime value number written on them. If staff imagine someone purchasing $5,000 worth of pizza, they might have a different reaction when an error occurs than if they see the person just as someone who comes in to purchase a medium-sized pepperoni pizza. Auto dealers really need to pay attention to this. The average American spends between $250,000 and $350,000 on automobiles in a lifetime.[22] Automotive call centers could bring up a total dollar amount that a customer has already spent and potentially what will be spent. That might influence how a call center rep talks with the customer.

Some people refer to selling more to existing customers as *customer share*; *market share* refers to selling to as many customers as possible.[23] For most companies, about two-thirds of sales come from existing customers.[24] At a minimum, local store employees may recognize their frequent customers by face, but that doesn't tell them the whole story about that customer. For example, in the early 2000s, the average Staples store customer spent between $600 and $700 per year.[25] If that customer also used a Staples catalog, he or she spent twice as much. Someone who used both the catalog and the store and also shopped online spent about four times as much as the store-only shopper.[26] Because of the volume a single customer can represent to a large retailer through several shopping media, and because no one can tell how much that customer is worth to the company by just looking at him or her, any customer complaints need to be handled very carefully and very quickly.

An IBM study suggests that if customers leave an establishment with an unresolved problem, less than half will repurchase. On the other hand, if customers feel their problems have been satisfactorily resolved, almost all will give the company another chance.[27] For every year customers are retained, they represent more in profits because marketing expenses can be amortized against long-term sales results.[28] Robert LaBant, senior vice president of IBM's North American sales and marketing, indicates that for IBM, "every percentage-point variation in customer satisfaction scores translates into a gain or loss of $500 million in sales over five years." He says that developing new business costs IBM three to five times as much as selling to its existing customers.[29]

When Vonage, a VoIP (voice over Internet protocol) telephone company, went public with its stock, it released information to the Securities and Exchange Commission indicating a customer churn rate of 2.11 percent per month as of March 2006. That means seventy-seven thousand customers terminated service in the first three months of 2006. Vonage acknowledges that expending marketing revenues is essential to acquire seventy-seven thousand new customers every quarter to maintain revenue parity. Vonage was forced to report, "Therefore, if we are unsuccessful in retaining customers or are required to spend significant amounts to acquire new customers beyond those budgeted, our revenue could decrease and our net losses could increase."[30] Vonage does not discuss the issue of retaining customers, but it does refer to the "significant amounts" required to acquire new customers. Since consumer research tells us that a high percentage of customers leave a business because of poor complaint handling,[31] what easier way is there to retain customers than better handling their complaints?

The Danger in Setting Goals to Reduce Customer Complaints

Rather than trying to reduce the number of complaints, organizations need to encourage staff to seek out complaints. If a company's goal is to have fewer complaints this year than last, it is easier to accomplish than you might imagine. Staff will get the message and simply not report complaints to management. How many times have you delivered a written complaint to the front desk staff of a hotel and wondered if your complaint was passed on to the general manager? Both authors have gone to the trouble to fill out response forms in hotels on a number of occasions, checked the box indicating that they would like a response to their complaint, and received nothing. Either this is extremely poor complaint handling or the complaint was never passed on in the first place. Glancing back after leaving the front desk, Janelle has actually seen hotel clerks tear up her feedback forms.

It's possible that the desire to reduce complaints results in the statement "We never get complaints." David Powley, an auditor for the ISO 9000 certification, says that when he hears that statement, he thinks the company probably would not know "how to recognize a customer complaint if it was staring them in the face."[32] Powley states, as do so many other researchers, that an "absence of dissent" doesn't mean there were no complaints. Opinions count, even if they are not expressed.

Setting goals to reduce complaints can end up casting a pall over an otherwise excellent service experience. One of the finest automobile manufacturers in the world makes the number of cars available to its dealers dependent upon high numbers on surveys that customers complete after purchasing a new car. After a very fine sales experience from top to bottom, the salesperson tells the customers that they will receive a survey to evaluate their experience. Sometimes the salesperson asks, "Is there any reason why you won't give me all 5s (the highest rating)?" or says, "Why don't you bring the form back to me and I'll fill it out for you to save you the inconvenience." Some salespeople are even blunt:

"We need 5 ratings from you in order to get enough cars to sell." When we have told the salespeople that we wouldn't give them straight 5s, they have bribed us for those higher ratings with free oil changes, tanks of gas, and in one situation, a complete set of upgraded tires. The genuinely pleasant experience of buying a new car just had dirt thrown on it. Organizations need to look carefully at the perks they attach to higher service ratings or lower complaint numbers. Staff members will figure out a way to deliver these numbers if it is in their interest to do so.

Shortly before Pan American Airways was sold to United Airlines, an angry staff member, in a letter to a newspaper editor, wrote that service had gotten so bad at Pan Am, customers simply stopped complaining. They knew it wouldn't do any good. This writer told about a chartered Pan Am 747 jet filled to capacity with a group going to a weeklong Club Med vacation. The plane arrived at the resort a day late—with none of the passengers' luggage! According to the frustrated former employee, not a single passenger complained.

Sometimes, a reduction in complaints can signal a positive trend. In such instances, the company is tabulating the number of complaints it receives about specific issues. For example, Brooks Brothers, Inc., enjoyed a positive reputation for producing high-quality clothing until the 1980s. Then management changed hands three times. The latest owners, Marks and Spencer, instituted new quality-improvement measures and saw specific complaints about the quality of goods reduced from 25 percent to 5 percent. That's significant.[33] Still, Brooks Brothers knows only that complaints about quality are dropping; the figures do not tell the company exactly how customers evaluate its products overall. In 2003, Adelphia, a cable television provider, had the highest number of recorded complaints in the city of Los Angeles. The company went to work on the specific issues involved and a year later had reduced complaints by 54 percent. One reason this worked is that the company also set goals to improve communications. In Los Angeles, this meant hiring Spanish-speaking customer service reps who are available 24/7.[34]

To Get the Complete Story,
Go After Hidden Complaints

Sometimes complaints are hidden from companies because of the structure of their businesses. As a result, companies have to be creative in how they hear about customer complaints. Some amusement parks, for example, outsource critical aspects of their business. Many subcontract their food services, allowing park owners to concentrate on park management. Subsequently, food complaints decrease, or at least complaints reported by the food services to park management decrease.[35] From the perspective of those who attend one of these amusement parks, however, that bad hot dog or surly treatment by a vendor is still seen as the park's responsibility. They don't know that the restaurant is no longer directly managed by the park. The park, in turn, learns little about the bad service and, thus, is unable to fix it.

Some companies conduct customer satisfaction surveys to learn more about hidden complaints. This is a good idea, to a point. But who normally participates in such surveys? Existing customers. Unless a company makes a point to ask everyone who used to buy, it is polling only those people who are still buying. These customers are still sufficiently satisfied to stay. Customer satisfaction surveys are not representative of your dissatisfied customers. They may give you some ideas, but you need to go after the customers who have left and find out why they left. Then the company can find some real gifts.

If companies look only at the people who ordinarily complain, rather than seek out additional feedback from noncomplaining customers, they may not have a complete picture of who is dissatisfied or why. People who complain tend not to be typical of the total population with unvoiced complaints. In the United States overall, the person most likely to complain is a younger, well-educated white male with a higher-than-average income.[36] This may not be the same person who is most likely to buy from a particular business. For example, this person isn't a typical McDonald's customer.

Word of Mouth and Complaint Behavior

Businesses are understandably interested in what the public says about them. Word-of-mouth advertising can make or break a business or product, and every dissatisfied customer who leaves a business represents a potential threat in the marketplace with respect to word of mouth. Complaints can work for or against your company in the following ways:

- People are much more likely to believe a personal recommendation than an advertiser's promotional statements.
- Effective complaint handling can be a powerful source of positive word of mouth.
- The more dissatisfied customers become, the more likely they are to use word of mouth to express their displeasure.

Let's consider these factors one by one.

People Are Much More Likely to Believe a Personal Recommendation Than an Advertiser's Promotional Statements

A General Electric study found that recommendations made by people that customers know carry twice the weight of advertising statements.[37] Perhaps you have seen a sale come to a halt as a person standing next to a shopper whispers, "I wouldn't buy that. I have one and it breaks easily (or the colors run or the quality is bad after a single wearing or it doesn't work the way they say it does or you can get a cheaper one somewhere else)." But the sale will likely be made if the person recommends, "Oh, I have one of those and it's great. I love it. And the guarantee is a very good one. Definitely get it, and you'll think it was one of the best buys you ever made."

Every bad word told and retold about a business becomes that much more difficult to overcome through marketing promotions. People are far more willing to listen to the advice of a good friend, or even a perfect stranger, than they are to believe a multimillion-dollar advertising campaign. John DiJulius, with John Robert's Spa in Cleveland, Ohio, talks about pulling out all stops to more likely create positive word of mouth when a customer has a complaint. One customer came into his salon for a hair coloring and ended up with a stained suit. DiJulius sent her a large check to cover the cost of the suit after a trip to the dry cleaner didn't work. He also gave her a free facial and pedicure. DiJulius estimates that he's gotten thirty additional customers from this gesture, and the customer is also now coming in for facials and pedicures on a regular basis. She says, "At first, I thought about never going back. Now I would never think of going anywhere else."[38]

Negative word of mouth can even affect an entire industry dramatically. Consider the insurance industry. Its image in the United States is at an all-time low. The Gallup Organization found that almost two-thirds of polled consumers believe that insurance companies overcharge auto, homeowner, and commercial-line policyholders. Gallup also found that an astounding 61 percent of Americans believe that profits are higher in the insurance industry than in other industries and that companies cheat on their financial reporting to hide excessive profits.[39] That's bad press. Each ineffective claim-handling incident discussed in the wake of a multitude of natural disasters, especially the devastation left by Hurricane Katrina (2005), convinces thousands of people that when they deal with their insurance agencies, their claims are going to be poorly handled.

If you have this belief about your insurance company, it does not matter how many times you are told that you're in good hands. You won't believe it. Robert Hunter, director of insurance for the Consumer Federation of America, says, "You could have 10 fender benders and one totally destroyed car, and guess which one isn't settled?" Insurance agencies consider a claim to be settled when some type of agreement has been reached. But Hunter points out, "An insurance company can say it's 'settled' even if the guy is still yelling and reluctantly takes what he is offered."[40] And television broadcasters love to put the yelling guy on the evening news.

Effective Complaint Handling Can Be a Powerful Source of Positive Word of Mouth

Spend some time on the Web reading all the personal service experiences that bloggers are having or are reading about on other blogs and repeating. Blogging sites are exploding in number. It's estimated that, while most will not survive, every single day one hundred thousand new blogs go up on the Web. Customer service stories are intensely interesting for bloggers. They are very human stories and do not carry with them the instant controversy that blogs on politics do. If you're not a blog reader, an interesting place to start looking is Vox, described as a free personal blogging service.[41]

Saska, a Vox blogger with a blog called Fiendish Glee Club, describes herself this way: "I'm a photographer, a writer, a reader, a gamer, a mother, and a geek. I refuse to grow up."[42] Saska posted a lengthy description of fantastic service she received from Nintendo. She bought a new Nintendo Wii on its 2007 launch day, and from the beginning the optical drive was noisy. When the noise persisted, Saska called Nintendo and was invited to come over to its offices since she lives close by and it would save her time. The service she received was "shockingly" good, and one small gesture after another added up to this: "So this is my Valentine to Nintendo. That was the most awesome customer service experience I have ever, ever had." And she has uploaded some pictures to prove her point.[43] It's a fun read, and to date ninety-five people have commented on her post, asking additional questions and making similarly strong positive statements about Nintendo. If you are thinking about the purchase of a video game unit, after reading this blog, you'd consider Nintendo. As it turns out, the Wii was the in-demand item for Christmas gifts in 2007.

The More Dissatisfied Customers Become, the More Likely They Are to Use Word of Mouth to Express Their Displeasure

If customers walk away angry with "expressed complaints that do not get handled," there may not be much a company can do to stop their negative word of mouth.[44] But if companies make it easy for customers to complain and then handle these complaints well, dissatisfaction levels will decrease, negative word of mouth will lessen, and positive word of mouth may be generated. If you read the complaints posted on the web, you'll see that they almost all involve complaints that were not handled well. It almost seems as if customers simply want to tell someone about their problems, and if the companies do not respond to them, they will find another audience.[45]

In the case of companies that have easy exchange policies, we expect the public to say fewer negative things about them. Costco is a good example because part of its reputation is "We'll take it back—no questions asked." Costco will even take returns without a receipt. In other words, Costco is saying, "Bring us your complaints. We want to fix your problems with any products we make available." Companies control negative word of mouth when they demonstrate to their customers that they are sincere about doing what it takes to create satisfaction.

The Negative Cycle of Poor Complaint Handling

Ineffective service recovery and an ineffective complaint policy can start a negative chain reaction leading to poorer quality service and products, as well as increased risk in the marketplace. Stated in its most damaging form, poor complaint handling starts with dissatisfied customers and ends up with customers and the business feeding into each other's negative attitudes. Here's the sequence that was applicable in the 1990s and still holds true in the 2000s:

1. Customers leave a business dissatisfied. They become "bad-will ambassadors," who voice their displeasure to others.
2. More and more members of the public begin to identify the business as a place where it does no good to complain because nothing will happen.
3. Customers stop complaining and the company loses opportunities to learn what it can do to improve services or meet customer needs. (Or large numbers of customers complain, so the organization walls itself off from hearing them.)

4. Product and service quality are, therefore, not improved, leading to even more customer dissatisfaction.
5. The customers who still patronize this business will come for the lower prices the company has been forced to set to remain competitive. Customers also arrive with the mind-set that product and service quality will be minimal.
6. Staff do not feel good helping bad-natured customers. In fact, the staff may start to call the customers names. (We have heard flight attendants on cash-strapped airlines say as the passengers march up the jetway, "Here come the animals.")
7. The staff feel more and more that they have "just a job," and a bad one at that. Those who can find employment elsewhere will leave, thereby depriving the business of their experience and skills. The staff who remain are less motivated and less capable of gaining the confidence, trust, and loyalty of customers.
8. This, in turn, leads to more customers leaving the business dissatisfied and telling everyone in sight just what they think. They will not charge a penny for this advertising. And so the downward cycle starts anew.

Many companies do not appreciate the real cost of losing customers. They can tell you exactly what they are doing to attract new customers and how much this costs them, but they may not have a clue as to how many customers they are losing, why they are being lost, or how much this costs them. In 1989, benchmarking data for the first time let the U.S. marketplace see which airlines were doing well and which ones weren't. Eastern Airlines and Pam Am had the highest complaint rates, and within two years both ceased operations. (In this study, complaints were identified as those that escalated to the Department of Transportation.) The next four on the list, TWA, America West, Continental, and US Airways, all sought out bankruptcy protection in the following years. Of these four airlines, only America West was able to reduce its cost per available seat mile. The airlines with the lowest complaint rates (United, Northwest, American, Alaska, Southwest, and Delta), while they have struggled since 2001, actually ended up with a better cost per available seat mile ten years after the original data was gathered. Here's what this data means: lower complaint levels suggest higher quality levels, which can translate into lower costs.[46]

Here's another example. The Better Business Bureau (BBB) in eastern Missouri and southern Illinois sent out news releases about thirty-two firms over the years from 1997 to 2006. The BBB warned consumers to be careful about doing business with these companies because of their high levels of unresolved complaints. Of the thirty-two firms, twenty-six are no longer in business. The BBB also found that 70.4 percent of the companies that resolved 10 percent or less of the complaints that were registered with the BBB also went out of business. The BBB concludes that not resolving complaints puts a business at risk for going out of business. "It follows that each unresolved complaint, each dissatisfied customer may serve as a stepping stone in that direction for any business."[47]

DISCUSSION QUESTIONS

- What are the ways you treat customer complaints as market information?

- What have you learned about your company by listening to customer complaints? Do your staff and customers know these examples?

- What are all the ways you count or measure customer complaints?

- If you count complaints, do you use a multiplier to account for noncompliance that is reasonable for your type of business? Do you compare these figures to the total number of clients you have? How much does it cost you to get new customers?

- How many customers have you lost in the past year? Who are these customers?

- How much are your customers worth to you over a lifetime of buying?

- What do your customers say about you in the marketplace? What is your plan to manage this public talk or word of mouth?

~ 3 ~

Capitalizing on Complaints

Restaurant personnel, in a high-profile Hong Kong magazine column, were quoted as describing complaining diners as "moaners . . . whiners . . . demanding . . . explosive . . . rude . . . self-centered . . . power grabbers . . . stupid . . . out-right cheaters . . . and devious."[1] Even researchers can't avoid calling customers names. One group divided problem diners into five categories: Bad Mannered Betty, Harold the Intimidator, Freeloading Fickle, Ignoramus Iggie, and Dictatorial Dick.[2] These labels are cute, but they also reinforce negative mind-sets about consumers. A University of Florida group divided complaining customers into the meek, the aggressive, the high-roller, the rip-off, and the chronic complainers. Nowhere in these designations was there a customer who just wants something that was promised or a problem fixed.[3]

Actually, most people who complain are not nitpickers; in fact, they represent a "rather broad sample of the buying public."[4]

To Capitalize on Complaints, You Must First Hear Them

It would be a wonderful world, indeed, if companies could produce services and products that always worked. According to product experts, however, a 10 to 12 percent problem rate may be the lowest that most industries can achieve.[5] It is safe to conclude that problems will always be with us. So companies need to learn about service recovery—the process of making right what went wrong. In order to engage in service recovery, a company must first know that a problem occurred, and there is no way that the people within an organization are going to find all the problems themselves.

To ensure that complaints are made, customer expectations need to be carefully managed, beginning with how they are formed during the sales process. Customers are more likely to communicate their dissatisfaction if they believe the products they are purchasing are basically of high quality and that any problems will be handled fairly and quickly. Under these circumstances, they will work as partners to regain satisfaction.

Here are the possibilities of customer behavior combined with organizational response.

No product or service failure	No product or service failure
If the customer speaks up, thank the customer for his or her praise	The customer complains; there's a chance to clear up the customer's confusion
Company action: Celebrate 1	2 **Company action:** Thank and educate the customer
Product or service failure	**Product or service failure**
The customer keeps quiet—to organization	The customer is dissatisfied and complains to the company
Company action: Ask for and encourage customer complaints 3	4 **Company action:** Thank the customer and engage in service recovery

Being in Quadrant 1 deserves a hooray, a celebration, maybe even champagne. On the surface, the situation looks good because from the company's point of view, things have gone smoothly, and customers seem to affirm this by not complaining or by paying a compliment. In reality, unless they ask, companies don't know exactly what percentage of customers are satisfied because most don't say anything. Given the penchant managers and product sellers have to blame customers for problems rather than take responsibility, it seems likely that when customers are silent, most companies will pat themselves on the back and say, "We must have done all right!" This could be a serious mistake. Some customers that the company presumes are in Quadrant 1 may actually be residing in Quadrant 3.

Quadrant 2 situations require gentle customer education. Sometimes customers do complain about things that are not the company's fault. For example, airline passengers may complain that it was the airline's fault that they missed their flight, when actually they misread their ticket. Even though these customers are not right, under these circumstances, they are still customers. Furthermore, customers aren't the only ones to make mistakes; employees make some whoppers themselves. From the perspective of the organization, it is a good idea to listen to these customers because there is a chance to learn from them. If tickets are commonly misread, perhaps it would be a good idea to redesign the ticket so fewer passengers misread them.

When customer service representatives take responsibility for what happened, at least to the degree that they apologize for the event, they demonstrate customer concern. If a business has a number of these kinds of situations, then it needs to be proactive and educate customers so similar incidents can be avoided. In late December 2007, a young Canadian oil-field worker got an $83,700 cell phone bill from Bell Mobility, a division of Bell Canada. It turned out that the young man, who was lonely working out in the field, used his cell phone to connect to the Internet. He thought this usage was covered by his $10 unlimited browser plan. This story received a huge amount of attention in Canada, and Bell Mobility, bowing to pressure, agreed to reduce his bill to $3,400.[6] That's quite a reduction, but it still left a huge sum for the young man, who lives basically paycheck to paycheck. Our recommendation: Bell should wipe the bill clean and use the opportunity to educate other customers that this "unlimited" browser plan isn't really unlimited after all. Perhaps it should also consider removing the word *unlimited* from its advertising. The reality is that most people do not read the fine print when they sign contracts of this type, so highlighted advertising words need to be consistent with the small "gotcha" words.

Quadrant 3 represents the biggest problem for companies: customers who do not say anything about their problems. When an organization concludes that if customers have not said anything, then there must not have been a product or service failure, it, in effect, denies the existence of Quadrant 3. We believe this to be the silent killer of many companies. One way a company can turn this type of dissatisfaction around is to make it easy for customers to sound off. In the financial services industry, for example, making it easier for customers to speak up through specially designated channels set up just for them increases customer satisfaction.[7] Having the direct telephone number of an assigned private banker means customers know how to contact the bank should something go wrong.

Another way to get more feedback from your customers is simply to ask them when you're already talking with them. Ask straightforward questions such as, "How is this feature of our product working for you? What's our response time like? Would it be better if we did this? What's the best thing about this product?" As Martha Rogers, partner at Peppers and Rogers Group, says when a company integrates customer input, "We get further and further up the learning curve, and after awhile, you're getting a product from me that you can't get anywhere else because you helped me create it."[8] John Huppertz, winner of an AMA Marketing award, looked at which of the following factors would make customers more likely to voice their complaints to organizations: liberal refund policies, employee empowerment, access to call centers, or reduction of in-store hassles to return merchandise. Looking at these four complaint-friendly approaches in the retail industry, which one do you think would have the strongest impact on customers' speaking up? Huppertz points out that all these factors made the organizations appear more complaint-friendly, but *only liberal refund policies* significantly affected customers' willingness to complain.[9]

Daryl Travis, founding partner with Brandtrust Consultants, strongly encourages asking customers for feedback. As he says, customers love to be asked, though not in surveys or in focus groups. Travis says, "You have to develop an insatiable appetite for that continuous feedback from the customers."[10] He advises organizations to not let any customers sit in Quadrant 3. When Gary Kelly took over the CEO's position at Southwest Airlines in 2005, he set up two daylong meetings (six groups in total) with passengers. Not quite the focus groups that Daryl Travis finds stifling but a way for passengers to bend the ear of the top guy at Southwest. After coming out of these meetings, Kelly said, "It helped me to prioritize the things we need to work on."[11]

Sun Microsystems, along with a number of other high-tech companies, sets up booths at trade shows. These booths are staffed by high-level managers, who, by talking with attendees, are able to gather a large amount of market intelligence in a short period of time at minimal cost. Ed McQuarrie, marketing professor at Santa Clara University, recommends that operational managers visit customers to hear what is going on. Don't just send out marketing reps or salespeople to sell. He says, "Customer visits represent a kind of home grown market research," where you have a real chance to hear from customers about their problems and how your products and services do or don't work for them.[12]

WinterSilks began selling silk garments in the early 1980s, first by catalog, then on the web, and now also in a single store in Madison, Wisconsin. The company has grown organically, relying primarily upon actively sought-out customer feedback to help shape its growth. Its outreach efforts touch thousands of customers. All accumulated information is summarized to sharpen the company's approach to business. WinterSilks creates a top-ten list of customer concerns and then actively works to address these issues. John Reindl, vice president of operations, says, "In terms of the payback, these efforts are very cheap. To become more competitive, you simply have to do it."[13]

With the growing, widespread use of self-service technology (SST), an increasingly large number of customers may not be able to get their needs met and may have absolutely no way to report this to anyone—

at least as far as they know. Just recently, Janelle stood in a large truck stop that featured multiple fast-food restaurants, a large retail shop, restrooms, and a game room. She began to count all the SST devices she could see from where she stood. She quit counting at forty-six. All the workers in the truck stop were busy with their own jobs, so reporting a broken SST machine probably would have done no good. Very few of the devices posted call-in numbers to use if they were out of order. Few people tend to call those numbers anyway. Most customers just find another machine to use or figure out some other way to get their needs met. Every machine that sits unused represents lost revenues. In situations like this, the SST device owners have to primarily depend on store operators to tell them what is happening with their machines.[14]

Take a look at the barriers that your organization has in place that may make it difficult for customers to complain. Do you make them write formal letters or call special numbers? How much documentation is required when customers want to exchange something or ask for a refund? How much time do you give them to report a problem? Some of these barriers, combined with unsatisfactory or no responses to complaints, have created a populace that TARP (the most widely quoted customer service research group) says doesn't believe anything will happen. For this reason, TARP's president, John Goodman, recommends that staff be taught how to recognize subtly presented complaints and then be encouraged to ask questions to find out what really bothers customers.

Handling Quadrant 4 situations, in which customers tell the company about their problems, requires great skill. Communicating with complaining customers is when maximum contact takes place, the most information from customers is gathered, and the greatest opportunity for service recovery and continuous improvement exists. If the company can fix the problem, take responsibility for the breakdown, and be polite and friendly, customers are more likely to give the company another chance.

One of our TMI-US colleagues is a professionally trained chef. She bought two very expensive steaks at a store in which she shops multiple times each week. (She likes foods fresh!) When she started to prepare the steaks the next night, they had already turned brown. She took them back to the store and talked with the woman who normally serves her at the meat counter. The clerk asked, "Did you leave them sitting out too long?" followed by the statement, "Your refrigerator must not be cold enough." Our colleague eventually got two fresh steaks but left with a "browned" judgment about her experience.

How could this have been handled differently? First, the woman could have thanked the customer for bringing in the steaks because clearly the grocery store needs to check with its supplier about such expensive cuts of meat. She could have apologized and maybe even put in an extra steak for the customer's trouble. After the exchange had been made, the clerk could then have asked some questions to make sure the issue was not an educational one, all the while apologizing for asking the questions. She might even have asked what the customer thought would cause these steaks to turn brown in less than twenty-four hours. At that point, the customer would have been in full partnership with the grocer. And the next time the grocer saw the steak shopper, she could have inquired about the meal she prepared. That's how long-term relationships get formed.

Companies benefit from customers who speak up, and this is why companies need to let their customers know they welcome complaints and feedback. This means that customer-facing staff must know how to recognize when something is amiss. For example, a friend called a long-distance carrier to complain about the billing procedure it used. At one point he told the service representative, "You aren't giving me good service." "Yes, I am," the representative replied, "I'm following the rules." This carrier definitely does not advertise its service promise that way: "We give you good service: we follow our own rules." The public would guffaw, but obviously someone within this organization taught this young woman, at least implicitly, that this is what she is supposed to do and say when questioned. Retailers estimate that 74 percent of dissatisfied customers can be retained if problems are rectified, but as we shall see, the overwhelming majority of customers never complain (or complain only when purchasing expensive items).[15] Therefore, retailers who are more adept at encouraging complaints have taken the first step toward service recovery.

Capitalize on Complaints by Identifying Your Common Service Failures

Service recovery does not happen automatically. Companies need to carefully think about possible errors and build in approaches to handle them (because they will occur). For example, hotels need to teach their cashiers how to respond to billing errors, problems with rooms, and overbooking. The airline industry must instruct staff how to handle late arrivals, late takeoffs, oversold flights, lost luggage, and cancelled flights. Grocers must know what to do and say when long lines form at check-out counters. Retailers need to know how to handle advertised bargains that have sold out, a lack of staff, and items that cost more today than yesterday.

Do all businesses put the spotlight on themselves to find their common service breakdowns and then plan how to handle them when they occur? For example, could any of the following happen at a dentist's or doctor's office?

- Patients are kept waiting two hours for appointments.
- Patients do not have their insurance identification cards with them.
- Patients are spoken to rudely by overworked technicians or office assistants.

If an organization actively solicits complaints and then tracks them, it can easily construct a list of the types of regularly recurring service breakdowns. Then the organization must plan its response. Some companies are better at service recovery than others. Those that are good at it educate their employees to anticipate customer problems, even something as simple as reminding customers that a product they just bought requires batteries. In companies that plan their service recovery, customer-facing employees know they have the support of the company behind them to fix things that go wrong. So when they sell something to a customer, they know they are selling a promise that will be delivered.[16]

Nordstrom may be better than anyone else at excellent customer service in the retail business, and yet Bruce Nordstrom says, "We don't want to talk about our service. We are not as good as our reputation. It is a very fragile thing. You just have to do it every time, every day."[17] A city-wide poll conducted in Phoenix, Arizona, a few years ago asked people to name their favorite department store. Nordstrom won by a significant margin, even though a Nordstrom won't open there until 2009. (There are several Nordstrom stores in surrounding communities, but none in Phoenix itself.) How did Nordstrom create such a legendary reputation? Part of the answer is Nordstrom staff who go way out of their way to deliver outstanding service—every once in a while. We have heard many organizations say they could never do what Nordstrom does for its customers. That's simply not true. Nordstrom couldn't perform these heroic acts all the time either. But "every once in a while" is manageable and has impact. Shoppers in New York City voted their Nordstrom outlets as being the best at making people feel special. A lot of that has to do with the stores' liberal (though not unlimited) exchange policy.[18]

And there's no better time to do something amazing than when customers want a refund. The most extreme story told about Nordstrom is a renowned example that may not even be true. It's a story about Nordstrom refunding money to an elderly customer for obviously used tires—even though the retailer doesn't sell tires. If you want to read the whole fascinating story and what it has done for the Nordstrom reputation, the most complete discussion is on the Snopes.com urban legends Web site.[19] The point is, you can build a reputation slowly but surely if you do everything well. But to get people in Phoenix, Arizona, to evaluate you as the best retail store when they don't even have an outlet there, you have to make a splash.

To Capitalize on Complaints, Get More of Them

The single most critical reason why customers complain is that they believe something will happen as a result of their complaints. It's useful to separate the dissatisfaction customers experience from the decisions they make to actually complain. Customers can be extremely dissatisfied and not say anything, or they can feel only minor dissatisfaction and speak up if they believe the company will do something for them. Enabling customers to converse with you starts with creating a culture where everyone inside the organization knows that customer feedback is viewed as a marketing investment and not a cost. Some simple methods include giving your staff preprinted forms so they can keep records of what customers tell them. Label the printed forms "Customer Gifts." Customers will see you are serious if you write down what they say. If you do not keep records of customer comments, they will be forgotten.

When you do something major for a customer, call your customer after the event. One restaurant owner calls the hosts of dinner parties larger than eight, even if they did not complain. He says, "We know with a big party we can lose control of what happens. The host of the party may not want to complain in front of others, and hosts tend to be important customers who spend a lot of money."[20] Many younger people prefer communicating via online chats, including Internet-based video chats. (If you google the words *live chat*, you'll find more than 82 million sites. And if that is overwhelming for you, go to Wikipedia [www.wikipedia .com] and search for *online chat* for a very complete summary of the subject.) Instant online messaging enables people to communicate one-on-one with a company representative in real time. Internet-based cash and coupon transfer technologies make it possible for compensation to be awarded immediately in online chats. Blogs are another way for organizations to speak directly to their customers, and they can be set up to drive traffic to their own Web sites.

Toll-free lines remain one of the best traditional ways to communicate directly with customers, especially one-on-one. Toll-free numbers have been available in the United States since 1967, when the service was introduced. Today, 98 percent of adult Americans use toll-free numbers; 52 percent estimate they make fifty or more toll-free calls a year. Making it easy for customers to successfully locate a toll-free number on a Web site significantly improves the success of any ad, whether online or in print.[21] Based on its research, AT&T says that 86 percent of customers would rather call a toll-free number than write a letter to a company, and 62 percent are more likely to do business with companies that have toll-free lines than those that do not.[22] In short, a company that does not have a toll-free line is at a competitive disadvantage. As a Minneapolis marketing consultant says, "It's the cost of doing business these days."[23]

Not all incoming toll-free calls, of course, are customer complaints. No exact data exists as to what percentage are complaints, but AT&T estimates that a "sizeable portion" of toll-free calls are complaints or customer feedback, especially when numbers are printed on products. AT&T prints a huge Toll-Free Business Edition Directory each year. Many of these numbers are designed for sales, but they can also be used for customer feedback. Any organization deciding to use toll-free numbers needs to carefully think through what it wants to accomplish.

If your organization arranges for toll-free lines and advertises them to the public without tight controls, more problems can be created than if the company hid itself from its customers. At a minimum, you must ensure that your staff can handle the volume of potential calls. One major furniture retailer learned this lesson. The retailer's CEO arranged for widely publicized toll-free lines to be installed. The first two weeks generated thousands of calls—many more than the system was equipped to handle, creating more upset customers. Customer dissatisfaction was beyond anything this company could have predicted. The lesson is clear: test-market toll-free lines.

TARP concludes that toll-free helplines are a great boon to companies—unless the calls are handled poorly. And that is a big "unless." As TARP warned over a decade ago:

> If the (customer service) system is not designed to effectively handle individual customer service contacts and to use that data preventively to eliminate the root cause of difficulties, the company may be better off not soliciting such contacts. TARP's cross-industry research has shown that an ineffective customer service system can do more market damage than not actively offering customer service.[24]

Deciding to market a toll-free, customer feedback/support line is a strategic decision; determining the details of responding to these calls are tactical decisions. Some companies do a poor job on the tactics. For example, if a voice-mail system is attached to a toll-free phone number, it must be monitored carefully to avoid what is known as voice-mail jail. This happens when callers get caught between repeating, looping menus and cannot reach a live person. TARP's president, John Goodman, says that there is major risk of damage to the company-customer relationship if no live person is reachable. Based on TARP surveys, Goodman says that customer satisfaction drops by 10 percent if customers have to leave their names on voice mail and then be called back.[25]

A review of extensive business literature on toll-free lines reveals the following complaint-related benefits:

- *Heightened consumer trust:* Customers think you are more solid if they can easily reach you. While Honda Motor Company will not say that its toll-free number alone created the success of the Acura, it does say that installing the line sent a loud and clear message to its customers: "We don't abandon you if you run into problems with our product."[26]
- *Immediate customer feedback:* Paul Walsh, former CEO of Pillsbury, says, "If we have a problem with a product we want to be the first to hear about it."[27]
- *Increased ability to reduce complaints about common problems:* If customers call to get information, an organization can teach them how to avoid other problems. Armstrong World Industries prints a toll-free number on its no-wax flooring that instructs customers to call Armstrong for information on how to remove the number. The number actually comes off easily with warm water, but while Armstrong has customers on the telephone, they are instructed on how to care for the floor so that wax buildup problems are avoided. Armstrong World estimates that this toll-free training course controls customer dissatisfaction and earns Armstrong a whopping $12,000 per customer over time based on customer retention. Armstrong sees its toll-free lines as revenue generating.[28]
- *Help in controlling legal action:* Sometimes calling right away can nip problems in the bud before customers begin to think of whom to sue.

- *Increase in market and product research information:* Callers on toll-free lines tell companies what they like, what they do not like, what works, and what does not work for them. Tapes of these calls can be played to product managers and factory employees so they can hear directly what customers think. Kraft General Foods puts toll-free numbers on most of its new product packages and says, "Our 800 numbers give us a great feedback mechanism for improving our products."[29]
- *Opportunity to sell additional products:* While most companies view product-support toll-free lines primarily as a way to strengthen client brand loyalty, it is also remarkably easy to introduce customers to additional products over the phone while they are calling with complaints: "If you liked (or didn't like) this product, could I also recommend . . . Most of our customers say . . . Would you like me to send you a half-price coupon to try it?" Most companies realize that the biggest hurdle in developing loyal customers is getting them to try their product in the first place. If they like it and it is priced right, they will probably continue to purchase it.
- *Enhanced ability to pay special attention to special customers:* By assigning special toll-free lines, companies can provide personal attention and special services to high-volume customers. United Airlines has a special toll-free number just for its Global Services fliers, those customers who fly more miles at the highest ticket prices on UA. UA personnel on that line will do more for their customers and resolve complaints more readily.
- *Generation of additional complaints:* A toll-free line says, in effect, "We're not afraid; we want more of your gifts!"

Capitalize on What Complaints Can Teach You About Your Marketplace

Complaints tell you what is meaningful to your customers. Extensive research conducted over the past twenty-five years reveals that customers mostly speak out about problems that matter to them, about issues they think can be solved, and about issues they want redressed. This view of customers runs contrary to what many service providers and managers think: that complaining customers want something for nothing. Complaining customers are the people who put money into the hands of businesses and are trying to—in the overwhelming majority of cases— right a perceived wrong. While it may seem paradoxical, to capitalize on complaints you have to welcome them rather than cringe when you're being taught about the marketplace.[30]

Here are a couple of examples. After listening to complaints, the tourist travel industry has learned that if positive memories can be created around food service experiences, an entire vacation is viewed more positively.[31] Darty, a French household appliance distributor, welcomes customer complaints that tell the company its products aren't the cheapest in the market. Its brand promise is that they will be, so customers are, in effect, conducting market intelligence when they complain that Darty's prices aren't the lowest.[32]

Frederick Reichheld underscores the importance of welcoming complaints when he says that in order to create value for your customers, you have to understand what their viewpoints are, what they want, and what they don't want. Hopefully, they'll tell you while complaining.[33] When we are customers, we hold a particular point of view, but when we represent a product, we appear to have another. As mentioned earlier, customers tend to be blamed by business representatives for product and service failures, while the company tends to get blamed by customers. When it does not acknowledge the customers' point of view, companies seriously underestimate the legitimacy of customer complaints. This makes it difficult for staff to see the link between complaining behaviors and the benefits they receive from customer feedback.

Presented with a set of complaint letters, a group of managers and a group of customers were asked whether they thought the complaints were legitimate. Over half the managers saw the complaints as unreasonable, while over half the customers supported the letter writers as having legitimate complaints. The managers concluded that the customers clearly wanted something for nothing, they were confused, or they were simply dead wrong.[34] If large numbers of managers believe this about complaining customers, is it any wonder they don't want to hear complaints? And wouldn't this attitude permeate the entire organization?

In another research study, the viewpoints held by apparel shoppers and automobile owners whose cars needed repairs were compared to those of apparel salesclerks and car mechanics. All four groups were asked whether a fictional service problem (a car breakdown after a repair) or clothing problem (split seams in pants) was caused by the customer or was the result of poor product quality or defective service repair. Eighty percent of the customers blamed the mechanic for a sloppy repair job, whereas 80 percent of the mechanics indicated that the driver or "other problems" were the cause of the auto breakdown. The split seams were attributed to the manufacturer's poor quality in 87 percent of the cases by the customers. But 64 percent of the apparel salesclerks blamed the customers. Customers bought the wrong size or they were too fat, said the clerks. The researchers also learned that the attitudes of the sales or service people were held only in relationship to the products they sold. In other words, the apparel salesclerks blamed the mechanics for the car repair problems, and the car mechanics blamed the clothing manufacturer for the split seams.[35]

An essential goal of complaint-handling education must include getting everyone in the organization (including the manufacturing side of the business) to understand how very infrequently customers will say anything. One of China's strongest brands is household appliance manufacturer Haier. The company was nearly dead when Zhang Ruimin was assigned the responsibility of turning this state-owned enterprise around in 1984. Zhang had a strong sense of quality management gleaned from all the reading he had done. He believed that customer complaints were major teachers for everyone in the factory. When a customer brought back a Haier refrigerator, Zhang was determined to get one that worked into the customer's hands. He went through the entire inventory of four hundred refrigerators and learned that about eighty of them didn't work at all. Zhang had his employees destroy the defective ones with sledgehammers. They were more than reluctant to do so. The average worker had to work for two years to be able to buy even a nonfunctioning one. Zhang told his employees, "If we don't destroy these refrigerators today, what is to be shattered by the market in the future will be this enterprise!" The refrigerators were smashed to bits.[36]

One hammer is still on display at company headquarters to remind everyone about quality. The story has taken on a legendary status similar to that of the Nordstrom tire story. Today, Haier is ranked as one of China's power brands, with $10 billion in annual sales.[37] In 2006, Haier joined the global top 500 list.[38] A lot of people believe that the Chinese population will buy only on price for nonluxury brands. But Haier clearly demonstrates this is not the case. And it all started with a complaint.

Capitalize on Gaining Strong Customer Ties, Positive Word of Mouth, and Additional Sales

When a customer turns over large sums of money to drive away in a new car, both the buyer and the seller are happy. But the sales process does not really test the mettle of the car dealer. It takes something going wrong to find out how the dealership operates under pressure. Is the dealer still going to smile when the customer reports problems with the car? Is the dealer going to be as responsive to needs as when the customer first inquired about the features of the car? In the automotive industry, customer treatment during car service transactions largely determines whether customers will return to purchase their next car.

Exceeding customer expectations, whether during the initial sale or when a complaint is made or maintenance is required, builds trust between buyers and sellers. This is particularly true in professional-client relationships. If people are pleased with how they are treated by their doctors, lawyers, dentists, psychologists, accountants, or other professionals, a bond is created that builds client loyalty and inspires referrals.[39]

Customers who return products to stores for repairs can be enticed to buy more if they feel good about how they are treated. One of our TMI employees recently called about a malfunctioning laser color printer. She was treated so genially and effectively that she made a spot decision to purchase a second color printer. She would never have done this had she been angered by the treatment she received from the repair department.

This next example was sent to us by e-mail.[40] An attorney for a major telecommunications company went bed shopping. When it came time to sign the ninety-days-same-as-cash, no-interest purchase contract, she asked questions that the salesperson couldn't answer. The manager was called over to help. The manager didn't like the tone of the questions and basically told the attorney that this was the way the contract was and if she didn't like it, she could go elsewhere. The manager then proceeded to yell at the salesperson, telling her that she should have said the same thing. The attorney walked away with the brochure for the Sleep Country mattress that she had wanted to purchase. She sent an e-mail to the owner of the boutique firm and told her what had happened. The owner herself responded the next day, apologized, and had the same bedroom set delivered to the customer at no charge!

Now most would agree that this is probably going overboard, and we wouldn't be relaying this story if there weren't more to it. The next day, someone else heard about this remarkable recovery example and told her mother, who was in the market for a new mattress, about Sleep Country. The mother, who had been planning on going to an upscale retailer, instead bought a similar set from Sleep Country to be delivered to her home the following day. Based on word of mouth, Sleep Country got this second sale that it would have otherwise missed. Sleep Country's Web site says, "Founded in 1991, the company achieves an unmatched level of customer service, excellent values and committed community involvement."[41] That would seem to be the case.

In a major study of seven hundred service incidents from the airline, hotel, and restaurant industries, researchers found that of all positive memories customers have of good service, fully 25 percent started out as some kind of failure in service delivery.[42] The lesson to management is critical. Businesses do not need to run away from service breakdowns. Each company representative has a chance to turn a negative situation into a positive experience for the customer.

Capitalize on Complaints by Creating a Strong Foundation for Total Quality Management

The late quality guru, W. Edwards Deming, described service recovery as putting out fires. "Finding a point out of control, finding the special cause and removing it, is only putting the process back to where it was in the first place. It is not improvement of the process."[43] As such, service recovery is not the same as quality improvement. The fundamental precept of Total Quality Management (TQM) is continuous improvement. Continuous improvement assumes you never achieve total quality; you only move closer to it. It is a process of adapting the company, its services, and its products to the ever-changing marketplace.

To discover what processes and products need to be changed to satisfy customers, companies need information. Complaints can be a major part of that information source. Continuous feedback tells employees how to improve services and expand product lines in ways they may never have thought of themselves. Treating complaints as feedback from a most valuable asset, customers, helps create a customer-focused culture. This, in turn, is the basis of TQM strategies. As Phil Crosby, author of *Quality Is Free*, puts it: "Satisfy the customer, first, last and always."[44]

Service recovery takes care of customers, makes them whole, and ensures that the organization lives up to its service promise. Customer complaints provide the information to improve the organization's quality.

DISCUSSION QUESTIONS

- Under what circumstances do you consider your customers' complaints to be unreasonable? How do you suspect your customers react when they sense you consider their complaints unreasonable?

- How does your company respond to customers who complain about things that are their fault? What are your most common complaints of this type? What is your plan for proactive service recovery or in-place customer education to handle these types of situations?

- Does your organization have any examples of when service or product breakdowns have led to stronger ties with customers?

- How do your customer-facing employees attempt to sell a positive image of your company while they resolve customer problems?

- How much does it cost your organization to resolve customer problems? What additional revenues are realized by retaining disappointed customers? How do you regularly measure these costs and revenues and communicate them through the organization?

- If you have installed toll-free lines, how satisfied are customers with the speed and effectiveness with which you handle those calls? Do you regularly call your own toll-free lines to experience the service you offer on them?

- Have you identified customers who will give you extensive and honest feedback about your products and services? What listening posts do you have set up to capture feedback from your customers?

- What systems are in place to capture customer complaints that staff hear? What are all the different methods you have in place to gather customer feedback?

- Are your feedback systems designed to capture primarily compliments or complaints?

- Which staff members regularly spend time with the customers? How is the information they gather channeled back into the organization?

~ 4 ~

Why Most Customers Don't Complain

"**Why don't** you complain?" It's a simple question with a surprising number of answers. We once heard over 150 discrete reasons from a single group of people as to why they don't complain. When you hear this many reasons rapidly tumbling from the mouths of people, you begin to understand why so many customers walk away without saying anything.

TARP concluded that complaints are actually declining, even when serious problems are faced. This is due to what the company calls "trained hopelessness." TARP's John Goodman says, "The customer has been trained by the system to accept problems as a general business practice—with the prospect of no change, why bother complaining?"[1] Perhaps underscoring Goodman's statement, RightNow Technologies, in its 2007 *Customer Experience Impact Report*, concludes that good service is still a huge differentiator. Fifty-one percent of survey respondents said that outstanding service is what makes them return to a company; 60 percent said that it is the major reason why they recommend a company. RightNow also found that a growing number of people said they won't go back to an organization after a bad experience: 80 percent in 2007, up from 68 percent in 2006.[2]

Here are some of the many reasons people have told us why they do not complain:

- I didn't want to spoil the mood of the party. I wasn't the host, so I didn't want to make a fuss. I was polite at the dinner table but grumbled in the washroom.
- It wasn't worthwhile mentioning it. No one would listen to me anyway.
- It wasn't that bad. After all, compared to people starving around the world, my complaint is nothing.
- They'll ask me for my PIN number, and I can't remember which one it is. I have dozens of account numbers.
- It was really clear: the person I was talking with was incompetent, definitely not top drawer. He wouldn't get the message right anyway.
- They might question my complaint, and I would need to defend myself.
- It would have cost more to complain.
- Their solution was to give me a long-distance number to call.
- I don't trust that they'll keep my complaint confidential.
- I complained once, and they recorded my call and then played it to everyone in the call center.
- I can tell by their body language when they don't want to hear from me.
- Most of the time they get it right. It was just this one situation they messed up.
- I felt sorry for the clerk.
- They told me I'd have to write a letter. Who's got time for that?
- The clerk helping me was really cute, and I didn't want to look like a creep in front of her.
- Other people might have gotten involved; maybe the headwaiter would have come over.
- I had a problem with a "female" product and the person helping me was a man. I was too embarrassed.

- I didn't know who to talk to.
- They would have been rude to me.
- It would have become a big deal.
- They probably would have treated me like a criminal.
- I would have had to wait a long time for a reply.
- I haven't been approved yet for the loan; I'll wait until after that.
- The complaint department was closed over the lunch hour.
- Forget it. I sent an e-mail on their Web site before and heard nothing back.
- They will tell me I need all my original documents, and I'm not sure where they are.
- I'd already thrown away the receipt.
- The person I wanted to complain about might have lost her job.
- I wasn't sure how to talk about this situation. It was too personal.
- Who knows? They might have spit in my food in the kitchen.
- I was partially responsible.
- I would have had to go up to the third floor to the complaint department. I didn't have time.
- I had a problem last week; they would think I am picky or a whiner!
- The last time I complained, nothing happened.
- I know the person. We go back a long time. No way do I want to complain to my friend.
- I'd rather just leave, never come back, and not say anything. It's easier that way.
- I'd probably just get more upset. It's better to just drop it.
- My daughter is a waitress. I know how hard these people work. I'm not going to complain about anybody doing that job.
- If I complain to my son's teacher, she might take it out on him in the classroom.
- If I complain about that person, he may come after me. You know how nuts people can get today.
- I had five problems. No way am I going to complain about all of them. They'll never listen. I'll just mention one of them.
- They could have made my situation worse.

It's a rather overwhelming list and makes one appreciate why large numbers of people who have complaints don't say anything.

How Complaint Handlers Tell Customers Not to Complain

Complaint handling that discourages customers from speaking up includes all or some of the following reactions: unfeeling apologies and nothing more, rejection, blame, promises that are not delivered, no response at all, rude treatment, being passed on to someone else, avoidance of personal responsibility, nonverbal rejection, a customer interview with repetitive questions, or a demeaning session that feels like an interrogation.

- *Apologies and nothing more:* A customer walks into a restaurant and leans against a freshly painted wall, leaving a paint smear on his coat. All the staff he talks to say they are sorry that this happened but make no attempt to remedy the situation in any way. "Sorry." The customer says, "They're very good at saying 'I'm sorry,' but they don't do anything. 'Sorry' isn't good enough."
- *Rejection:* The rejection usually starts with an apology. "Sorry, but there's nothing I can do. Next!" If the customer protests, she hears, "Look, I said there was nothing I can do. Now may I help the next customer?" Customer reaction: "They will take my money. That they can do, but they won't help when something goes wrong."
- *Blame:* The customer is blamed for the complaint. "You must have handled it wrong." "You should have complained earlier." "You brought the wrong guarantee." "You didn't send the guarantee card in." Customer reaction: "Their guarantees don't mean a thing."
- *Promises that are not delivered:* The service rep promises to correct a mistake in a timely manner but does not. This may be in sharp contrast to advertisements. Customer response: "They definitely don't walk their talk. I wonder what else they don't do."

- **No response at all:** This happens more frequently than you imagine. Company representatives do not return telephone calls or respond to written complaints. Customers sometimes call back several times, each time being told they will be helped, and nothing happens. The customer says, "Forget it. These people just want my money. Then they're gone."

- **Rude treatment:** Basic politeness goes out the window; many customers are handled brusquely. People are insulted; in extreme cases, they're made to feel like criminals. "No one else has complained about that," the company representative may say. (This does not mean that someone has not felt like complaining; it just means no one has complained yet.) Customers promise themselves, "I'll never have anything to do with these people in the future—unless I'm on my deathbed and need them."

- **Being passed on to someone else:** "I can't help you. You have to go upstairs [talk to someone else, write your comments down and send them to another planet]." "We are just the distributor; you'll have to contact the manufacturer." The customer laments, "Why do they make it so difficult? Don't they want me to be their customer?"

- **Avoidance of personal responsibility:** "I didn't do it. It wasn't my fault." "I'd like to help you, but I don't handle this." "I just work here; I don't make the rules." "I didn't serve you; it was my colleague." "It was our suppliers [our delivery service, the mail carrier, our stupid policies, my ridiculous manager, the phases of the moon], and what did you expect anyway? It was on sale." The customer judges, "These people are buck passers. No one wants to take responsibility, so they give me some junior assistant who can't do a blasted thing!"

- **Nonverbal rejection:** Sometimes people being complained to frown, act impatient, and in effect tell the customers they are wasting their time. The reps give the impression that they have better things to do than to listen to customers and their measly complaints. This is never said out loud, but the atmosphere sings this message loud and clear. The customer concludes, "They say they want to hear my feedback, but they sure don't make it pleasant for me."

- *Customer interview:* The customer is asked a long list of questions before any attempt is made to help. "What is your name? Your address? When did you buy this article? Who helped you? Who told you that? Did you pay cash? Where is your receipt? Do you have a customer registration number? What is your mother's maiden name?" Maybe the company needs the answers to some of these questions, but they are not a good way to start the service recovery process. The customer thinks, "They are holding me hostage when I just want to get my money's worth." Frequently, the customer interview leads to customer interrogation.

- *Customer interrogation:* The customer is subjected to the third degree, which stems from doubt about the customer's motivations, competence, or right to complain. "How can I be sure that what you say is true? Are you sure you bought it here? Did you follow the instructions? Did you read the thirty-page fine-print document that lists all the exceptions? Did you even read any of the instructions? Are you sure you didn't drop it?" The interrogation frequently ends with, "Anyone can make a claim like that. You just wouldn't believe the number of people who tell us all kinds of stories." The customer says, [censored].

If customers are poorly treated when they complain, the service failure they experienced is magnified. Customers are not dense. They feel the rudeness directly from frontline staff. They also pick up on subtle clues that tell them not to complain. Sometimes several clues come at them at once. Emotionally, the customer is out of balance, and even a little product or service problem becomes a huge service failure. If customers persist in complaining in the face of all these disincentives to complain, they may be on their way to creating serious problems for the company.

How Company Systems Tell
Customers Not to Complain

Companies tell their customers not to complain by making it difficult for them to know where or how to complain. Experiment by visiting a number of business Web sites and see how many display their telephone contact numbers in such a way that you don't have to dig halfway through the earth's crust to find them. Charles Underhill, with the Council of Better Business Bureaus, Inc., told a conference in The Hague about visiting twenty major Web sites prior to his speech and not finding a single site where the word "complaint" or "problem" was used. Underhill blames this approach on marketing departments that don't like to admit that customers are anything but satisfied.[3] Zappos.com makes a point of putting its 800 toll-free number on every single page of its Web site. It may be the only e-tailer that does this. If it's not the only one, it is definitely one of the few.

Complaining frequently has a high hassle factor attached to it. Customers who go out of their way to publicly attack businesses tend to be alienated from the marketplace. Some feel unfairly treated and move to this position of alienation. Consider the following example, which is a typical example of someone who attempted to complain to an organization and ended up telling huge numbers of people because of how he was treated.

Mitchell Gooze is a professional speaker,[4] a fact that becomes important a little later in this story. Gooze bought an LG VCR/DVD combo player/recorder. LG is a Korean firm that used to be known as Lucky Goldstar. It describes itself as a major global force in electronics information and communications products. Gooze's DVD combo worked great for about nine months and then stopped operating. About a month later, Gooze got around to calling the 800 number listed on the company's Web site. (Janelle tried locating the number herself and after about thirty clicks could not find it, but then she wasn't quite as motivated as Gooze.)

Gooze was happy with the company's response except the amount of time it would take to fix his DVD player. The device was under warranty and Gooze could send it back, but it would take three to five weeks to fix. About a month after he sent it back, LG called saying that it couldn't repair the device because he hadn't sent in $69 to cover the service charge for warranty service. Gooze had not been told about this. He gave LG his credit card so he could get the device repaired while the company still had possession. About a week later, his device was returned to him, still broken. He called LG again and was informed that the credit card hadn't gone through. He asked how he could possibly have known that since he was told that it was okay. The rep told him that he should have checked his credit card bill and suggested resending the device, but he would need to send $199 (more than the original cost of the device) because it was no longer under warranty, now being over a year old. Gooze protested at the unfairness of this statement since he had originally sent it when it was under warranty. He got nowhere fast.

Gooze didn't give up easily. He asked to speak to a supervisor but was told that LG had no supervisors in the United States and that whomever he talked with would tell him the same thing. Gooze, a very pleasant man, says that at that moment, he became an "assassin." There is no way to contact LG in the United States except by calling this one 800 number, so through its systems, LG has effectively cut itself off from what is happening with its customers. Gooze now features this story in a keynote speech and has written about it in his e-zines.

LG is getting punished in another way as well, and the sad thing is, it'll never know about it unless someone in Korea reads this book or hears one of Gooze's speeches. Gooze bought a new DVD player— definitely not the LG brand. His son recently set up a household, and Gooze helped him get started by buying about $5,000 worth of new non-LG appliances. For a sum of $130, LG has lost thousands of dollars in sales from just this one customer. Gooze said that he would have liked to buy LG appliances because he likes them. But he'll never buy LG again. As he says, "You love it when they act like they're human and hate it when they don't."

Whenever an organization fails to follow through, a message is sent about complaining. And when customers are betrayed on a guarantee, an even clearer statement is sent as well. Explained below are some of the ways customers are told not to complain.

People Do Not Know Where or How to Complain

Many retail shops do not have clear signs telling customers where Customer Service is located. Sometimes service reps are not available to hear what customers have to say. Customers who have feedback to provide a manager may be told to go to Customer Service, which handles product exchanges and is not organized to feed complaints or suggestions for change back to management.

Customers may finally find a telephone number but they have to go through a phone menu that has nothing to do with handling problems or they reach a company operator who has no idea where to direct the complaint. The operator may connect customers to anyone, who will then send them to someone else who also does not know where complaints are to be directed. Customers finally get frustrated and demand to talk to the top person in the company, which is undoubtedly not necessary to solve their original complaints.

You can experiment yourself. The next time you are shopping in a mall, go into a few large department stores and ask where you can make a complaint. Ask around and find out how many people who work in the store know where to send you. See how many make an effort to handle you directly and immediately. Call companies in your area and tell the people who answer the phone that you have a complaint about one of their products and ask to whom you should speak. Or call a large company, perhaps a Fortune 100 company, and ask whomever you reach on the phone for the address where you can send a complaint letter. Based on our experience, unless you get very lucky, you probably are not going to get quick, knowledgeable answers to your questions. Then conduct a similar test with your own organization.

Complaining Has a High Hassle Factor Attached to It

Customers may be required to talk to someone who can handle a complaint during specified hours. These hours may be when customers are normally working. Customers may be asked to fill out complicated forms, or the forms may not have room to list special problems or complaints. On the web, a series of drop-down menus may force customers to choose options that do not describe their situations, and no "other" option is available.

Some companies are at greater risk for giving the impression that complaining is a major bother. For example, many high-tech companies farm out product support to subcontractors. Customers are unaware that they are not speaking to the company that produced the product. For example, customers may call the support line of a software company to report a product defect, which starts the clock ticking on a thirty-day free support period. But what if the customers do not need support at this time and only want to report a bug in the software? They are told that they have reached product support, not the manufacturer. To report a software bug, they have to contact the software company directly. However, the software company does not know where to direct the caller to complain. (Can all of this happen? It did to one of the authors.) What then happens to the customers' motivation to provide feedback to the software company? Companies that subcontract their support must carefully coordinate their complaint policies so they are seamlessly executed by outside vendors.

Companies Do Not Follow Through

Sometimes all the right systems are in place to help customers, yet after the airing of a complaint, nobody acts on it. Customers get discouraged in the face of failed responses and are likely not to complain in the future. There are several explanations why customers get no response to their complaints. Sometimes a customer-facing employee will hear a complaint and then not pass it on. Many customer-facing staff have never been told to pass along customer feedback, so they do not even think it is part of their job. In fact, many of them have been told to tell customers to contact Customer Service directly when they have a complaint. When pushed to pass along the complaint, staff may say, "No one listens to us."

Organizational behavior experts have found that just as customers do not like to complain, staff do not like to pass complaints up the organizational hierarchy. Staff apparently feel that when they pass on bad news to management, they are criticizing company policymakers. So they downplay the complaint, blame the customer, or simply do not pass the information along. In fact, Professor Alan Andreasen at Georgetown University writes that just as customer-facing staff do not like to pass complaints along, managers do not like to hear about customer dissatisfaction.[5] Perhaps the manager frowns or appears annoyed when hearing a complaint. How many staff want to face that? Changing these attitudes about complaints throughout an entire organization will eventually get the word out to customers that the company wants to hear their opinions.

In a broad-based survey, service employees were asked about the amount of encouragement they receive from their managers to report customer feedback or complaints. About a third of the employees felt their managers encouraged them to report customer feedback. But more than 17 percent said they received no encouragement at all, and another 23 percent reported receiving only a little encouragement.[6] When we ask managers directly whether they want to learn what their customers say, they all report encouraging their staff to speak up. Something isn't lining up with the research.

Surveys of consumer affairs department employees suggest that the more complaints the department receives in relation to other kinds of consumer communications, the more isolated that department will become from the rest of the company. Consumer affairs departments become the keepers of the dirty secret of customer dissatisfaction. This kind of vicious circle of consumer complaints suggests that the more complaints a company receives, the less the company wants to hear them, which no doubt means that the company is less energetic in managing them.[7]

Guarantees: A Hassle or an Encouragement to Complain?

Guarantees can be a huge subset of high-hassle complaining. Frequently, guarantees have so many requirements that most people give up before trying to implement them. Customers may be required to send in the registration card right after purchase. Many times the original packing is required to return the item. In most cases a receipt is required, and sometimes a credit card receipt is not sufficient. Customers are forced to send the product to a distant location. Only part of the product may be covered by the guarantee. The guarantee may apply only if certain restrictive conditions are met. It sometimes takes eons to repair the item—so long, in fact, that customers give up and buy a new one rather than wait. It's safe to say that customers perceive many guarantees to be marketing ploys, which they can be. They make customers feel as if they have some protection, but the reality is that guarantees often are not used unless the product is very expensive. Nonetheless, 91 percent of consumers interviewed in one study said that return guarantees were an important part of their decision about where to purchase.[8] It's likely that a majority of customers never intend to cash in on the guarantee, but the promise makes them feel more secure about their purchases.

Jon Schwartz, aka Vinny Verelli, had an interesting experience with Iomega. Years ago, he purchased one of the company's external drives that used removable media to back up his considerable number of large music files. He ended up having numerous drives replaced—all according to the fairly generous guarantee. So, the guarantee worked insofar as replacements were obtained. Unfortunately, the cost of getting these replacements made the guarantee virtually useless. First, Schwartz had to spend hours on tech calls. Technicians would run him through all the prescribed tests and then say, "It's a bad drive. Send it in." As an experienced Iomega "bad drive" person, Schwartz knew this. He even bought a second drive in anticipation of one going bad so he'd have a backup for the bad drive. The refurbished drive would soon go bad, and he would then switch to his backup, which eventually also went bad. This went on for five years; Schwartz couldn't switch brands because he had his music files on Iomega's storage disks, which could be read only by Iomega drives. When CDs became available and Schwartz could back up his files on them, he did and vowed never to buy Iomega products again. Ever.

Nice people and guarantees that work aren't sufficient to maintain customer loyalty. Products have to work as well. Just replacing a product for another that causes problems doesn't make happy customers. As researchers at Deakin University indicate, focusing on the process of recovery by itself isn't sufficient. "Relying purely on the guarantee compensation to recover the customer may not satisfy the customer."[9] No doubt Jon Schwartz would agree with them.

Here is a sample of a real guarantee.

Customer Satisfaction Policy

We are committed to your total satisfaction. Unopened product accompanied with original sales documentation may be returned for a full refund within 30 days of purchase. Opened products cannot be returned unless defective, with some important exceptions; please ask your representative. Defective software may be returned for replacement within 30 days of purchase when accompanied with original sales documentation . . .

Before returning any product please call our customer service department for a Return Merchandise Authorization (RMA) number and instructions.

We want to know how this policy results in total satisfaction as promised in its opening sentence. How many people buy a product and then not open it before finding out it is not what they want? And what if the product is not defective but the customer wants to return it anyway? You might say, "Wouldn't a software company go bankrupt if it took back opened software that was in good operating condition? What if computer users have already installed the hardware on their computer?" Actually, most software companies can tell when a product has been installed if the computers are online, which they almost always are. The companies can simply render their software unusable over the Internet.

We say to all companies that have guarantees like this: "Fine. But be prepared for some off-the-wall complaints when you guarantee total satisfaction." Promising total satisfaction is generally misleading and can make an already alienated buyer even more cynical. Personal taste makes total satisfaction very difficult to deliver. For example, how do you guarantee total satisfaction with the temperature of a hotel swimming pool? Pools can easily be too hot or too cold for different people.

A famous German designer company guarantees that it will fix any of its writing implements free of charge—forever. This sounds great until you learn there is an automatic $20 service fee for each repair, and your pen or pencil must be shipped by insured transport, adding an additional 20 percent to the total charge. This "free service guarantee" amounts to about 15 percent of the total cost of the pen. When you are buying the pen, the guarantee is proudly marched out, but nothing is said about the cost of implementing the guarantee.

Effective Guarantees

What is an effective guarantee? It must, above all, assure customers that if they are dissatisfied, the company will be there to help. From a marketing point of view, a guarantee is a statement to consumers that the company trusts its own work so much that it's willing to guarantee it. Consumer uncertainty is reduced. Even for companies that have reputations of the highest quality, an explicit guarantee is still preferred by consumers. They like matters spelled out for them. Offering an explicit guarantee may not necessarily drive more traffic to your door if you already have an outstanding reputation. But, even if you are doing a great job and consumers know this about you, you'll have more communication with your customers by offering a concrete guarantee.[10]

An effective guarantee does not mean that customers will always get a brand new product or money back whenever they express dissatisfaction. But it does mean that they will have the feeling that the company is there to help them achieve satisfaction with a new hotel room, a functioning computer, or a fresh hamburger. Jochen Wirtz at the National University of Singapore has empirically tested which is the best type of guarantee to offer: an effective guarantee that describes the attributes being guaranteed or a "no-holds barred" guarantee. An effective guarantee does not have to be unconditional, but it needs to be specific, simple, and clear. A guarantee of this type says to the customer: "Give us a try. If we do not live up to your satisfaction, we will make it up to you by refunding your money or replacing or fixing the product. We will not abandon you."

His conclusion: full-satisfaction guarantees are no better than attribute-based guarantees. The major reason for this, Wirtz reports, is that consumers are uncertain about what a full-satisfaction guarantee covers, and this leads to a "discounting of their expected value."[11] This point is important, and we have included it in this book because many managers are reluctant to offer guarantees when they are nervous about customers who cheat. More managers need to understand that guaranteeing specific attributes is just as effective as, in essence, writing a blank-check type of guarantee, the kind that frankly this scares most managers. This also means, as Wirtz suggests, that organizations should conduct research to find out which attributes consumers would like guaranteed. Good advice. Here's an idea: maybe it's what they complain about.

Family Fare, mentioned in the introduction, guarantees a clean washroom. If it's not clean, the customer gets a free cup of coffee. Family Fare doesn't have to give out much coffee, and it's not that the company minds giving away the coffee. The guarantee affects staff behavior so that even executives will mop restroom floors if they are dirty.

Some products may demand restrictions on their guarantees. When such restrictions are in place, however, companies have to be careful with the use of the phrase *total satisfaction*. Car companies, for example, cannot replace a used car with a brand-new one at any time at any customer's demand. But a fast-food hamburger chain can easily replace an unsatisfactory hamburger.

Carl Sewell, a car dealer and the author of the perennial best-selling *Customers for Life*, offers a satisfaction guarantee that has limits but is still effective. Sewell Village Cadillac has relationships with customers whose families buy dozens of cars from the dealership, and it doesn't want to say no (within limits) to customers like that.[12] Sewell says that if a customer buys a car from Sewell Village Cadillac, takes it home, and shows it to his or her spouse, who hates the color, he will gladly take the car back, no questions asked. But if someone buys a car, drives it around for ten days and then learns he or she could have bought it cheaper at another dealer, Sewell will not take it back. A deal is a deal, Sewell says, and the dealership's satisfaction guarantee does not include refunds in such cases.[13]

Easy product exchanges have contributed to customers' becoming champions of Nordstrom, the high-end retailer, even calling themselves Nordies. Nordstrom customers spend more, pay higher prices, and tell everyone they know to shop there. Nordstroms no-hassle guarantees and refunds more than compensate for their higher prices. In the early 1990s, Nordstrom sold more per square foot than any other department store in the United States. When Nordstrom began to develop the chain out of the Seattle area, pundits had already predicted the demise of the large, full-price department store. Almost immediately, Nordstrom shot to the front of the pack with high profits and astounding customer loyalty. If you give customers what they want and handle their complaints when they emerge, it is possible to be successful in almost any market.

Many hotels are beginning to jump on the guarantee bandwagon. Those that do are enjoying a marketing edge as a result.[14] Eric Pfeffer, president of Howard Johnson Franchise Systems, uses statistics to support his hotel's guarantee. He says that a guest with a complaint that is satisfactorily resolved is 92 percent more likely to return to the hotel. A guest whose problem is not solved is less than 50 percent likely to book a room again.[15]

Empowerment is the key to making guarantees work. Customer-facing employees have to know about the company's guarantee, feel comfortable with complaining customers, and understand that delivering satisfied customers is their most important job. McDonald's uses a video training session with role-played examples to teach managers and front-line staff how to carry out the McDonald's guarantee.[16]

Components of an Extraordinary Guarantee

Christopher Hart, who introduced the notion of a "high-octane" guarantee, claims that every company that offers an extraordinary guarantee outpaces its competitors and dramatically improves its financial performance.[17] "In its strongest form, a guarantee of this type promises exceptional, uncompromising quality and customer satisfaction. It backs that promise with a payout that has few strings attached and is intended to fully recapture the customer's goodwill."[18]

The purpose of an extraordinary guarantee is not just to make sure your customer's spending with you is safe but also to make sure your organization learns from satisfaction failures and then plugs those holes. It's clearly not an approach for every organization, but for those that take a step in that direction, the results can be phenomenal. Hart relates one example: Northeast Delta Dental. As a result of its extraordinary guarantee, this dental insurance company charges 20 percent higher fees, and its market share has gone from 25 percent in 1995 to over 80 percent in 2006.[19]

Tom Jones, CEO of Epsilon, a database marketing company, once wrote a refund check of $210,000, the entire client's fee. The company had instituted a guarantee promising unconditional satisfaction or a 100 percent refund. Jones says he returned the client's money to put pressure on his team internally; it wasn't done as a marketing ploy. He wanted his entire team to find out what it had to do to offer that level of service. Jones states, "Call me crazy, but I was excited. There are few moments of opportunity where a CEO can create major change through a single, symbolic act. This was one of them." The customer didn't even want to take the money back. Jones insisted. You can imagine how this news spread throughout Epsilon. Jones says, "That $210,000 was the best investment I could have made."[20] Jones is hitting on a point that other people have made: a service guarantee also acts as an internal change agent. It gets employees to focus on meeting the terms of the guarantee and helps define the terms of staff empowerment—namely, do what it takes to deliver the terms of the guarantee.[21]

Christopher Hart describes an extraordinary guarantee as a marketing investment in an organization's good reputation. He says it has three parts:

1. *The promise:* a clear "no-holds barred" pledge with no weasel words
2. *The payout:* a clear statement of what customers will get that leaves them thinking "wow"
3. *The payout process:* a clear statement of a hassle-free process to collect on the guarantee[22]

In Hart's opinion, the process also needs to be proactive ("We found a mistake, even if you didn't") and empathic ("We're sorry and we don't want this to happen again").

When customers ask to have your company's guarantee implemented, be sure to use the opportunity to win back their confidence. Don't just fulfill the terms of the guarantee. Janelle once asked for money back on a "no-questions-asked" guarantee, and the money was handed over, no questions asked, no comments made—and no effort made to win her future business. This was a wasted opportunity. At a minimum, the representative could have said, "We realize we have a 'no-questions-asked' guarantee, and so we respect your not telling us why you were dissatisfied. But it would be very helpful to us to learn why. Your feedback could help us with the rest of our customers." A statement like that would have recaptured a lot of Janelle's confidence.

Finally, a word of caution about guarantees and complaints. Domino's, the famous pizza maker, used to guarantee that if a telephone-ordered pizza was not delivered in thirty minutes, the pizza would be free. Many readers may be aware that Domino's got into trouble with this guarantee because the company was held liable when some of its drivers had accidents while speeding to meet the thirty-minute guarantee. Domino's also discovered that many people ordering pizzas felt guilty cashing in on the guarantee when the pizza was just a little late. Domino's slowed down its speedy drivers (now the guarantee is an estimated thirty minutes) and emphasizes its Total Satisfaction Guarantee: "If for any reason you are dissatisfied with your Domino's Pizza dining experience, we will re-make your pizza or refund your money." Domino's keeps its unique selling point and still receives customer feedback about its delivery service. Today Domino's, described as a megabrand, operates in more than fifty-five countries, is the world's leading pizza restaurant chain, has over 145,000 employees delivering more than 1.3 million pizzas per day, and earns gross revenues of $1.4 billion per year.[23]

What About the Cheaters?

Hart is careful to point out that you can't just make an offer of "100 percent satisfaction or your money back" without putting in-house processes into place. He points out that most extraordinary guarantees are gutted by financial and legal departments that want to put in so many exceptions to the guarantees to protect their companies that the guarantees are no longer extraordinary.

Our experience from working with companies is that it doesn't take an entire legal department to prevent a guarantee from being put in place. It takes just one skittish manager who is afraid of all those cheaters running wild in the marketplace just waiting to take advantage of guarantees. After all, we are fully aware that people do shoplift, as evidenced by all the security devices placed on clothing. And most retailers have security cameras attached to their ceilings to catch sticky-fingered shoppers. We are also aware that a lot of people think the problem of stealing is much worse than it probably is. Whenever we bring up this topic in a workshop, people will tell us, "Oh, you can't offer such a guarantee. Everyone will cheat." So we ask them, "Would you?" And they say, "Of course not." We then ask, "How come you're so different from all the people that you think are cheaters?" It's something to think about.

Stretching guarantees to a maximum, some people buy a product, use it for a period of time, and then return it for a full refund. Hart writes about a Hampton Inn policy that encouraged customers to regularly take advantage of the inn's guarantee of 100 percent satisfaction or no charge. A truck driver allegedly said he liked Hampton Inn because he could stay there for free.[24] TMI sells leather calendar binders and has gotten its share of people who used these products for twenty years and then asked for replacement binders because the stitching came undone.

Jochen Wirtz, quoted above, has looked extensively at consumer cheating on service guarantees. He has identified situations that inspire customers to cheat and situations that make the customers afraid to cheat. He has measured the likelihood to cheat against what is to be gained. Wirtz also examined personality variables, comparing those who have strong tendencies to cheat anywhere with people who never engage in cheating behaviors. Remember our earlier statistic: somewhere between 1 and 4 percent of customers cheat with their complaints. Here's what Wirtz discovered: people who are your loyal customers and are satisfied with what you do for them and tend to have pretty good morals in place are the least likely to cheat. No surprise there. This implies that customers who have no loyalty toward you, who don't like what you have done for them (perhaps feeling that you owe them something), and who tend to take advantage of situations where cheating is easy, are the people most likely to cheat.[25] The lesson to be learned from this is to get to know your customers and do well by them. If you discover that some of your customers are going to cheat regardless of what you do, such as the truck driver who stayed at the Hampton Inn, it might be a good idea to fire those customers. (Hampton Inn could tell the customer that he can no longer book rooms because it is impossible for the inn to satisfy him.)

What does all this suggest? You can offer full money-back guarantees without fearing that your loyal customers are going to cheat at any higher level than they currently do. And you will reap the benefit of customers' feeling more confident about doing business with you. If customers feel this confidence with you, they will be more likely to give you repeat business, which will drive down the chances that they will cheat because they'll feel guilty if they cheat while they are regular customers. If you are still worried about cheaters, Wirtz recommends setting up your strongest guarantees for your most loyal customers. "Perhaps service guarantees could be incorporated into a firm's membership or loyalty program and even be positioned as an additional benefit of that scheme."[26]

The Difficulty of Complaints
in Unequal Relationships

Some industries must deal with dependent or unequal relationships—real or imagined—with their customers. How do patients complain, for example, when the person they complain to may be responsible for helping them get well? The health-care industry is by no means the only industry that faces this complaint challenge. How do parents complain about teachers when those teachers can then take it out on their children? How do policyholders complain to insurance companies when their files might be deliberately lost or moved to the bottom of the pile to be processed? How can staff members or political appointees complain to their boss or the head of government when they fear losing their jobs? How can hotel guests complain in the middle of their stays when they feel threatened that things may not go right for the rest of the trip or that staff may discuss their behavior in unflattering terms at morning meetings? How can spouses complain to their partners if they're afraid they will be abandoned? How do people getting their hair styled complain when the stylist may take revenge on whatever hair remains? How many people risk complaining to tax authorities such as the U.S. Internal Revenue Service if they might trigger an audit? And how can suppliers complain to merchandising departments when they fear losing accounts if they say anything?

This lack of parity is the bedrock of relationships between employers and employees. Only recently has whistle-blower legislation in the United States and other countries attempted to protect people who speak up.[27] Most analysts seem to agree that even with protective legislation, career damage is significant for anyone who alerts the public about corporate or government misdeeds.[28] Institutions that are based on dependency relationships with customers have to be particularly careful in how complaints are received if they are to be received at all. Research demonstrates that in these situations, consumers prefer to say nothing at all rather than alienate the provider that they are dependent on.[29]

Any business that provides more personal services, from a hospital to a beauty salon, must strongly communicate that it wants to hear from customers. Roadblocks that stop people from complaining need to be removed, and when customers (even when they are patients, clients, or patrons) do complain, they need to be assured in words and behavior that nothing negative will happen to them. The health-care industry needs to pay particular attention to this issue as it has only recently adjusted its mind-set regarding patients as customers. If you scan the thousands of documents on this subject on the Internet, you will find a great deal of disagreement among health-care professionals on whether patients should even be considered customers. Many medical people object because they say it turns medicine too much into a "business." To deny the business side of the health-care industry, however, is to ignore reality. Most medical doctors function as legal corporations these days.

If pushed too far with bad treatment, customers who have complaints will assume they have nothing to lose and resort to legal action. Vanderbilt University advisors say, "Patients frequently tell us the reason they went to a lawyer was because their health professionals showed no concern, no warmth, wouldn't listen, wouldn't talk or wouldn't answer questions."[30] By any standard, that's horrible complaint handling. Dr. Philip Greenland suggests a simple question to remind the health-care industry of the importance of empathy in dependency relationships: "What if the patient were your mother?"[31]

An elderly woman—we'll call her Lucy—was hospitalized and unfortunately had her chart confused with another patient's. As a result of this mix-up, an unwarranted medical procedure was performed on Lucy, and her lung collapsed. A collapsed lung is extremely painful and dangerous, especially for a person in her late seventies. A few days later, with staff tiptoeing carefully around the issue and lots of questions being asked by her children, Lucy was finally told about the mistake. Hospital staff also told her that her stay would need to be extended for at least another week, and they did not offer to waive those charges. Lucy's children were aghast. They insisted that their mother take legal action in what was an obvious case of malpractice.

Lucy was clear: she didn't want to sue. Her reasoning was that the staff had made a mistake, she didn't want to upset them by calling attention to what they had done, and they shouldn't be sued for a mistake. "They didn't mean to do it," she said. And she really liked her primary care physician and didn't want to make him feel bad. The hospital's legal department had a policy in place that prevented staff from talking with patients who were going to sue, though there was no indication that Lucy was planning that. As a result, the hospital staff were warned that they should not talk with Lucy about the collapsed lung—or about anything else either.

After a few days of zero communication from the staff, except minimal daily greetings, Lucy went from feeling isolated to rejected to insulted to annoyed and finally to angry. You can guess what Lucy finally decided to do. She was awarded a tidy sum from her legal action. If the hospital staff had continued to communicate with her, apologized, and observed basic courtesy after such a traumatic incident, legal action would have been avoided in this case. Research conducted by A. J. Kellett found that physicians who own up to a problem, apologize, and then explain what happened are sued significantly less frequently than physicians who do not apologize. It would have worked for Lucy![32]

DISCUSSION QUESTIONS

- What are the ways, both direct and subtle, your company tells customers not to complain?

- How does your company value the departments or people who handle customer complaints?

- How ready are your staff to pass along complaints to upper management? What clues, if any, do your managers send to customer-facing staff not to pass along bad news?

- What system does your company have in place to ensure that once a complaint has been heard, it is passed along to an appropriate person or committee so the organization can learn from customer feedback?

- What dependency or unequal relationships exist within your organization? How are people who feel dependent upon someone else able to give appropriate feedback without being threatened?

- What kind of guarantees do you offer? Do your guarantees make it easy for customers to complain? Does everyone in the organization understand your guarantees and know how to implement them?

- When customers ask for your guarantees to be implemented, do your staff use the occasion to try to regain the customers' confidence?

- In what ways does your organization create customer dependency relationships that may discourage complaints?

~ 5 ~

In the Mind of the Complaining Customer

 When customers have problems with products they have purchased, few will bother to complain if the products are low in price. The research group TARP found that somewhere between 1 and 5 percent will complain to management or headquarters—that is, to someone who will or can do something about the problem.[1] About half the customers who are dissatisfied will just walk away and not return. What about the other 45 percent? They will complain to customer-facing staff. So, if service representatives are inclined to take care of customers and are empowered to do so, there's a good chance that many of these customers can be retained.

For small-ticket items, only about 4 percent of disassatified customers complain to retail outlets; if they purchased a large-ticket item, about half of dissatisfied consumers will complain to customer-facing staff and between 5 and 10 percent escalate to local management or corporate offices. Having readily accessible toll-free numbers will double the number of calls to corporate offices. But TARP estimates that senior executives receive only one out of one hundred to five hundred complaints that come into headquarters.[2] TARP, incidentally, has replicated its research in almost every industry and in more than twenty countries, and these figures hold across the marketplace and around the world.

The types of problems people encounter affect whether or not they will complain. People are much more likely to complain (between 50 to 75 percent) if the problem causes monetary loss. If customers have a problem with service, they are even less likely to say anything compared to having a problem with a product. In other words, customers don't particularly like complaining about people and their behaviors. The types of staff behavior that might do more damage to loyalty in the long run (such as incompetence, poor quality, and mistreatment of customers) are less likely to be brought up (between 5 and 30 percent).[3]

Dissatisfied Customers Speak Out to the World

If customers do not say anything to the company, does this mean that they do not speak up? Absolutely not. And they are much more likely to talk when they aren't in the presence of someone who will confront them directly. These statistics are perhaps the most significant. Dissatisfied customers will tell between eight and ten people about the bad service they received. One in five will tell twenty people.[4]

Many people are puzzled by the statistics generated about complaining customers because they do not always seem to match up. Part of the variance in the statistics can be accounted for by whether the product is expensive or inexpensive, whether customers purchased services or products, how much competition the product or service faces, whether customers bought nationally recognized branded products or generic products, the level of dissatisfaction experienced by customers, the socioeconomic group of the customers, the relative costs and benefits of complaining, the tendency on the part of individual consumers to complain, and the importance of the purchase to the customers. These are a lot of variables, so we should not expect all the research to come up with identical numbers, especially numbers that are unique to various industries. In general, however, the huge amount of research continually demonstrates high levels of consumer dissatisfaction about which customers consistently do not complain. As researchers for a study published in *Harvard Business Review* concluded, "While we cannot claim that our figures have no upward or downward bias, business should be alarmed at the amount of unresolved dissatisfaction that apparently exists in the marketplace."[5]

We recommend that rather than attaching yourself to any specific set of statistics, know that throughout the years the overall statistics have not changed much, and they do not look good for businesses trying to learn about the degree of dissatisfaction that exists after customers face problems. Read some of the research that is easily available on the Web to find out what has been learned about your industry. For example, if your company is a utility, you can look at complaints sent to the New York State Office of Consumer Services. Every month since June 2000, this office has produced a well-formatted PDF utilities report. You can even compare your statistics against other utilities.[6] You can also find statistics about managed health care, railroads, Internet content, special education, homebuilders, the media, airlines, insurance, small businesses, and citizen complaints about the police. These statistics have been gathered in the United States (in some cases, state by state), Northern Ireland, Australia, Canada, Hong Kong, Malaysia, the United Kingdom, London, and many other areas. In addition, the Better Business Bureau tracks complaints by industry. And this is just in English!

Noncomplainers Must Be Factored into Complaint Statistics

Even though complaints can tell a business how it is performing in the marketplace, many companies hide the bad news of complaining customers from themselves. If it's true, as frequently cited, that twenty-six out of twenty-seven service customers do not complain in such a way that people in charge hear about what goes wrong, then to get an accurate count of dissatisfied customers, service companies should multiply the number of complaints they receive by twenty-seven.[7] One hundred formal complaints equals a potential twenty-seven hundred dissatisfied customers in the service industry.

Find out how many people tend not to complain about your service or product offering. Then choose a factor estimating how many dissatisfied customers the complaining customer represents. For example, perhaps in your industry, 10 percent typically complain, so each complaint represents nine others from customers who aren't saying anything. (TARP provides numbers that should make the hair rise on the back of most executives' necks—for example, if corporate offices receive twenty complaints about a policy, that could mean between six hundred and one thousand customers are unhappy. John Goodman in his speeches says that he has observed situations where the ratios were as high as two thousand dissatisfied customers to one complaining customer whose message gets through to corporate offices.)[8] Now make another guess, based on your research or on customer trends, about how many of those nine you will lose because they didn't speak up. Then you can begin to estimate potential revenue gains by fixing service problems.

If you think that your customers are part of the group that always speaks up and that none of this applies to you, you really ought to look at your industry carefully. And remember, most industry complaint statistics require that the complaint be filed in a particular way. Normally, customers can't just tell agencies their complaints over the phone. If you believe that your customers don't complain because you offer such great products and service, you ought to think that one through as well. Janelle and her husband had this brought home to them while traveling in Germany and stopping at a charming country inn. Janelle's husband, Jeffrey, a very experimental eater, chose an exotically named fish on the menu that the waiter assured him was excellent. The fish came to the table basically raw, with the head still attached. Janelle and Jeffrey began to discuss the issue of how people don't complain even when they are completely dissatisfied while Jeffrey hid the fish in a potted plant nearby—so the waiter wouldn't feel bad. When the waiter returned, he saw that the fish plate was completely clean—even the bones were gone! "How was it?" he asked. "Fine. It was delicious." So the restaurant never learned that it's probably not such a good idea to recommend that particular fish to Americans.

We've told this story to dozens of people, always to their great delight. Dissatisfaction is a more popular topic of conversation than satisfaction. The fish story wouldn't be nearly as appealing if we talked about the most fantastically prepared fish in the whole world. If a line forms at the refreshment counter of a movie theatre and the line moves quickly, most people will not praise the speed of the line: "Wow, look at this. The third movie I've been to this month, and the snack line moves so fast. This theatre is really something. It makes up for the price we're paying for this bag of popcorn." But if the line is slow, perfect strangers will grumble to each other about how the theatre isn't staffed adequately on top of what a rip-off the price of the popcorn is. This may remind them of how expensive movies are today, especially compared to twenty years ago. They may even start to complain about government policy. And no one will think this is in any way abnormal. It is so much fun to complain when there is no one around who can do anything about the problem.

Inner- and Outer-Circle Complaint Behavior

If you watch carefully, you'll note that people talk about products differently to their inner circle (family, close friends, and work colleagues) than they do to their outer circle (people they stand next to in lines; people they meet for the first time at a luncheon; people they have never met but who are listening to them in a meeting; people sitting next to them on planes, buses, and trains; or people to whom they are peripherally connected). People feel comfortable telling their mail carrier, to whom they may rarely speak, about the lemon car they just bought. In fact, some exaggerate their stories, just a little, to get the maximum effect. "Can you imagine such a thing? I was shocked!" We have seen speakers stand before audiences without a word of introduction and tell everyone how an airline lost their luggage, the plane was late and overbooked, and they ran out of pillows and blankets. And the audience, laughing in shared recognition, will accept this as a suitable beginning for a speech.

Listeners generally relate to these tales of woe and are eager to talk about their own horrible experiences. In a worst-case scenario, if someone tells his or her story well, a listener may turn around and retell the experience to another group of people. All these people become bad-will ambassadors for a product or company and seriously undermine the effectiveness of expensive marketing strategies. "Yes, I've heard the same thing. (Therefore, it must be true.)" You can also be sure that the story is not retold as it was heard. Generally, the retold complaint example becomes more extreme, dressed up so that listeners are sure to roll their eyes.

Some people go so far as to relate bad consumer experiences that happened decades ago. The company involved may have changed hands or improved its customer service, but the public is still discussing the company as if it currently performs as it did twenty or thirty years ago. The Jaguar automobile company is a case in point. Jaguars used to have major repair problems. It used to be said that if you bought a Jaguar, you needed to buy two so you would have one to drive while the other was in the shop. Today, *Fortune* magazine describes Jaguars as being among the most dependable cars manufactured in the world.[9] It took a long time for that old reputation to mend. Incidentally, blogger Joe Sherlock explains how listening to and addressing vendor complaints substantially contributed to Jaguar's improved quality. "Ford, appalled at the poor quality of vendor components supplied to Jaguar, initiated frank discussions with suppliers. Ford got the equally frank feedback that crap was supplied because Jaguar was a crappy customer and very slow in payment. Ford traded prompt payment . . . in exchange for improved component quality."[10]

Consider the Chevrolet Prizm as an example of where reputation matters. The Prizm and the Toyota Corolla were both built at the NUMMI plant in California by the same workers. The Prizm consistently sold for less than the Toyota Corolla, even though it was essentially the same car. Yet Chevrolet had to add incentives to sell the Prizm. And after a few years, the Prizm lost value in the resale market when compared to the Corolla. Consumers in the know understood that these two cars were the same; resale ads normally mentioned that the Prizm is a Corolla, the best-selling car in the world. How did the Toyota Corolla maintain an advantage over its twin but tainted Chevrolet sister? Toyota has been better at providing what most car buyers want—the basics—and then standing behind its cars when problems occur. Over the years, consumers have told a brand story about Toyota's reliability, reasonable price, value in the resale market, and excellent after-sales service. The Chevrolet story has been considerably more mixed. Consumers remember the failures and tell each other until they become reality, even if in this particular case it wasn't.

In contrast to the large numbers of others to whom people relate negative stories, those who are pleased with a car purchase will tell only eight other people. And these will likely be people in the person's inner circle. People more readily tell friends and family about positive purchases because those who are close to them will more likely be happy for them without showing a lot of jealousy. For example, if a woman buys a new car for her family, she will feel comfortable telling her friend, "Hey, I just got a new car. You have to see it. It drives like a dream. The children love the color of the leather seats, and we got it for a great price. I've been waiting a long time for this." This is a normal interaction among friends. The friend won't be thinking, "What a turkey. Here we're going to see a movie and she wants to show me the color of her new car." If the proud car owner doesn't know the other person very well, however, it's unlikely she will brag. Pleased recent buyers generally don't extol the virtues of their cars to strangers unless they are asked.

TARP found that if companies can get customers to complain directly to them, they can minimize the damage. Customers who complain about their dissatisfaction are also more likely to repurchase, even if their complaints are not handled satisfactorily. In fact, TARP, along with a large number of other research groups, concluded that customers who don't complain are the least loyal customers, while those who complain may be or become the most loyal customers.[11] The reason for this goes back to basic psychology. If you receive a significant discount for something you purchased because you received poor service, you can brag about this and not incite jealousy. After all, you had to endure some pain to get the benefit. If your friend says, "Oh, you're always so lucky," you can respond, "I'd rather not have gone through the ordeal they put me through. I'd rather not have had the problem."

This is probably the strangest conclusion generated in the complaining customers arena. A company actually has a chance of increasing positive word-of-mouth advertising if it recovers well for dissatisfied customers.[12]

Complaints and the Reciprocity Principle

The reason why customers are likely to say positive things after a problem has been fixed for them is best explained by the social psychology principle of reciprocity. Humans like to return favors (reciprocate) when something nice has been done for them; in other words, "you scratch my back, and I'll scratch yours." This principle applies in every culture across the world. It translates into consumer behavior this way: even if I have had a problem with your company, if you do something nice for me, including something as simple as giving me a free hamburger or sincerely apologizing, I will be likely to give you more of my business and tell others what a great company you are. In other words, customers will reward businesses for taking care of them.

Reciprocity provides the justification for businesses' being proactive when errors occur. Acting proactively to create a feeling of reciprocity puts the service provider in the driver's seat. If the organization takes care of the customer's complaint but only after making the customer jump through hoops, the sense of reciprocity is muted. A financial services survey of six thousand North American households found that "the number one [determinant] of customers' willingness to buy again or buy more products from the company" is customers' feeling that the company has acted as their advocate or in their interest.[13]

John O'Neill and Anna Mattilla, at Penn State University, surveyed 613 hotel guests and concluded that customers like being upgraded to nicer rooms. No big surprise there! It's like winning a minilottery. But the reason they are upgraded affects satisfaction and loyalty. If the upgrade occurs because an honest mistake was made, customers tend to be satisfied and are even more likely to return to the same hotel. Reciprocity in action. However, customers don't like it when the hotel has a policy to overbook figuring there will be last-minute cancellations. The flying public doesn't like the overbooking practices of the airlines, but they've gotten used to them. So far, however, consumers don't think hotels should overbook, and O'Neill and Mattilla conclude that if a guest with a reservation believes that the hotel regularly overbooks its rooms, an upgrade isn't nearly as satisfying. The researchers advise hotels to be careful about their overbooking practices because they open themselves up to punishment by guests who won't return.[14] It matters whether customers believe that the hotel is to blame for the problems they face, even if they're upgraded to a royal suite.

Reciprocity is not a technique used to manipulate customers. Rather, if all the people in an organization take the attitude that they are going to give their best to customers, then reciprocity will naturally emerge during the customer-business relationships. If reciprocity means "I'm smiling at you, so you better smile back," the positive power of natural positive human behavior is lost. A good example of a company that creates a lot of natural reciprocity is USAA, the military insurance company. One way it does this is to advise customers not to buy insurance just because they want it if the USAA representative feels they do not need that coverage. Reps will talk people out of inappropriate purchases. That sends a very strong message of customer advocacy.

At some point, good customer service has to be about simply offering it because it's good for customers, whom we want to take care of, and also because it makes service providers feel good to help their customers. In our personal relationships, a lot of tit-for-tat behavior goes on. For example, I'll iron your shirt if you take out the garbage. That type of personal negotiation is unspoken and enables a couple to take care of each other without negotiating behavior exchanges. In commercial relationships, we ultimately have to get down to economic basics. Utilitarian ethics, on which modern economics is based, argues for the greatest good for the greatest number. At every interaction point with a customer, someone has to answer the question, "What should I (or my company) do?" If the company does something that results in an enhancement of the feeling of reciprocity, we are probably behaving in the best way for everyone, which is the definition of *cooperative economics*.

Levels of Complaint Reactions: Driving Our Customers to Anger

One of the most complete research studies on dissatisfied-customer behavior was conducted at Case Western Reserve University.[15] Thousands of households were contacted to determine if they had had a dissatisfying experience in one of four areas: grocery shopping, automotive repair, medical care, or banking services. Of the hundreds of households interviewed in depth, approximately 30 percent recalled a dissatisfying experience and were eager to talk about it. The researchers wanted to know what these people did about their bad experiences and divided their responses into three categories, or "levels of reaction."

- *Level 1:* Complain to the company. The customers spoke up and told the salesperson, retailer, or provider directly about their bad experience.
- *Level 2:* Complain to other people. The customers told people they knew but not the company about their bad experience; they also stopped buying from the company in question.
- *Level 3:* Complain to a third party. The customers went to a third party such as a lawyer to initiate legal action or a newspaper to tell of their experience in a letter to the editor, or they issued a formal complaint to an agency such as the Better Business Bureau.

The interviewed subjects fell into four clusters and were identified as Voicers, 37 percent; Passives, 14 percent; Irates, 21 percent; and Activists, 28 percent.

Voicers

The most desirable of dissatisfied customers, from our point of view, are the Voicers, who tell the organization when they have bad experiences. They assist the company in trying to improve services and products.

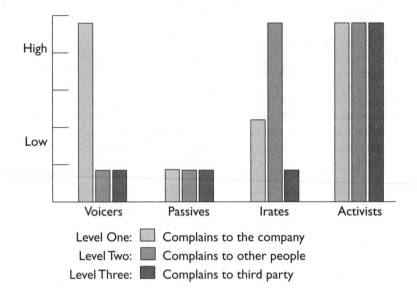

The Voicers will let the company know when something does not please them, and they generally do not go out and tell a bunch of other people about bad service or products. Voicers are actively interested in getting redress for their situations. If the company does not handle them well, they may become Activists. Companies must convert all their dissatisfied customers into Voicers and then satisfy them. They are truly helpful to any organization.

Passives

Many companies set goals to reduce the number of customer complaints they receive. Such companies might choose the Passives as the preferred group of customers. A company can provide problem-ridden service or products to this group and they will keep coming back, at least for a while. Furthermore, they will not tarnish the company's reputation by telling anyone else. Employees can feel good about their services and products, oblivious to the customer experience.

Unfortunately, such a group does not help with positive word-of-mouth advertising. Because these customers are passive, they may not say anything negative, but they definitely are not going to be cheerleaders either when things go right. We also do not know how far these people can be pushed before they move to one of the other levels. Passives could just as well be called fence-sitters, waiting for something else to go wrong before they act. Maybe they are the three-strikes-and-you're-out kind of people, or perhaps they are the slow burners. It takes them awhile to heat up, but once they do, they do major damage to a company's reputation or switch suppliers. Perhaps they grew up in a culture where complaining is looked down on, such as in Japan, where the virtue of *gamen* (accepting whatever fate throws in your path without complaint) is highly prized. Unfortunately, companies do not know much about these shoppers because they have little chance to communicate with them.

Passives also do not share their insights as to how the company can improve its products and services to meet customer needs. Companies interested in providing higher-quality products and services must adopt strategies to get this group of customers to feel comfortable speaking up when they are dissatisfied or have ideas.

Irates

The Irates are dangerous to an organization's reputation; in many cases, they will not say a word to the service provider or company. But they will tell lots of people about their bad service and generally will stop buying. The company thereby loses the opportunity to regain these customers' loyalty. They just leave, talking all the while as they take their business elsewhere!

Some industries generate more Irates than others. Retail stores that sell relatively inexpensive items will rarely hear complaints directly. It is not worth the trouble to complain about a $1 or $2 item. Travelers also rarely complain to the travel industry. The TARP report quoted earlier found that 55 percent of travelers who have problems with airlines, hotels, or rental-car companies endure in silence. Jean Otte, former vice president of quality management at National Car Rental, explains it this way: "Many feel that complaining won't do any good, and the rest are too damn busy or don't want to be humiliated."[16] But put a group of frequent travelers together, and you will quickly learn one of their all-time favorite topics is the bad things that can happen while traveling. Monopoly businesses have to be particularly aware of this phenomenon.[17] Customers tend not to complain because they don't have anywhere else to go, but they readily engage in negative word-of-mouth as payback.

Activists

The Activists are potentially the most lethal of the four groups, particularly if they are dissatisfied with the company's response and are out for more than redress. They may be seeking revenge while spreading the word of the company's bad service to everyone and never again patronizing the company. Activists can even damage a company's stock price. As a case in point, a study measured the impact of Activists' escalating their complaints to the Complaints Service of the Bank of Spain, a government body. When the Complaints Service annual report is released, the stock market reacts negatively to those banks with the most complaints. This may be because the market knows from experience that there is a negative relationship between complaints and performance. In Spain, at least, complaint handling should clearly be considered an investment rather than an expense in the banking sector.[18]

The Case Western Reserve University study found a larger number of Activists (28 percent) than most other research studies. Perhaps this is because automotive repair was one of the services included in the study. Consumers have been educated to complain to state government agencies when they have car repair problems. A much more common statistic of Activist behavior that gets reported is closer to one in twenty-seven, or 4 percent.[19] With the exception of car repair, most people do their complaining to their inner and outer circles and nowhere else.

Starbucks seems to attract an inordinate number of Activists. In late 2007, some 337,000 Web sites appeared when we searched for "Starbucks complaints" on Google. In the 1990s, Jeremy Dorosin of Walnut Creek, California, bought two espresso machines at a Starbucks and both malfunctioned. Dorosin began his campaign against Starbucks by taking out ads in the *Wall Street Journal*, asking, "Had any problems at Starbucks Coffee?" He signed the ad, "One mistreated customer" and asked other mistreated customers to call a toll-free number that he set up at his own expense. Starbucks has tried to settle with Dorosin a number of times, but Dorosin describes its offers of settlement as always being too late and only in response to his Activist behavior. Dorosin's latest demand is that Starbucks fund a nonprofit center for runaway children in San Francisco. He says he does not want any compensation for himself. A Starbucks spokesperson has called Dorosin's requests "ridiculous" and labeled Dorosin himself an "ego."[20] Dorosin says he is not a contentious person and had never made a consumer complaint before he went after Starbucks.

Now a man calling himself DaVido is pestering Starbucks with his song, "Java Jitter," inspired by Starbucks. DaVido wants Starbucks to sell his song in its stores. The company keeps saying no. He keeps going into its stores, dancing, singing, and filming. He keeps getting thrown out. He keeps putting his videos up on the web, including on YouTube, where his original video, "The Starbucks Rejection Tour," has been watched by huge numbers of people. His music is catchy. Seth Godin, author of *All Marketers Are Liars*,[21] says, "So if I was in Starbucks' shoes, I'd say this is great because we got 10,000 people who would love to sell their CDs. Let's let them sell them on the website and we'll take the five best-selling ones and bring them into the store."[22] A major complainer is telling Starbucks that it has become like Nashville or *American Idol*, and it might be a good idea to listen to DaVido's song and Godin's idea. Starbucks refuses. DaVido seems to be more energized every time he gets thrown out of a Starbucks, which to date has been over two hundred times. As he says, he's not going away. Whether people love or hate him, when you read all the comments written about him on the Web, it's striking how thoroughly DaVido engages people. One thing is clear, Starbucks needs to figure out a strategy to deal with the likes of Dorosin and DaVido because the brand and all it stands for seems to attract this intense kind of energy.

If an industry allows complaints to go unanswered until large numbers of people become Activists, then government agencies tend to step in and take charge. It's not going to happen to Starbucks, but where the government acts as the watchdog, politicians will step in. Fines have been imposed for selling incorrect policies and using misleading advertising in the insurance industry. Banks have also been allowed to move into the expanding marketplace of lifetime financial investments, directly affecting the insurance industry's market share.[23]

One final word. Some businesses categorize their customer complaints into two response groups: public and private. Public responses are complaints to the company itself and complaints to third parties; private responses are behaviors such as boycotting of the company or product and negative word-of-mouth. Many businesses see private responses as nonassertive behavior by customers, and as a result, these responses are considered unimportant and undeserving of attention by managers.[24] Irates who complain on the Internet would be categorized as private complainers. In other words, many companies ignore the Irate group, while in this book we consider them dangerous to the health of a company!

How Are Activists Created?

As a group, Activists are consumers who tend to be the most alienated from the marketplace. In this case, alienation can be described as a mindset that when something goes wrong, normal complaint channels will not work so other methods of redress must be chosen. Something very personal happens to Activists that prods them to engage in behavior that frequently is costly to them and, at a minimum, occupies a great deal of their time. Customer research shows that alienated consumers generally agree with the following statements:

- The provider of the service cares nothing about the customer.
- Shopping is an unpleasant experience.
- Merchants forget about the customer once he or she has purchased something.

- The customer is the least important part of the business.
- The customer does not get to decide which products are available for sale.[25]

Even though Activists tend to be alienated from the marketplace, this does not fully explain how these customers come to believe that normal complaint channels will not work for them. Activists in most cases are created over a period of time, it's like loyalty in reverse. Loyal customers aren't created overnight, and neither are Activists. Consumers move from one category to another depending on how they are treated when they initially voice their complaints. They may even move from Activists back to Voicers if they are treated well.

A well-known ice cream company runs the risk of legal action whenever the extras (nuts, raisins, cookie chunks, etc.) it puts in its ice cream cause tooth damage or, in the worst case, choking. This particular creamery had a policy that once a case became known to the company, its service department was to cease communication with the customer and let the legal department handle the case. The customer service people thought this wasn't the best service and proposed an experiment. They would contact the injured person, apologize, and continue to check in with the person, even though legal action might have begun. A year after this experiment began, the creamery's insurance company reimbursed the creamery a quarter of a million dollars because of the sharp reduction in legal claims.

What Do Customers Want When They Complain?

Remember the reciprocity principle discussed earlier in this chapter? If you do something for someone, he or she will likely reciprocate by doing something for you. Most customers want only what they were denied and perhaps an apology. So if a company gives them a token of atonement beyond what they expected, they will likely reciprocate by continuing to do business with the company and perhaps say something positive. Numerous research studies suggest that companies' success in tapping into this reciprocity behavior—in other words, getting the customer to repurchase—varies widely (between 40 and 80 percent).[26] Companies can create a feeling of reciprocity by taking customers' complaints seriously and offering one or more of the following:

- A price reduction, or no charge at all, if this is appropriate
- A sincere apology
- A free product or gift
- A coupon for future price reductions
- Assurance that something has been changed inside the organization so this will not happen again

This does not mean the company has to give the store away. Customer complaints can be solved in ways other than a refund—in fact, consumers do not always want a refund. For example, fewer than 10 percent of diners expect even a bill reduction, let alone a free meal, if a specific dish they ordered was unsatisfactory.[27] But they would like the dish replaced or reheated or cooked a bit longer. Tearing up the bill or giving out a coupon for a free meal may be handing over money needlessly. Some things customers complain about, such as a noisy environment, antismoking laws, lack of free parking, or an inconvenient restaurant location, can't be fixed in any case. Customers dissatisfied with issues that cannot be fixed may not have any intention of becoming a long-term client of the restaurant, so offering a free meal will not create long-term customers in these cases. But give them a coupon for a free dessert or a half-price meal and at a minimum the restaurant will receive some cash back for their apology. The customer may also bring a dining partner whose future business can be enticed.

Customers want different responses depending on what happened to them. One useful way to figure this out is to sort complaints into two groups:

- Complaints about issues that can be fixed
- Complaints about situations that cannot be fixed, but about which customers, nevertheless, want to be heard and have their feelings acknowledged

Understanding and then categorizing customer complaints into these two groups is useful in determining how to satisfy customers. For example, if you buy a computer that does not work, you want it fixed or replaced. You may not care why the problem occurred: you just want your computer fixed or replaced with a new one that works as promised. It would also be nice if the company representative is courteous and pays you some attention, but mostly you want your problem solved as quickly as possible.

Some situations cannot be fixed in the same way that your computer can be replaced. For example, if you order a gift through a mail-order house in plenty of time for it to arrive for a friend's big birthday bash and it's late, this situation cannot be remedied. Nothing can be done retroactively to get that gift there on time. An airline representative may have ignored you, thereby making it impossible for you to catch your flight. You cannot get to the event you missed as a result of not catching your plane. A lab technician may have lost your blood sample, requiring you to return to the lab at great personal inconvenience and have blood drawn again. The lab cannot recreate the blood sample that disappeared. In these cases, customers want to be emotionally compensated, and part of this includes being told what caused the service breakdown.

In the field of health care, one survey revealed that however else they are compensated, 87 percent of customers want to know that the problem won't happen again. Of the group that doesn't want a repeat, 79 percent want to know specifically how procedures will be changed. They also want more disclosure from hospital staff and expect staff to admit when a mistake has occurred. There are more people who want a full explanation of what happened (65 percent) than those who want an apology (41 percent). A relatively small 7 percent want some type of financial compensation.[28]

Customers respond more favorably when they learn the company had no control over what happened: "I'm so sorry your special-order package hasn't arrived. The entire East Coast delivery system isn't working today. Have you heard about the blizzard? It's causing problems for everyone." The same is true when they learn that the product or service failure is an exception: "This is so unusual. This just never happens. In fact, I'm very shocked by this. Thanks for telling me."

In any case, an explanation goes a long way toward satisfying upset customers.[29] Sometimes a company can offer an alternative solution: "I'm sorry, we don't carry that product. Perhaps another company has it. Would you like me to call for you?" By contrast, customers who are "dumped" because the company cannot help are infuriated: "There's nothing we can do. Now, excuse me, I need to help the next customer." Implying that customers are the cause of their own misfortune is also a mistake: "I'm sorry, but it's not our fault. If you had only come in yesterday, we might have been able to help you." Customers want the company to put some effort into keeping their business. When a company has wounded them in a way that can be only emotionally recovered, customers want a sincere apology more than anything else.

Some airlines are effective at handling complaints that cannot be fixed. Japan Airlines uses a strategy it calls a Service Irregularity Message, in which it patches things up with a customer while he or she is still on board the plane or in the airport terminal. The airline tracks any problem a passenger has had through the entire flight, which means that a problem that occurred in reservations might be addressed on board, in the transit lounge if the passenger is connecting to another flight, or upon arrival at the final destination. Making amends means a lot more if it is done quickly than if the customer has to wait to receive a letter three weeks down the road. Scott Friedman, a humorist who speaks to corporations around the world, talks about holding a reservation on Cathay Pacific and being told that because of a shift to a smaller aircraft, he was going to have to fly on a different carrier. As it turned out, there was a seat on Cathay for Friedman but on a different flight leaving from another gate. A gate attendant personally escorted Friedman to the other gate, making him feel very special indeed. Small courtesies after small insults are remarkably memorable and remarkably healing.

Some complaints are about the rude or heavy-handed behaviors of company representatives. We would argue that these are also situations that cannot be fixed in the same way that a company can fix or replace a broken computer or other tangible product. Impersonal or rude behavior can be made better by an apology, but the rude behavior has already occurred, and sometimes it is delivered publicly so the customer has been both insulted and embarrassed. In cases like this, customers may appreciate a price reduction, but they probably want to see conciliatory behavior. Such service wounds cannot be erased, but they can be eased. A heartfelt apology and a statement of embarrassment by the company goes a long way to recovering the emotional balance of the abused customer. Nancy Friedman, in *Customer Service Nightmares*, shares a letter from a woman who argued with a billing clerk about the charges to cover the expenses associated with the birth of her premature infant. The clerk eventually told her that if she didn't want problems, she should have had a healthy baby.[30] Serious service recovery needs to be delivered in such a situation. Just reading about this situation makes one cringe. It's hard to imagine how it felt to be on the receiving end of such a comment.

When Christopher Hart, originator of the extraordinary-guarantee concept, analyzed data from PlanetFeedback.com, he found that having a service-provider issue is much more likely to affect a customer's future willingness to recommend a brand than having a product problem.[31] The emotions generated when talking with a service provider are likely to be more pronounced and therefore memorable than if the customer is trying to get a product to work. It makes sense. After all, getting angry with an inanimate object is rather pointless. Most of us save our anger for people.

Some industries do not understand this distinction of fixable and unfixable complaint categories and end up handling complaints poorly as a result. In a joint research project, three business school professors from across the United States looked at how one teaching hospital with two thousand staff "handled" and "managed" complaints. The researchers defined *complaint handling* as fixing the situation directly with the customer, whereas *complaint managing* was defined as fixing policies or the way the hospital does business so that future customer care is improved. The researchers found that hospital administrators preferred to "manage" complaints they were informed about but were unlikely to recommend direct follow-up with the complaining patients. As a result, customers rarely received apologies for the negative interactions they experienced. The patients also never learned what was done to ensure the problem would not happen again, even though many quality changes had been instituted, thanks to their complaints.[32]

One of the major findings of this study was that complaints about quality of care (adequacy and delivery of medications, assistance with bed pans, etc.) were viewed by hospital personnel as more important than complaints about their attitudes. Hospital personnel tended to create an "us versus them" attitude toward customers who complained about them. They were inclined to excuse bad attitudes on the part of their fellow employees by saying, "Anyone can have a bad day."[33] Furthermore, because customer-facing staff—or as our organization, TMI, likes to call them, "the fingertips of the organization"—felt uncomfortable dealing with complaints about attitudes, they tended to push these problems upward to managers, where they took longer to be resolved. Managers had the same reaction. They saw complaints about personnel as accusations, disapproval of what they were doing, or whining. Small wonder that most managers prefer to "manage" complaints about policies, which is much less direct and confrontational, rather than "handle" complaints about people.

A Special Note About Older Complainers

We haven't specifically discussed older consumers. We do know that, according to research, the elderly do not complain as much as younger people. But once they make up their minds to complain, they seem to take very strong positions, and many are willing to fight for what they consider to be fair.[34] As the world's population—particularly in developed nations—is growing proportionally older, there are greater numbers of elderly consumers. While we have conducted no research on this topic ourselves, in our discussions with clients, we hear that elderly complainers are more emotional when something goes wrong and that they don't always understand the rational side of the problems they seek help with.

Perhaps because every day is increasingly precious to them, service issues strongly affect their overall emotional well-being, or perhaps they have stopped caring what others think about them. Emotions are a part of every complaint, but they can be remarkably strong among the elderly who decide to complain. The big question for organizations is whether their customer-facing staff are equipped to deal with the intensity of an older person's highly emotional complaint. An emotionally upset elder is not going to be satisfied just by having a problem solved. The emotional impact of having the problem in the first place must also be addressed, and we recommend that it be addressed before any attempts are made to solve the problem. This requires careful listening, great empathy, and assurances to the person that he or she will be treated fairly and that the problem will be solved.

DISCUSSION QUESTIONS

- Based on the research that has been conducted and the types of products or services your company sells, how many of your customers are likely to be experiencing dissatisfaction and then communicating this to their inner and outer circles?

- How many of your complaining customers repurchase from you? What special efforts do you take to win customers back when they complain?

- What are the indicators that the following belief is widespread throughout your organization: when a service breakdown occurs, your organization has a chance to retain customer loyalty by satisfying the customer's needs?

- How does your organization work with the principle of reciprocity? What do you offer customers when a service breakdown occurs?

- What does your organization do to get the Passives to speak up? Does your organization have any cases of Activist behavior? If so, how did this happen? How could you have prevented this extreme response on the part of the customer?

- What products and services do you sell that can or cannot be fixed? How do your customer-facing people handle these different kinds of service or product breakdowns?

- What kinds of service problems cause your customers to immediately cancel their business relationship with you without complaining?

≈

PART TWO

Putting the Complaint Is a Gift Strategy into Practice

How you talk about complaints shapes how you think about them. If you want to behave as if complaints are gifts, it helps to speak the language of complaints as gifts. This second part of the book begins by explaining the Gift Formula, an eight-step response to complaining customers. With practice, this approach can become second nature. Just as we thank a friend for a birthday gift, so too can we respond to a complaint as if it is a gift.

We will also look at strategies to increase goodwill. When complaint handlers interact with customers, especially if the customers are likely to deal with multiple people or departments within an organization, those customers need to feel better at the end of the interaction than when they started it.

Sometimes situations get out of control, and customers lose their patience with a company. We outline five principles that are fundamental for handling upset customers. We recommend that companies teach their employees the five principles and then layer their own language on top of these principles. For example, we recommend that service providers use language that allows for some level of personal relationship with upset customers. That is a principle. Companies can recommend the most appropriate language to make this happen.

Written complaints are a special category of complaints. In most cases, though not all, written complaints are red flags because of the effort required to write them. But if a company is prompt in responding and uses the Gift Formula for written complaints, most customers can be enticed to give the company another chance.

Finally, we briefly look at what organizations can do to protect themselves from the global shout that so easily occurs when complaints are written about and discussed around the world on the Internet. By no means are organizations defenseless against modern technology.

~ 6 ~

The Gift Formula

Complaining **has** never had a positive meaning. It comes from the Latin verb *plangere*, which originally meant "to hit"—metaphorically "to beat one's breast." Today a complaint is the utterance of pain, displeasure, or annoyance. It also is an illness or ailment, and in legal terms, it is a formal charge or accusation. In English slang, to complain is to quibble, raise a fuss, yammer, squawk, bitch, bewail, moan and groan, bellyache, carp, nag, pick at, give someone a hard time, find fault, gripe, whine, and fret.

Small wonder that no one likes to receive complaints. Yet this is the method by which customers tell us how to run our businesses and organizations! After we have worked like the dickens to deliver a service or a product that we believe in, customers have the gall to let us know our efforts do not suit their purposes or meet their needs. It's almost as bad as someone sitting down to a dinner you prepared and wrinkling his or her nose. Are we to welcome these kinds of statements and confrontational behaviors? Yes. That is precisely the point. To paraphrase Marshall McLuhan's words, the medium is the complaint. Customers may moan and groan—seemingly unfairly—but their messages are vital information to any business.

The metaphor we use in this book is that of complaints as gifts. Complaints provide a feedback mechanism that can help organizations rapidly and inexpensively shift products, service style, and market focus to meet the needs of their customers—who, after all, pay the bills and are the reason why we get to hang a sign over our door. It's time for all organizations to think of complaint handling as a strategic tool—an opportunity to learn something about our products or services we did not already know—and as a marketing strategy rather than a nuisance or a cost.

When someone gives you a real gift that you instantly hate, your first thought is, "Yuck. How could anyone think I want this? Whom can I give this to?" Yet you still manage to put on a polite face and thank the gift giver. This situation is so common today that we actually have a new English word to describe what to do with forgettable gifts. It's called regifting, and an online encyclopedia even spells out *regifting* etiquette.[1]

We must become so comfortable with the idea that a complaint is a gift that we don't hesitate in our responses, even if we receive a clunker gift. If our attitude is deeply ingrained, as in the case of saying "Thank you" when we receive a gift, then when someone complains to us we will truly welcome the complaint as something of value. We will not have to think our way through it; our natural response will be as if we have received something wonderful.

How can we do this? First, the company must talk the language of complaint giving as gifts. The idea needs to be reinforced at every meeting, on wall posters, and in all conversations and educational and training sessions about customer service. Second, the company's policies, compensation systems, operational systems, communication systems, mission, vision, values, and managerial behavior must be aligned to support the gift-friendly philosophy. (Check the www.tmius.com Web site for downloadable PDF files on how to align your organization with the Complaint Is a Gift philosophy.) Finally, we must learn some fundamental techniques for handling complaints. This can be done by using the following Gift Formula.

Eight-Step Gift Formula

The Gift Formula is a step-by-step process that, in its most impactful form, is delivered in a set order. Nevertheless, you may find occasions when it will be more appropriate to vary the sequence or to modify the steps with your own equivalent language. The steps are as follows:

1. Say, "Thank you."
2. Explain why you appreciate the feedback.
3. Apologize for the mistake.
4. Promise to do something about the problem immediately. Take responsibility.
5. Ask for necessary information.
6. Correct the mistake—promptly.
7. Check customer satisfaction.
8. Prevent future mistakes.

Say "Thank You"

Don't invest any energy wondering whether customers have a legitimate complaint or not when you first hear them speak. Simply acknowledge that you are about to receive valuable information—a gift. We need to create immediate rapport with our customers, and to do that we must meet them on their ground. There is no better way to make someone feel welcome than to say, "Thank you." You'll probably be surprised at the reaction you get.

Most people never start by thanking someone for a complaint. Rather, it is deeply entrenched in languages and cultures around the world to start with an apology to verbally presented complaints. When people write complaint-response letters, however, they invariably start their letters with an expression of thanks, such as "Thank you for writing to tell us about . . ." If this is a logical way to begin a written response to a complaint, why shouldn't it work for an oral response?

Try an experiment. Ask someone to thank you after you express a complaint. Notice your emotional reaction upon hearing "Thank you." After we had covered the Gift Formula in a recent TMI workshop at a hotel, a participant walked out of the meeting room and saw a particularly bad mess in the hallway. The participant grabbed a passing hotel employee and told him. "My gosh, that's horrible. Thank you so much for letting me know!" The staff person responded with a grateful look on his face. "I'll get it cleaned up immediately." The rest of the participants happened to witness this exchange so they got to see firsthand how good it feels to be thanked for delivering bad news instead of feeling guilty for pointing out the problem.

Your expression of thanks should be as natural and spontaneous as the gratitude you express when you receive a present. Make sure your body language demonstrates that you appreciate the complaint and that you support your customers' right to complain. Eye contact, an understanding nod, and a friendly smile can work wonders. Remember, a smile comes through even on the telephone.

When we demonstrate using the Gift Formula in our seminars or workshops, people tell us that they feel uncomfortable the first time they begin their response to a customer's complaint with "Thank you." They say it feels fake and unnatural. But then we talk with the people who just heard the thank-you, and to a person, they say that it sounds great, that it makes them relaxed, that it lowers their emotional arousal. And so we say to the participants, as we will say to you now, "Thank you sounds better to the listener than it feels to say." Try it, and see what happens.

We've heard some remarkable stories over the past twelve years from people who have experimented with first thanking their customers. By far the most amazing of these stories is from a colleague who lives in a part of the world where kidnappings for ransom are not all that rare. Close to the time our colleague was to give birth to her first child, her husband was kidnapped. Shortly thereafter she received a call from the kidnappers, who demanded ransom money. They told her that her husband hadn't been harmed—yet. Our colleague didn't say anything for a very long moment. She knew that the next words out of her mouth would no doubt be the most important words she ever said in her whole life. The Gift Formula passed through her mind, and with as much sincerity as she could muster, she said, "Thank you for not harming him." She hesitated again and then continued, "You see, he's going to be a father soon." Remarkably, the kidnappers released her husband unharmed and gave up their request for a ransom.

Thanking a customer is not enough to take care of the complaint by any means, but it is the basis for a positive conversation. The key is to remember that you aren't just fixing a problem. As blogger Olivier Blanchard says, the thank-you just takes customers back to neutral. "Neutral isn't where they were when they first took your product home."[2] You have to touch them emotionally in order to engage them after a mishap.

Explain Why You Appreciate the Feedback

"Thank you" by itself can sound empty. You need to qualify your gratitude by saying something about what hearing the complaint does for you. For example, it will allow you to better address the problem or fix your processes or make sure such a problem never happens again. "Thank you for telling me" or "Thank you. I'm happy you told me so I can fix this for you (or repair the damage we have done)" or "Thank you. I'm happy you shared this because it gives me a chance to improve our quality—and this is what I intend to do" or simply, "Thank you for letting me know. We're better than this."

Although you'd never want to say the following statement out loud, the complete thought that needs to run through your mind goes something like this: "Thanks for telling me about this situation. You can't believe how many customers just walk away without saying anything, even though they're really dissatisfied, and we probably lose their business. Not only that, they say nasty and damaging things about us to others without giving us the opportunity to resolve their problems. And we definitely want to do that because we value our customers' business. We're trying to keep every customer we can for the long haul so we can develop our business and get better at serving all our customers. That's why we really do appreciate your taking the time and trouble to come up to us and say something. Thank you, thank you, thank you." That's the Complaint Is a Gift mind-set.

If you can keep this attitude clearly in mind, then the short version, "Thank you for telling me about this," will communicate the entire philosophy.

Common complaints involve prices, and most people tell us they are among the more difficult to handle. Frankly, many customer-facing staff tell us in private that they agree with their customers' complaints about prices. Sometimes, staff will even say something like this: "I agree. The prices here are outrageous. I never shop here. Go down to Costco, and you can get it for half the price." In order to get your staff to never say anything like that, you have to give them something else to say.

Customers rarely say, "I'd like to complain about your prices." Rather they'll say something like this: "Your prices are really high compared to (someone else)." Or, "Wow, your prices have really gone up in the past year." Or sometimes they'll get quite direct: "You must be kidding! You're charging this much?" All of these statements are complaints, and it gives you an opportunity to use the Gift Formula. "Thank you so much for asking about our prices. It gives me a chance to explain." Then, of course, you need to know how to justify the value the customer receives from buying at your price point. We've covered this topic in many of our workshops and have found that most people cannot explain their company's prices. They've never thought much about them. To organizations we say, prepare a price-justification statement and make sure that everyone who has customer contact knows how to speak from the document. To customer-facing staff we say, whenever you hear a complaint about prices, ask your manager or supervisor how you should explain price questions.

Steve Trollinger, director of client marketing for J. Schmid & Associates, says that when you "stop [special pricing] offers cold turkey," you can expect your call centers' phones to ring.[3] So be prepared. Whenever prices change (for example, if bargain pricing is no longer available, but it was available last week, last month, or even last year), discuss with your staff how to speak about this increase in fees or reversion to earlier prices. It's also possible that some customers should be given those earlier lower prices. If this is the case, then your staff should know when to make exceptions.

Apologize for the Mistake

It's important to apologize to customers, but it shouldn't be the first step. You create greater rapport with customers by saying "Thank you. I appreciate your telling me about this." Then comes the apology: "May I apologize? I'm really sorry this happened."

Too many people begin their complaint responses by apologizing, frequently before customers have even had a chance to explain any details. The apology is important, but it has no punch when it begins the conversation. These service providers don't even know what they are apologizing for yet. Then there are those who never apologize—lots of them. Surveys reveal that about half of service providers do not apologize at all at any point in the exchange.[4]

Many companies, customer service books, and service experts advise service employees to apologize first.[5] If this is your company's approach, then you may have to do as your company says. We believe, however, that beginning with "Thank you" underscores and reinforces to both the speaker and the listener that a complaint is a gift, and that's a very good way to begin. It's a more logical approach and encourages additional customer feedback. The authors have noticed that hearing "Thank you" makes us feel that the person saying it is going to do something for us. "I'm sorry" leaves us feeling that an apology is all we're going to get, and that's why the person is apologizing.

Incidentally, when you apologize, use *I* as much as possible instead of *we*. "We're sorry" does not sound sincere. The other people you are apologizing for don't even know what is happening, and customers are aware of that.

Customer service representatives have asked us why they should say they're sorry when the customer is clearly at fault. "If I apologize, then aren't I, in fact, taking responsibility for something that may have been the customer's own doing?" Think about it this way. If you know someone who has experienced a death in the family, a natural, courteous expression is "I'm so sorry." You're not taking responsibility for the death by expressing your sorrow. You're saying you are sorry that this has happened. It has nothing to do with blame or fault. In the same way, when we tell a customer we're sorry about something that happened, it doesn't matter who did what to whom or who caused something to happen. We simply wish it hadn't happened. The customer will appreciate your concern.[6] If you're not sorry, maybe you've been working too hard and should take a little break.

One solid reason for apologizing is that it's been clearly demonstrated that when customers are offered a well-delivered apology, they're much less likely to switch to another supplier when they have problems. Customers also say that whatever problem they faced was not so bad once they got that apology.[7] It's clear that apologies are much more than simple words. They're a concrete offering.

One more note about your language. We recommend that you don't say, "I'm sorry for any inconvenience caused." *Inconvenience* is quite a weak term. It means troublesome, bothersome, or uncomfortable. Sometimes the "inconveniences" caused by organizations are much more than troublesome. They are major. Janelle once spent three and a half hours on hold to get help from a computer company. When the line was finally picked up, she was quick to tell the man she had been waiting to get help for three and a half hours. He responded, "I'm sorry for your inconvenience." Three and a half hours on hold is not an inconvenience. It's outrageous and unbelievably bad service. When Janelle strongly pointed out that this was much more than inconvenient, the service provider hung up on her.

We've heard airline employees tell passengers who have sat on airplanes for eight hours waiting for their flight to take off that they're sorry for the inconvenience. We've heard restaurant owners apologize for the inconvenience when they made a mistake about a large group's reservation, recording it for Saturday and not Friday. We've heard hotel staff apologize for the inconvenience when they forgot to make a wake-up call and as a result the traveler missed an international flight. And many service providers don't understand why customers don't accept their apologies as sincere and adequate to make up for what happened to them.

Our best recommendation is to simply stop using the word *inconvenience*. Chances are, you don't know the half of what this "inconvenience" caused for your customer. And take it off any signs such as "Sorry for the inconvenience caused" or "We apologize for any inconvenience." Here's what you can say: "I deeply apologize for what happened. I am so sorry for the problems this caused and probably a bunch of other problems you haven't even told me. Please accept my apologies. This shouldn't have happened."

Most people will accept an apology delivered sincerely and appropriate for the situation at hand. Don't overplay your apologies, but frankly, some of us need to spread broken glass on the floor and crawl through it for some of the problems we cause our customers.

While customers are speaking, send all the clues you can that you're intensely listening, including taking notes or telling the customers that you're entering their information as they speak. Don't even think about multitasking, such as responding to e-mail or finishing paperwork from a previous call, as you are listening. Customers will pick that up, even on the phone. If nothing else, they will hear you clicking on your keyboard, and they'll notice your hesitations when you respond to them. North Carolina University researchers found that product knowledge and demonstration of listening in a retail setting were two characteristics that strongly influenced whether customers had a positive or negative response when they complained.[8]

One last word about apologies. While they are important, they can also be overdone. After all, once the customer understands that you didn't want the problem to happen, it's time to move on to what you are going to do. Consultants at Katzenbach Partners in New York found that average performers at call centers apologized a great deal about what they couldn't do, while "high performers always offered something."[9] And that leads us right into step four.

Promise to Do Something About the Problem Immediately

Once you've apologized, don't ask for anything right away. Don't start to interview the customer. Tell the customer that you're going to take care of him or her (step four). "I promise you I'll do my best to fix (or look into) this situation as soon as possible." Hearing this makes customers relax because they know you're going to do something. Then, of course, you have to do something.

Service recovery has two aspects: emotional and tangible. The emotional aspect is helping everyone feel better about the situation that created dissatisfaction. The tangible aspect is doing something to fix the situation. Tangible responses are steps that will cost money or time. The Gift Formula's first four steps are part of the emotional response; they cost nothing. Unfortunately, companies can easily discount their significance.

A few years ago a Big Eight accounting firm conducted a client survey and received a surprise. Customers said that although technical expertise in auditing or consulting was important, it wasn't the most important thing they considered when choosing this particular accounting firm. They expected the expertise; the empathy and personal concern shown to them was what made them stay.[10]

When you start to use these step-by-step procedures, they may feel clumsy. Your language may not be smooth, and you will probably need a little time to get all your words out. But with practice, your phrasing will become easy, sincere, and appropriate. "Thank you for bringing this to my attention. I appreciate your telling me because now I can fix it. I really apologize for the trouble this caused. It must have been frustrating to open the package and find two pairs of blue slacks when you counted on a blue one and a brown one. I'll get this settled as soon as possible. By the way, those are beautiful slacks."

Now you need something from the customer.

Ask for Necessary Information

"In order for me to give you fast service (or to help you), could you please give me some information?" Don't say, "I need some information, otherwise I can't help you." You're the one asking for help from your customers. They're the ones who brought you the gift.

Ask only for what is necessary. You must know in advance the information you need to help customers. This needs to be part of your company's complaint-handling system. Make certain you ask for enough information or you'll have to call back for more—or force customers to call you again when nothing happens. Sometimes in this step you will learn what's really bothering your customers. They may have told you one thing, believing they have accurately presented the problem, but by asking a few questions you may discover their real problem is a bit different.

Ask what it will take to meet their needs or to satisfy them. Or ask them if they'll be satisfied if you do something specific for them that is related to their problem. Sometimes they only want to let you know something happened; they don't necessarily want anything from you.

Correct the Mistake—Promptly

Do what you said you would do. A sense of urgency is greatly appreciated by customers and puts you back in balance with them. The Gift Formula will not be adequate if you don't fix problems to the customers' satisfaction or you fix them slowly.

We've talked about speed throughout this book. Without question, it's important. Rapid responses say you are serious about service recovery. When somebody does something for us with speed, it sends a message. If I run across the room to get the paper you want, I'm telling you that I know this is important to you. If I amble over to get the paper, pause and talk with someone else, and then slowly walk back to you, I'm suggesting that you and your request aren't very important to me. Customers read speed in the same way.

Check Customer Satisfaction

Follow up. Call your customers back or send an e-mail to find out what happened. If you are face-to-face with them, ask them point-blank if they are satisfied with what you did for them. If you do this, your customers will likely fall out of their chairs. Very few providers do anything like this. If appropriate, tell them what you are doing to prevent this from happening in the future so they feel good about having helped you with their complaint. Thank them again for their complaint. You are now in partnership.

You might say that this will take too much time or involve too much of the company's resources. Actually, all it takes is a (usually) very brief telephone call. But it's a telephone call the customer will remember for a long time. You may reach the person's voice-mail system or answering machine, in which case you can leave a message. You don't necessarily need to speak to the customer in person.

If the customer tells you that everything still isn't okay, you have been given a second opportunity—a second gift, if you will—to fix the problem. Think of it this way. Your customer had a problem and told you about it. That was one disappointment. Whatever you did to fix it didn't do the job. That's a second disappointment. The customer has been let down a second time, even though an effort has been made by your organization. Believe us, it's better to know if your first efforts invested in this customer worked or not!

If there's a chance to affect the relationship so customers feel they are in partnership with you, the time (and money) invested to make a follow-up telephone call is well spent. At this point, what you're doing is no longer complaint handling. It's marketing that started out as complaint handling.

Prevent Future Mistakes

Now it's time to manage the complaint. Make sure the complaint is addressed throughout your organization so this kind of problem can be prevented in the future. And remember, fix the system without rushing to blame staff. Punish your processes, not your people.[11] Staff members are more likely to pass along complaints if they know the complaint helps the organization improve and is not used to blame staff.

In order for the complaint to truly be a gift for the organization, the root causes of that complaint must be identified. As a customer satisfaction executive with Hewlett-Packard (HP) in Cupertino, California, says, "We can say we're listening, but it's not until we take action that things really start happening."[12] HP logs its customer complaints as a means to audit trends and then uses this information to drive its quality program.

If your company has a slow turnaround time for invoice approval, resulting in both internal and external complaints, this system needs to be redesigned so customer service can improve. Merely apologizing to customers for slow times or threatening staff to make them work faster may create more problems. Michael Hutton, an airline consultant, says, "Airlines have taught their staff to say sorry in five different ways, but they have not asked themselves what they have to do so that they never have to say sorry again."[13] Most industries, with few exceptions, react to complaints as one-time transactions rather than using them as a free source of information to improve quality. Complaints are not fully utilized if they sit in a complaint-handing center; they must be used as a feedback mechanism to help the company improve itself.

Does the Gift Formula Work?

When we wrote the first edition of *A Complaint Is a Gift*, we had examples of people using this philosophy only after they had attended one of our workshops. Since the release of the book in 1996, we have been honored to receive dozens of e-mails from people who experimented using the Gift Formula under a wide variety of circumstances. Here are a few examples.

- *A customer violates programming protocol.* John, a technology analyst, was on vacation when a customer went directly to one of John's staff programmers and asked for changes to a program. The programmer did not check the impact of these requested changes, which conflicted with existing commands when the software was launched. The customer's system crashed, and everything was down for two days—except the customer's anger. On the morning John returned to the office, the customer came in ready to drop John and his company as his service provider. John had been advised about the situation and said he wasn't nervous in the least because he'd been using the Gift Formula two years. "I don't need to prepare myself emotionally since learning to see a complaint as a gift," John said. He thanked his customer, apologized, and took total responsibility for not coordinating the changes—even though he had been on vacation. The customer came around very quickly, confessing that he had circumvented the established process by going directly to the programmer himself. The customer then apologized to the analyst. John wrote in his e-mail that he always deals with emotions first and then tackles the substance of the complaint. He believes that with this approach, the blame gets distributed more justly. When we asked John if he was surprised by the customers' reaction, he wrote that at this point, he'd be surprised if it didn't happen. He's seen it happen so many times using the Gift Formula.

- *Her staff practices arm flapping while learning the Gift Formula.* An owner of twenty-four businesses around the United States, Suzanne teaches her staff to use the Gift Formula. To loosen her staff up while they are learning the Gift Formula, she has them put on Groucho Marx glasses and walk around the room flapping their arms. Suzanne says these warm-up exercises make everyone sound friendly while they handle complaints. Suzanne says they receive thank-you messages from their customers when they call to complain. "They thank us for being so helpful and for caring about them."

- *Self-esteem is way up.* Frank, a hospital administrator, distributed 150 copies of *A Complaint Is a Gift* to his staff and used the book as a topic for discussion in their weekly meetings. Frank says that before they started using the Gift Formula, complaint handling was draining his staff. Now his staff are excited to receive customer feedback. He also reports that the self-esteem of his frontline workers has gone way up.

- *A customer holds on to anger for years.* When a former customer called with a question, she brought up a long-festering complaint.

Catherine talked with the caller, who was still mad that no one had even tried to solve the problem at the time it occurred. Catherine said she used the Gift Formula, taking total responsibility for what had not happened all those years before. The caller then apologized for being so rude herself and agreed to restart working with this transport company!

- *A complaint is lodged over smoking.* Tessa received an e-mail complaint because smoking is allowed in a restaurant that Tessa manages. She used the Gift Formula in her reply by e-mail and heard back from the customer almost immediately. Tessa's civil tone, her quick response, and her apology had affected the customer dramatically. The customer's tone changed, and she offered realistic suggestions about what could be done to protect nonsmokers in the restaurant. Tessa says that all the customer's suggestions will be shared with the restaurant owner to use until the city bans smoking in restaurants.

- *You can't keep your pager number, but we'd like to keep your business.* A large telecommunication company had thirty-five hundred customers in Austin, Texas, who were all going to have to change their pager numbers. Cynthia describes this as an "ugly situation no matter how you slice it." She went to Austin to answer all the calls coming in from a lot of very angry customers. She used the Gift Formula, validating their concerns right up front, and says it worked every single time. She took close to eighty calls over a two-day period and not one customer canceled. She said that many customers started by saying, "I'm just callin' to tell you that there is no way in hell you are changin' my number on me. If you do, I'll sue your %#@!" Cynthia kept them all.

Practice Examples

Listed below are some situations with which you can practice the Gift Formula. Focus particularly on steps one through four until you become fluent in the language of the Gift Formula.

- Step one: "Thank you . . . "
- Step two: "for . . . (explanation for why you appreciate the customer's complaint).
- Step three: "I'm sorry."
- Step four: "Let me help you" or "Let me see what I can do to take care of this."

It would be best to practice with another person so you can experience being on the receiving end of this language as well. Hearing someone thank you for a complaint may be the best way for you to understand how powerful the Gift Formula is. Practice with these examples (or use others relevant to your particular organization) as many times as necessary until the words come easily.

If you decide to share the Gift Formula with your staff or colleagues, begin by first explaining the Complaint Is a Gift philosophy. If you start by teaching your staff the Gift Formula without explaining the philosophy behind it, the formula will make little sense. It will seem like a scripted technique rather than a philosophy about complaint handling. Then go through the Gift Formula, and finally, give everyone an opportunity to practice with each other using the examples below, which include both phone and in-person complaints.

- *On the phone:* "The clock I ordered doesn't work."
- *In person:* "I called your operator, and she gave me the wrong instructions on how to get here. I've been driving around for two hours."
- *On the phone:* "I just got home and discovered that two of the glasses I purchased are broken. They must have been packed poorly."
- *In person:* "I've been waiting in this line for ten minutes. You need more people at the check-out stands."
- *On the phone:* "I'm really mad. This is the third time I've been put on hold and made to wait for more than ten minutes."
- *In person:* "Your prices are too high. I don't see why I should pay so much when I know other stores have a better deal."
- *On the phone:* "I just got a second bill from your company. I know I already paid this."

- *In person:* "There's someone smoking in the nonsmoking section. You need to do something about that."
- *On the phone:* "Your company told me that someone would be out to fix my washing machine this morning. It's already two o'clock, and no one is here yet."
- *In person:* "Your newspaper ad shows these shirts available at a good price, but you don't have any left. I think you did this just to get customers into the store."
- *On the phone:* "I called your service number three times, and no one has gotten back to me. In the meantime, I can't use my computer."
- *In person:* "You can't find anything in this store. I have been walking all over three floors trying to locate the buttons, and everyone keeps sending me to another location."

Once you feel comfortable with these examples, take some real-life complaints of the type you hear in your own business, and practice the Gift Formula until you don't have to think your way through the steps. Experiment with different ways of saying the phrases. You can even try flapping your arms!

DISCUSSION QUESTIONS

- What information do you need from your customers to help them with their problems?

- What questions do you ask of complaining customers that could be eliminated?

- What questions do you ask complaining customers that annoy them? How can you tell? How can you handle this so your customers don't get upset?

- In what specific situations would it be difficult for you to use the Gift Formula?

- How frequently do you check back with your customers who have complained? Who keeps track of this?

- How do you ensure that complaints are made known throughout your organization?

- How do you track what happens to the information you learn from your customers' complaints?

~ 7 ~

Creating Better Customers
with Goodwill

Janelle was invited to present a Complaint Is a Gift workshop in Budapest, Hungary, in 1999, ten years after the Republic of Hungary was formed. In the middle of the workshop, a middle-aged woman raised her hand and asked if there was some way to "teach customers to be better customers." She added that she didn't want them to complain so much. About half of the several-hundred audience members were in their twenties and had spent the better part of their current careers under a capitalist system. This younger group broke out laughing. Their perception was that customers get to behave the way they want to.

Janelle has often thought about that woman's plaintive question. Her first reaction was to dismiss it as a remnant of the socialist economy, but the more she thought about it, the more she has wondered, "Indeed, why can't we have better customers?" In the Eastern Bloc, government-run enterprises definitely had good customers. They were good or they didn't get served and couldn't buy anything because of the extreme shortage of goods. Shoppers, it is told, would join long lines outside stores not even knowing what was being sold. And when they could buy something, they bought as much as they could because they never knew when that particular item would again be available. But this isn't the kind of "good customers" Janelle was thinking about.

What if you make the assumption that most consumers are good people or at least have a good side? Then why couldn't that side be encouraged to appear when they have a complaint? Clearly, that's challenging. But what if we could make it more likely that customers show up in a somewhat positive frame of mind, even if they have been stung by errors, shoddy goods, lackluster greetings, accents difficult for them to understand, promises not delivered, or long waits.

The question isn't quite how we teach people to be better customers. This may be part of what we get if we can teach customers how to get their needs met without irritation, including how to navigate phone menus with the least amount of frustration. The better question might be, how can we interact with our customers so that whoever last deals with a customer leaves that person better off, with appropriate expectations and the feeling that he or she is safe in our hands? Then the next person from our organization who helps that person gets to deal with a "better customer." Researchers give us reason to believe that customers come to complaint situations with a set of memories that impact what they think will happen at the next complaint event. Customer complaints are not discrete events by any means.[1]

Other than the Gift Formula chapter, this chapter is the closest one to a "how to." We cover a variety of approaches referred to by Professor Amy Smith as a "bundle of resources."[2] The complexity of complaints and the multiplicity of customer emotions and motivations make this bundle necessary to having a chance of retaining customers after we have failed them. We are categorizing a variety of techniques into three action ideas:

- Maintain a focus on fairness
- Move from problems to partners
- Manage mishaps to create broader customer tolerance zones

Maintain a Focus on Fairness

We're going to start with the most complex of these ideas because it is the foundation for the other two. We're also going to attempt to simplify a concept that has been researched in some very elaborate ways in a number of different fields. Our endnotes provide a variety of sources you can read, if you like, for a more complete explanation.

Fairness is a value that strongly resonates with almost everyone. Fairness has a lot to do with how people judge who is morally responsible for an event. According to Fairness Theory,[3] people engage in "counterfactual thinking."[4] That's a term that means imagining what could have happened, what should have happened, and how it would have felt if it had in fact happened: coulda, shoulda, woulda. When complaining, customers create an entire three-act play, counterfactualizing to come to a conclusion that may make it unlikely that they will ever buy from you again. Incidentally, one of the good reasons for asking customers what they think "shoulda" happened is to uncover their counterfactualizing.

Academic researchers are clear that whether or not customers feel they have received justice (been treated fairly) is an important part of their evaluation of their total complaint experience.[5] Typically, the researchers cover three types of justice as they relate to complaint handling: procedural, interactional, and distributive. *Procedural justice* refers to the process of handling the complaint. Was it fast, flexible, and accessible? *Interactional justice* covers the way in which people are treated when they complain. Sometimes customers feel they were given what was fair but still feel mistreated. For this reason, it is never a good idea to compensate customers in a nasty, petty manner. *Distributive justice* looks at the outcome. Did customers get what they felt was fair? Sometimes what they want is an apology. Customers typically get angry when they feel they did not get what was fair, and remarkably, they feel guilty when they feel they received more than they deserved. Most customers like to believe that they are being compensated with something that is in the ballpark of what they paid.[6] Domino's Pizza, for example, caused many of its customers distress by not charging them for their pizza if it hadn't arrived within thirty minutes. Thirty-one minutes, and the Domino's customer got a free pizza. Domino's listened to its customers' feedback and changed its guaranteed delivery time to forty-five minutes or $3 off the purchase price. The customers could accept that, and Domino's was still able to promise rapid pizza delivery.[7]

Early in life, children say with a great deal of indignation, "That's not fair!" In fact, unfairness is one of the first judgmental concepts they learn to express. As we age, our language is peppered with phrases about fairness: What's the fair thing to do? All's fair in love and war. Play fair, fair dinkum (Australian), or fair and square.

In customer service, *fair and square* means that everyone is treated according to the same terms. Customers don't have to worry about bias of any sort if a business is fair and square. Most of our customers are unknown to us until they become our customers. So they start off with the notion that they'll get fair treatment compared to all other customers. They expect that they won't have to pay higher prices and that if something goes wrong, they'll receive equitable treatment. *Fair and square* also means that if you promise something for which the customer has spent time or money, you'll live up to your word. Finally, when customers receive service they think is unfair, they almost always judge it as poor quality.

If the norm of fair treatment is violated, some people will fight to the death to restore "justice." The American Revolution began when citizens perceived that British taxation policies were unfair. Customers under similar circumstances are certainly more inclined to become Activists. They want to get even. Some are willing to pay a high personal price for justice.

Trust and fairness are intimately related. The basis for trust is perceived fairness. Without trust, a shaky foundation exists to solve customer complaints.[8] A body of research literature supports the point that when customers perceive themselves to be treated unfairly, they experience immediate emotional reactions, which dramatically affect whether or not they are satisfied. In addition, customers remember service encounters that have an element of unfairness in them longer than encounters that are not seen as unfair.[9]

Here's an example that highlights the issue of unfairness and will no doubt be long remembered by the customer. A passenger's luggage was lost. That part of the story is both so commonplace and so individually impactful that it is frankly almost boring for experienced travelers to hear about, so we'll skip the details. The interesting part for us is how the passenger expressed her dismay so sharply in terms of fairness. "I was surprised at the pettiness and inability of [the airline] to verbally commit to reimbursing what I needed on my trip. When I was a passenger on your flight, I took full responsibility for my actions. I arrived at the airport with an hour to spare, checked my luggage with my name clearly labeled on the inside and out, behaved in the usual and expected fashion, dressed appropriately for the flight, followed all rules, and promptly paid 100% of my ticket price. Now, I expect the same courtesy, taking of responsibility, and prompt 100% reimbursement in return."[10] Good luck!

"All's fair in love and war" is a phrase first used in 1578; it was a concept used to justify cheating. This is not what we want our customers to believe. Unfortunately, many of them do after being abused by our policies or having their time wasted by products that don't work. No doubt customers who engage in destruction of company property think they are just getting even. And many probably also justify shoplifting by telling themselves that the organization they're stealing from is still making lots of money from them because of price gouging. Customers who benefit from a mistake (more money returned to them than is due or billing that doesn't accurately reflect the true price of goods or services) and who don't notify the organization to return the money or pay the amount that is fair probably go through a conversation with themselves to justify their behavior.

How common is consumer perception of unfairness? Apparently rather commonplace. In one study, customers were asked to evaluate the fairness of a variety of service recovery procedures. Less than half of the participants judged the procedures to be fair. Fair service recovery procedures were those rated as clear and easy to understand, quick, and hassle free.[11] This would seem to match the research literature on what makes for an effective product or service guarantee.

Unfairness is perceived in a variety of situations. Before reading the list below, make a quick list of what you think is unfair when you do business with an organization. Here's what people in our workshops have told us is unfair. Some of these may surprise you.

- Customers have to repeat information they have already provided.
- A service window closes just as they get to the front of the line.
- They have to wait a long time for an appointment.

- They are ignored or overlooked and someone else gets attention.
- They are told, "You should have . . . ," and there is no way they could have known.
- They are overbilled and then have to fight to get the billing corrected.
- The product they purchased fails a day after the warranty expires.
- One person gives them information that another person refuses to honor.
- The fault is clearly the organization's, but no one will take responsibility.
- Customers are blamed for something they weren't told about.
- No one seems interested in them if they face a problem, but the organization is very friendly when it comes to taking their money.
- Customers have to provide documentation that is clearly in the organization's database.
- Products break down.
- Guarantees are not honored.

When faced with situations like this, customers not only have a complaint, they are also emotionally aroused. Many of them are fed up, and there is really only one way to punish an organization: become a *former* customer. They can also tell everyone else not to do business with the organization.

The extensive research done about fairness can help us walk through a lot of these tough issues. Here's what some of it says about customer behavior in the face of unfairness.[12]

1. When customers think they are not technically competent, fairness becomes even more important to them. They are at the mercy of their suppliers. Is your product complicated? If so, fairness is more important to your customers.
2. When customers have given a lot of their business to an organization, fairness is important to them. They think, "How can they treat me this way? Don't they know who I am and how much business I have done with them?" Do the bulk of your customers tend

to be repeat customers who have done business with you over a long period of time? If so, fairness is more important to your customers.

3. When customers purchase products that they can't evaluate before purchasing (a haircut, a massage, health care, entertainment, software packages), fairness, in how they are treated is very important to them. They have been forced to rely on their trust of you and your advertising. Can your customers evaluate your product before they purchase it? If not, fairness is more important to your customers.

4. When customers feel that your service recovery is too slow or they had to devote an inordinate amount of time getting a problem fixed, they're likely to judge it as unfair, even if you give them a full refund. How quick are you at fixing customer problems? If your service recovery is slow, fairness is more important to your customers.

5. When customers know you will stand by your guarantees but you make them go through a lot of hassle to be redressed, they will think of you as unfair. How much hassle do you create for your customers when they ask for a refund? The more hassle you create in order for them to get refunds or redress, the more important fairness is to your customers.

6. When customers don't have a lot of options to go elsewhere, they feel more vulnerable on the issue of fairness. They expect you to behave without bias. This can happen with utilities that are monopolies or government agencies. Does your organization have much competition? If not, fairness is more important to your customers.

Fairness Susceptibility Quotient

It's a good idea to be fair to all your customers, but some people are more easily offended than others when fairness is not delivered. A quick way to determine which customers are more likely to be sensitive to fairness is to assign them a ranking on the fairness susceptibility quotient chart below.[13]

1 Customer not knowledgeable
Product complex, expensive
 	
Customer feels most vulnerable
High anxiety
Fairness element most critical
Product guarantees important
Greatest opportunity to build loyalty
	2 Customer knowledgeable
	Product complex, expensive
	
	Relatively high degree of customer
	   control
	Fairness element somewhat critical
	Customer demands still high
	   because of product cost

3 Customer not knowledgeable Product simple, low priced Customer may need some help Fairness element not too critical	**4** Customer knowledgeable Product simple, low priced High degree of customer control Fairness element least critical

When customers are not knowledgeable and are dealing with a complex and expensive product or service, they are likely to feel vulnerable and anxious. The fairness element is most critical under these circumstances, and product guarantees are most important. In fact, fairness becomes the single most important predictor of perceived service quality when customers feel they're at the mercy of someone else's knowledge.[14] When customers are in this position and they complain, they offer the greatest opportunity for loyalty building if the fairness issue is handled well. When customers are knowledgeable and the product is complex and expensive, fairness is not as critical, though it's still important because of product cost. These customers feel that they have a relatively high degree of control, so they can take care of themselves if they detect unfair supplier behavior.

When the product is simple and low priced and customers are not knowledgeable, they may still need your help, but because of the low cost of the product, fairness is not as critical. And, of course, when customers are knowledgeable and have purchased a simple, low-priced product or service, fairness is the least important among these four scenarios.

Make a list of your customer types based on the products and services they buy from you and assign them a fairness susceptibility rank. Depending upon their ranking, you then need to emphasize the following four behaviors when you sense that your clients feel you aren't being fair. (Sometimes, they'll tell you!)

- *Don't blame.* If your customers think you have been unfair with them and you blame them, you are throwing gasoline on a fire. As Eric Hofer wrote in *Working and Thinking on the Waterfront*, "Fair play with others is not blaming them for anything that is wrong with us."[15] Even if customers did something to contribute to the problem themselves, keep focused on solving the problem rather than pointing out where they were at fault. They will appreciate your not rubbing their nose in their mistake.

- *Keep assuring your customers you want to do everything you can to help them.* When customers feel they have been treated unfairly or their susceptibility quotient is high, knowing that the person helping them at that moment is concerned about them will go a long way toward reducing their feelings of vulnerability. Tell them they are important to you and you are very sorry about what happened. Apologies are particularly important when customers feel they have been handed an unfair deal.

- *Offer complete explanations.* This is the time for careful explanations as to what happened and why. If you can keep your complaining customers as loyal customers, the extra time you spend while handling their complaints and problems will be worthwhile. An Australian study found that after companies had made mistakes, simple explanations generated much higher levels of customer satisfaction and loyalty than did explanations that sounded like justifications. Let go of your need to justify anything when you have a severely upset customer.[16] Think about how much it costs to acquire new customers. When you are so fortunate as to be talking with an upset customer, you have the chance to "create a loyal customer," in Peter Drucker's words. If you can't give complaining customers what they want, explain the reasons for your policies and procedures and try to help them in some other way.

- *Ask lots of questions.* First, ask your customers why they think the situation is unfair. Be gentle in how you ask because this is a very direct question. You could say, "I want to understand exactly what you are thinking. I sense you think this is unfair. Can you tell me why?" You may learn a great deal from the responses you hear. You may not be able to give your customers exactly what they want, but you can give them the gift of your listening to them. You and your customers are exchanging gifts. You get their feedback and they receive full information. While you're talking about fairness, be sure to ask, "What would it take for you to feel that you have been treated fairly?" Even if you can't do what your customers ask for, you can at least pass this information on to your organization. If a large number of your customers feel the same way, everyone in the organization can learn from this situation.

What's our bottom line here? When customers face a problem, they want certain things if they are to walk away with their positive perceptions of the organization still in place. First, they want money, goods, or coupons when a product failure occurs; they don't necessarily feel that they should be given free items if someone is rude to them or makes them wait. Second, speed is extremely important when a product or service failure occurs; speed is not as critical when customers feel they are owed an apology. Third, apologies are most important when something upsets customers in terms of how a service representative behaved toward them; apologies aren't a very good remedy when customers face a product failure. Fourth, if an organization has a clear, strong guarantee, then customers tend not to focus on distributive justice (how they are compensated) and instead focus on interactional and procedural justice.

The key point to remember is that any service failure creates an imbalance in the exchange relationship and it needs to be rectified in a way that matches people's sense of fair play. One researcher, for example, found that when a problem happened in a hotel setting, customers preferred to get a 50 percent refund if the service provider was seen to be adhering to company policy. They didn't like feeling that something special was being done for them in violation of company policy. If a small token of compensation was given to them, they liked to think that the service providers decided to give them this gift (such as a drink coupon) on their own initiative and weren't just fulfilling company policy.[17]

Move from Problems to Partners

The authors both travel a great deal to deliver speeches and to be with clients. As a result, we spend a lot of time in hotels. Janelle once was placed in a smoke-filled room with a nonfunctioning television set and broken furniture. And this was at a high-level branded hotel. She called the front desk and was told to come back to the lobby to get a key for a new room. Janelle asked that the key be delivered to her to save her the trouble of carting her luggage all over the large hotel. The desk clerk agreed, but after fifteen minutes, no one had arrived at Janelle's room. She called the front desk again and was told they forgot! So, Janelle suggested that she meet the hotel employee at the new room, thereby saving her a bit of time. She waited for over five minutes in front of the second room before someone showed up. The front desk had sent this person to the unacceptable room. By this time, you can imagine that Janelle wasn't feeling fairly treated and she complained clearly and loudly.

The hotel representative listened, looked at Janelle, and said, "Oh my gosh. That's not right. Thank you so much for saying something. I personally apologize that we've treated you so badly. I'm going to check out this new room to make sure we've got you in a comfortable, suitable room. Then I'm going to go back and take that other room out of service. No one should have to endure a room like that." Janelle stood there, mouth agape, surprised to hear the Gift Formula used on her so effectively.

After analyzing that experience, we developed the following model of what happens to customers when their perceptions are turned around.

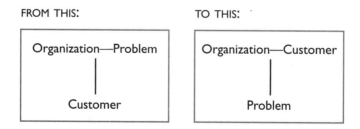

FROM THIS:

Organization—Problem
|
Customer

TO THIS:

Organization—Customer
|
Problem

When customers begin their complaint, they see themselves in conflict with the organization. It's a position of deficit because, in the customers' eyes, the organization and the problem are one and the same. If you use the Gift Formula at the beginning of the interaction, such as the hotel employee did with Janelle, you strongly influence the customers' state of mind. When you thank them and apologize for mistakes, customers will more likely see themselves in partnership with you, united against a common enemy: the problems that they face. Everyone involved in complaint situations will benefit by taking customers from the left-hand box to the right-hand box as quickly as possible. Once customers see that you and they are linked in a common effort to solve the problem, customers become "better."

We always need to emphasize the mind-set that complaints are gifts, and there is no better way to begin your conversation than by thanking customers for their feedback. You can take a few additional steps to help customers shift from seeing you and the problem as married to viewing themselves as partners with you.

- *Warn your customers about danger spots.* If you know something can go wrong, take customers into your confidence and let them know where they can get in trouble. Make sure they know when they need to come back to you or they'll possibly get into deeper trouble. If you do this right, you'll have partners and better customers the next time they call with a problem to be solved.
- *Let your customers know the ways they can influence the speed of service they receive.* Tell customers when you are least busy. Teach them how to navigate your phone system. Tell them what to have ready the next time they call so they'll save time. Make sure they have your name so if they call back, they can mention it when talking with a different person. All these behaviors make them feel they are in partnership with you. And customers operating from the box on the right are definitely better behaved customers.
- *Tell your customers you want to fully understand what is happening, that you want to get to the bottom of whatever problem they are facing.* Partners want complete understanding, so tell customers you're

going to ask what may appear to be dumb questions and that you are doing this to make sure you aren't missing anything.

- **Don't hide information.** Tell customers how they can help themselves, if necessary, on your Web site. Or e-mail them documents that will help them. Make sure you have read these documents yourself so you aren't just sending something that someone told you to send. Make sure they're the right documents.
- **If you possibly can, give customers your direct-line telephone number so they don't have to go through a phone menu.** Or send them an e-mail so they can write to you if they have additional questions. It's all about good partnership, and partnership helps to create better customers.

By the way, after Janelle got settled in her new room, she sought out the general manager of the hotel to praise the way this service recovery had been accomplished. She complimented the staff person who thanked her for the complaint, and she asked the manager whether he taught his staff to thank customers for their complaints. The manager replied, "As a matter of fact, we found this book"—he held up the first edition of *A Complaint Is a Gift*—"and we've been working with it here in the hotel!"

Manage Mishaps to Create Broader Tolerance Zones

Customers have two pictures of service in their mind when they complain:

- Desired service: what they would like to receive
- Adequate service: the minimum they'll accept without negative feelings or complaints

The zone of tolerance (or "goodwill," as referred to by some) resides between these two pictures.[18] It can be broad or narrow. When customers think they received desired service after delivering a complaint, their tolerance zone is very broad. When customers think they received poor treatment while complaining, they operate in a very narrow tolerance zone. When customers operate in a broad tolerance zone, they are more accepting. Long waits aren't quite as annoying. Unfriendly service isn't such a major affront. Product unavailability isn't intolerable and, therefore, a reason to switch suppliers.[19]

Maritz Research looked at thousands of hotel satisfaction surveys and states that most guests are less likely to return after a mishap about which they complained. This primarily seems to be because most hotels aren't very good at responding to complaints. Maritz says that hotels are at least four times more likely to not recover well for guests than they are to exceed expectations. Maritz concludes that "wise hoteliers focus on proactive rather than reactive service strategies as a means to drive guest and meeting planner loyalty to their properties."[20] We agree with Maritz Research that proactive strategies that expand customer tolerance zones are important. It is, in fact, the main point of this section. At the same time, we think hotels should also focus on handling complaints well so that they also build goodwill.

Even though many consider "goodwill" one of the softest issues in the business world, the reality is that when customers have a narrow zone of tolerance, you have less flexibility with them. They are, as a result, a lot harder to please. When operating in a narrow tolerance zone, customers look for things to go wrong—and they'll find them. Sometimes the zone of tolerance is so narrow that only the best complaint redress will be minimally acceptable to your customers—if you want to keep them.

While organizations always need to work at broadening customer Zones of Tolerance, it's important to remember that the customers are keeping tally in their brains of the amount of goodwill they are experiencing as well. Customers expect that the longer they stay with an organization, the broader the company's zone of tolerance should be toward them. This means that if customers make a mistake, they expect the company to forgive and not penalize. For example, if a regular customer who has tolerated numerous flight delays and cancellations makes a mistake and orders a nonrefundable ticket for the wrong day, this customer expects the airline to show greater tolerance about the mistake. If a long-term, loyal customer forgets to bring along a receipt, the customer expects the company to not be a stickler about the receipt rules.

Occasionally, the zone of tolerance shrinks to such a degree that absolutely nothing will satisfy your customers. As a complaint handler, you have very little room in which to maneuver when this happens. With our friends and families we tend to enjoy broader Zones of Tolerance, so there is greater trust and opportunity for forgiveness. In fact, parents tend to have an infinite zone of tolerance with their children. They would never walk away from them. This isn't always the case between spouses. And it definitely isn't the case between customers and their favorite companies or brands, unless perhaps they happen to have a gigantic logo of the company (like Harley-Davidson) tattooed all across their backs. That tattoo represents a very broad tolerance zone.

Academic researchers who have studied the zone of tolerance seem almost embarrassed to say that something as simple as friendliness expands customer tolerance zones.[21] Being friendly with customers is basically the same as being friendly with your friends, which typically involves giving them a lot of attention. Friendliness includes simple acts of courtesy such as using a customer's name, smiling, and looking for connections. Tolerance can be expanded when customers are honored by direct communication with the CEO. Blogger Bruce Nussbaum, who has been tracking Delta's service to see that it lives up to its marketing, recently got a personal letter from Delta's CEO. A recent Nussbaum blog is headlined "Delta's CEO Sends Me a Personal Letter Apologizing for Bad Service—That's Actually Pretty Good Service."[22] Friendliness builds trust and inspires forgiveness. Surprisingly, asking customers who have faced problems to complain also seems to increase satisfaction compared to not asking customers to complain.[23]

This is an important point for customer-facing staff to remember. The simple act of inviting a customer who has faced a problem to fill out an evaluation form or go to the company Web site and send feedback to the organization or letting the customer know that you will pass on his or her complaint apparently builds tolerance. Pret, the high-quality, fresh fast-food UK outlet chain, invites its customers to complain with a clever, friendly card that is available at the checkout station. Printed with the brand statement "Pret, Passionate about food," it reads: "My name is Steph. I'm the General Manager at this Pret Shop. My team and I meet every morning. We discuss the comments you've made, the good, the bad and the ugly. If we can deal with it ourselves, we will. If we can't, I'll forward this card to Julian Metcalfe back at the office. I know he'll do what he can. If you have a minute, please do ask to speak to me or one of my team right now." That's about as inviting as it gets. On the back side is a lot of space to write down what happened—no boxes to be checked. Pret wants to read its customers' words.

When customers have a high fairness susceptibility quotient, friendliness becomes even more important to keep their negative emotions in check. Friendliness is not as emotionally important to customers when they don't depend on your product or service. They can always go somewhere else, so they are less dependent upon you to help them maintain a positive mood. If they are dependent on your service, they need friendliness to feel secure.[24] Without this friendliness, customers become less tolerant and more difficult.[25]

Businesses should try to nurture stories about them that are so positive that they are discussed publicly and create broader tolerance zones when customers read them. The *Wall Street Journal Online* recently ran a lengthy story about a United Airlines pilot, Denny Flanagan, who works at having fun on his flights and does some truly extraordinary things with and for his passengers. People who hear about him say they wish all of United Airlines' personnel were like Captain Flanagan. The reality is that the negatives are going to happen, so whenever an organization can get positive press online, it's good. Anyone who is inclined to believe that United offers good service will be convinced by reading about Captain Flanagan. As one passenger said, "If other folks in the airline industry had the same attitude, it would go a long way to mitigating some of the negative stuff that has come about in the last four or five years."[26] This is a very clear statement of the positive impact of a broad tolerance zone.

One way to become aware of the zone of tolerance your customers think they're in is to listen to them when they interact with your customer-facing staff. Ronald Zebeck, president of Metrics Companies, a direct marketer of consumer credit products, says his marketing people hate him because he makes them listen in on their call-center phone lines four hours a month. He doesn't ask them to take any calls but just to listen. Why do this? As Zebeck says, "Because there are those gaping chest sound kind of sound bites that come across in those phone calls that make a big difference."[27]

Part of the power of making everyone inside an organization aware of the zone of tolerance is to create a customer approach in which all customer-facing staff have a minigoal for every customer interaction. That goal is to have the customer leave with a broader tolerance zone so the next person who interacts with that customer starts off with a "better" customer.

DISCUSSION QUESTIONS

- How does the issue of fairness emerge when customers complain to your organization?

- Can you determine which type of justice (procedural, interactional, or distributive) is most important to your customers or under which circumstances one type of justice becomes more important?

- Where do your products or services fit on the fairness susceptibility quotient scale? How does this influence your service behaviors toward customers?

- What behaviors can you engage in that will quickly move your customers from seeing themselves as standing in opposition to your organization to a view where they see you operating in partnership?

- What specific "friendliness" behaviors can help broaden your customers' tolerance zones?

~ 8 ~

When Customers
Go Ballistic

No one likes to see customers scream at company representatives, but it happens. A 1976 study of consumers said 32 percent reported experiencing a serious customer service problem in the previous year. By 2003, after the establishment of huge call centers, that number had risen to 45 percent, and of those consumers more than two-thirds reported feeling "rage" about how their problems were handled.[1] Not only can screaming customers leave service providers shaken, but the customers may be embarrassed by their public display of emotions; to cover their embarrassment, they may become more self-righteous. Viewers are uncomfortable, wondering if they should take a stand—and on whose side.

It is essential that service providers be trained to handle volatile situations. Faced with the threat of possible attack, our natural inclinations are either to fight or to flee. Neither of these behaviors is appropriate in a business environment (unless someone is truly threatening), but they are natural responses that we suppress. Hollywood capitalizes on this frustration with movie scenes in which the overworked, underappreciated, trampled-on employee who finally can't take it anymore calls the customer a foul name, insists he or she is not paid enough to take the abuse, and walks right off the job. Almost all movie audiences spontaneously applaud such scenes.

Some approaches, such as the Gift Formula, can help calm upset customers. We have seen the Gift Formula work successfully with some extremely wrought-up customers. Shortly after the first edition of *A Complaint Is a Gift* was released, we heard from a veterinarian with a customer who was furious that a treatment for his cows did not do what it was supposed to do. The customer believed he had been sold an inferior product, but what really fed his anger was his belief that the vet simply didn't care. The vet realized that the emotions had to be handled first. Once that issue got sorted out, the two of them were able to analyze what was happening. The vet kept saying over and over again to his customer, "I'm so glad you brought this to my attention." Each time, it helped calm the customer.

It's important to remember that the vet's customer was dissatisfied. That is clear. The customer was also angry, and that difference needs to be acknowledged. Dissatisfied customers may give you a second chance if their needs are met. But if they are angry and dissatisfied, there is a much greater likelihood that you'll not see them again. And if customers are both furious and dissatisfied when they leave you, it's extremely difficult to get them back.[2] Therefore, if your organization is measuring only dissatisfaction, you may be getting a very incomplete picture of future consumer intentions. One way to get more information about the emotional state of your customers is to ask staff at call centers to check a box from negative five to positive five indicating the intensity of customer emotions. Zero in the middle would represent no significant emotional effect. Five on the positive side would indicate a customer who hangs up delighted. Five on the negative side would indicate a customer who was furious and perhaps swore before hanging up. Managers could call the people with high negative numbers to see if there was some way they could still reclaim them as customers.

On occasion, customers are beyond wrought up. They are ready to explode, and it takes a mature, self-aware person to be able to handle a situation like this. Frequently, customer-facing staff are just beginning their careers and have had limited experience with maintaining a professional presence while handling explosive customers. Sometimes even highly experienced staff have difficulties dealing with angry customers.

A medical doctor in one of our workshops told us he did not like it when his patients got upset. "I don't understand why they get upset with me," he said. "I had one patient who felt I wasn't sensitive to him. I don't get it. I saved his leg, didn't I?" The other doctors in the audience applauded his remarks. Janelle pointed out that saving a leg is indeed a very important part of the professional services a doctor can provide. But it's not sufficient. "Perhaps," Janelle said, "your patient thinks of himself as more than just a leg. Perhaps this patient experiences himself as a total emotional being."

We'll go out on a limb and say that the service you offer is only as good as your complaint handling when customers are frustrated and angry. Authors Wolfgang Seidel and Bernd Stauss support this idea when they say, "From the customer's perspective, the actual problem solution is not judged independently from the way the [organization] treats the customer in case of a complaint."[3] Ongoing practice in handling complaints is essential to create a foundation for professional action when staff are placed in situations in which their natural inclination is to leave or to do combat.

In this chapter, we discuss five principles that underlie techniques that can be used to handle difficult customers. These principles are based on extensive psychological research: corralling the energy of anger, pacing the customer, valuing language and timing, forming partnerships, and getting personal. While these are the same principles we wrote about in the first edition of this book, we have updated our examples.

Corralling the Energy of Anger

A common reaction to stress is hostility, which can be so extreme that it is physically expressed toward others. Laboratory animals become aggressive when they are overcrowded, shocked with electricity, or *fail to get what they want*. When people get frustrated, they are likely to take it out on somebody as well, frequently an innocent bystander. It is easy to see why staff who deal directly with customers but who may have had little to do with the cause of the anger sometimes feel as if a verbal ton of bricks has been thrown at them by upset customers.

The aikido concept used in Japanese martial arts is a useful one when dealing with anger. *Aikido* means "the way of unifying with life energy."[4] Aikido is about blending with another's energy so it doesn't knock you over and then channeling that energy in the direction you want. Masters of aikido do not resist the physical force of their opponents; rather, they turn with it and let it pass them. Approaching anger this way keeps you from becoming defensive and lets you treat upset customers with a degree of detachment as you try to solve their problems. Detachment, by the way, doesn't mean not getting involved. It means not letting your emotional buttons get pushed.

Aikido offers an approach that protects the one being attacked from harm, while showing concern for the attacker. When you think about this in relationship to complaining, ballistic customers, it makes a lot of sense. Service providers need to be protected from customers' negative energy while at the same time showing regard for customers. Morihei Ueshiba, founder of aikido, put it this way: "To control aggression without inflicting injury is the Art of Peace."[5] This is a good way to look at how to handle out-of-control customers.

Angry people generally will not get any angrier if you handle them well. But if they are pushed, controlled, or treated rudely, their anger can escalate. Of course, you don't want this to happen. It's better to corral the person's emotional energy and, hopefully, transform it with a positive service encounter. (Consider couples. Frequently, the most intense love they experience is after a bitter fight that turns from anger back to attraction.)

What Exactly Is Anger?

Anger is strong emotional energy, so strong that it can leave anyone close to it shaken. Nonetheless, our job is to help customers channel this energy so they walk away feeling good about what just happened. Almost all anger is identified as being caused by something from the outside, even when it may be internally generated (such as by getting up late, forgetting to bring a receipt, or being annoyed with a family member).

Psychologists today generally categorize anger as (1) a response that is stimulated when physical self-preservation is threatened, (2) a feeling that emerges spontaneously as part of a person's character traits, or (3) a reaction to perceived harm or unfair treatment. Character traits can influence how customers talk to a service provider or how easily they allow their irritation to show. Someone might be naturally irritable, antagonistic, peevish, bristly, pricklish, miffed, offended, piqued, rankled, ruffled, stirred up, annoyed, chagrined, exasperated, impatient, or petulant. (Take a look in a thesaurus and you will find a lot more synonyms for *angry* than there are antonyms.) Anger, however it is expressed, is more readily displayed by certain customers whose character traits incline them in this direction.

Anger can effectively manipulate others, and it's fairly commonly used that way in customer service interactions. Customer Care Alliance, a Virginia-based organization, found that 8 percent of frustrated consumers admit to cursing at service representatives; 28 percent say they have yelled.[6] And once certain customers benefit from this type of behavior, it's hard for them to not repeat it because it works, even if intermittently. Customers who act with more certainty can frequently get the organization to do something for them. Giving in to customer-displayed anger, unfortunately, teaches more customers to get angry. Therefore, it's not beneficial for service providers to fuel customer anger.

Anger, as a topic, has been around for a long time. Even ancient philosophers wrote about anger. Seneca, the Roman stoic philosopher, told his readers to find inner peace by simplifying their lives and avoiding anger-provoking people. That might be difficult in today's busy call-center environments! Seneca advises that if you can't avoid angry people, take the negatives being thrust at you and see them in the most positive light (use the Complaint Is a Gift Philosophy), or put yourself in the other person's shoes (listen with empathy). Finally, Seneca says that when dealing with angry people, the best thing to do is not overreact, even though that is a natural protective behavior. He's actually recommending the soft aikido response to others.[7]

Stages of Anger

It's useful to look at ballistic anger as having stages similar to the stages of grieving: denial and shock, blaming (of themselves or others), bargaining, and finally, acceptance.

In the denial phase of major anger, you'll hear customers say, "There's no way this could be true" or, "There must be some mistake." Be alert when you hear these types of statements. They are likely the opening volley. Customers are attempting to control their anger, and you are glimpsing the beginning of a potential major volcanic eruption. In this stage, you have a chance to avoid this eruption if you can answer the customers' questions, look competent, and provide as much information as possible. Emotionally, it's a very good idea to support the customers' initial reaction. "You're right. There must be some sort of mistake. Let's check it out." Get them involved with you in figuring out what happened. If you are looking at information on a computer screen, tell your customers what you are doing or seeing. Don't exclude them from the process. Keep them involved. It helps defuse their anger.

In the blaming phase of anger—generally the most difficult part of the anger process for service providers—customers go on the attack. "I'm not surprised. This happens all the time. Your people are so incompetent." Even though they may not say it, they are definitely including you in this group of low-performing idiots. This is where it gets hard to not take it personally. Keep looking at the gift you are being given, even though it is wrapped rather poorly. Keep reminding yourself that there's a gift in there. All of us who help our customers want to be appreciated for our efforts, and when we are being blamed it's not easy to remain friendly. In fact, it generally makes us itch to go on the attack. If we appreciate that these blaming statements are part of the anger of dissatisfied customers who are at least still communicating with us, then we may not get quite as defensive. While customers are in the middle of this phase of anger, it's best to actively listen rather than attempt to say anything.

When customers are angry, they also tend to become very loud. They do this because they want you to know that what they are angry about is important to them. If they think you are going to brush them off, they tend to get louder. It's a nonverbal way to let you know that they want you to listen to them.

If your customers look as if they might have the wherewithal to continue shouting for an extended period of time, you might try the following statement. You can use it to your advantage primarily because it starts with two negatives and then finishes with a positive. It's like good comedy in that it grabs attention in a positive way. The listener has to figure out what you just said, and we've seen it turn people around instantly. Here's how it goes: "I don't care how angry you get with me [the first negative], it's not going to stop me [the second negative], from doing everything I can to help you [the positive]." You need to practice this statement a little until you can say it fluently and with some meaning.

In the bargaining phase of anger, customers begin to seek a way to solve their problems. Their anger is starting to subside, and they are using the rational side of their brains. This is our opportunity to partner with them. It's at this point that we can become more active in the conversation, but we must stay focused on solutions rather than problems. In the blaming phase, customers remain glued to their problems. In the bargaining phase, we have the chance to move the conversation to the issue of how our customers' needs can be met. Customers will enter the acceptance phase if their problems are resolved or they hear a promise that they'll be resolved in the future.

An understanding of anger's stages helps explain why sometimes our methods to control upset people do not work. We too rapidly try to jump over the stages to get to problem solving, but angry people must express all four stages to come out on the other side—just as they do in the grieving process. People are not rational when they are in the denial and blaming stages. They become rational in the bargaining phase and finally have a chance to internally integrate their mixture of thoughts and feelings in the acceptance phase. Don't try to fix your customers' problems too quickly. Give them a chance to express the emotions they feel.

Anger, like a volcanic eruption, bursts forth and then it subsides. When you are around people who are erupting, the best thing you can do is to let them express their feelings. It's quite impossible to stop an erupting volcano. You can only observe it and listen to it. One way to indicate that you are listening intently is to take written notes. If customers make a negative remark about that, tell them, "I want to make sure I get everything you are saying down on paper. I want to get it right and not forget anything you're saying." As the service provider, you want to be available to help the customers as their anger lessens. Telling them not to be angry almost never works. We know that anger carries a lot of energy. Angry customers, as compared to worried customers, for example, tend to engage in more negative word-of-mouth or even switch suppliers.[8] This energy merits our patience and respect.

Once your customers start to become rational again, you can help move them to a more positive emotion. In *Beyond Culture*, anthropologist Edward Hall describes an *action chain* as a set sequence of events between two or more people. For example, if someone says, "Good morning. How are you?" to complete the action chain someone has to respond, "I'm fine, thank you." If the appropriate response is not forthcoming, the first person feels that something was not finished. He or she will feel cut off and incomplete. If an action chain is interrupted or stopped, it will likely be repeated, says Hall.[9] This means that if you do not acknowledge customers' anger or somehow respond to it, they probably will just get angrier. The applicable rule is, never break an action chain unless you have a very good reason for doing so. For instance, if listening to customers means they will miss their flight, then break the action chain and get them on the plane without patiently listening to their tirade. You can always apologize later.

In order to complete an anger action chain, you need to acknowledge your customers' anger. We have observed service providers saying to angry customers, "I can't help you if you don't settle down." In fact, we know of many companies that advise their customer-facing staff to say those exact words. From our point of view, that represents a break in the action chain, and customers will remain upset in most cases. A better response would be, "I know you're angry. I would be, too."

By the way, we might point out that when a customer gives you a complaint/gift and you say "Thank you," an action chain has been started. Typically, the common completion to a thank-you action chain is "You're welcome." Even if the customer never *says* these words, at some level within their consciousness, they are searching for or feeling them. "Thank you" and "You're welcome" form one of the most polite action chains that people around the world use with each other.

The first step in handling angry customers is to simply hear them out. Listen intently. Don't interrupt; it will only make angry people get louder, exacerbating their already stressed internal state. They obviously have something to say, and the quicker you let them do that, the faster you can move to problem solving. When you do talk, speak to what the customers were talking about or you negate their message, which only leads to more anger. So listen carefully and don't start talking about a different subject.

How do you do this? One way is to focus on their upset but not necessarily on their words if they are trying to bait you. "When did you start treating your customers like dogs?" is a statement designed to pull you into an argument. You could respond by saying, "I'm very sorry that we've obviously offended you." If the customer says, "If you cared even a tiny bit about your customers, you wouldn't have such stupid policies," they are baiting you to say, "But we do care about our customers." You are then put in the position of defending yourself, which will only give customers more ammunition to continue doing battle. "Then why . . . ?" And the battle will rage. A better way to respond is to ask a question about their attack. You could say, "What happened that makes you think we don't care about you?" This will surprise them. They expect a defense, not a question. If you do not defend yourself, it is more difficult for customers to continue with their assault. Remember aikido.

It's also critical to accept angry people for who they are and what they are expressing right now. People tend to get stuck when they sense you don't accept where they are at the moment. People get angry only about things that are important to them. If they sense you don't find their issue important, they will get louder, as we mentioned earlier. They want you to hear. Your acceptance can help them change and soften their tone.

Questions help move people to a position of rationality rather than emotionality. Generally, three open-ended questions posed one after another will help angry people become more rational. If you've been pulled over by a police officer because you were speeding, you may remember that the officer started with a series of questions. The first typically is, "Do you know why I pulled you over?" The driver's answer tells the officer what his or her next step should be. If the driver says, "Yeah! Because you don't have anything better to do with the taxpayers' dollars," then the police officer knows that this is a potentially difficult citizen and acts accordingly. If the driver says, "Why? Was I speeding?" then the police officer goes to the second question: "May I see your driver's license, please?" This is followed by the third question: "May I see your car registration or insurance papers?" Police officers don't wake up one morning and simply start asking questions of speeding or reckless drivers. They are trained to do this; they are attempting to determine whether the driver is rational. Police officers are under a lot of stress themselves and may find it difficult to control their own anger. (And most people who have just been pulled over to the side of the road by a police officer are emotional!)

For those who are acquainted with transactional psychology language, the rational brain is referred to as the "adult tape."[10] Questions activate the rational brain, and in most cases, three questions in succession will take people out of their emotional, reactive, limbic brain and engage their cortex, whereby they can use rational thought. In order to become an expert at asking questions of angry people, you need to test your questions. Develop alternative second and third questions and possibly more if your initial questions do not yield a rational response. You need to know that your questions do not increase frustration, and the best way to find out is to get feedback in practice environments. Ask questions that make sense and demonstrate that something positive is going to happen. Remember, we are trying to convert the energy in the anger into a positive response.

If you absolutely must set limits—such as to wait for their turn or to stop interrupting—do so in such a way that customers do not lose face, the Asian concept that allows people to retain their dignity or position status, especially in public. Sometimes it helps to remove customers from crowded areas so their emotionality does not cause them shame. Customers can then express their anger privately, which also prevents your company from looking out of control. It's never smart to treat adults like children, but we're amazed at how frequently we have observed service providers order customers around by saying, "I can't help you unless you all sit down" or, "You must to form a single line." You'll have many ballistic customers if you publicly patronize complaining adults.

If you're dealing with someone who is furious and he or she is going to explode regardless of what you do, remember your audience: the rest of your customers who may be watching to see what you do. In most cases, they'll be sympathetic to you unless you also become aggressive, such as the grocery-store example we related in chapter 1.

There is one final approach to consider if you have customers you know to be always angry and never satisfied. Oren Harari says don't tolerate abusive, destructive, or violent customers.[11] Such customers can be very time consuming, especially in relationship to the revenues they bring to the organization. They can also be very upsetting to customer-facing staff and other customers. Consider "firing" these customers. Firing customers needs to be done carefully because you don't want to create Activists (described in chapter 5). Tell them with great courtesy that based on your history with them, your service seems to make them angry, and, for that reason, you never seem to be able to satisfy them. And then suggest that perhaps other providers might be able to meet their needs better. In this way, you are positioning your release of them as being in their interests—you want the best for them and, clearly, it's not with you.

Chip Bell and Ron Zemke, with Performance Research Associates, differentiate between customers from hell and customers who have been through hell. Bell and Zemke say it's important to remember that sometimes a customer who has been through hell ends up looking like a customer from hell.[12] One way to avoid falling into this trap is to remember that customers who complain are not necessarily customers from hell. However, if you treat them as if they're from hell, they may end up meeting your expectations because you put them there.

Pacing the Customer

Pacing, in neurolinguistic psychology, means to get in step with some-one. This is done by mirroring the person's behavior, so that the person sees a reflection of himself or herself. When we pace another's smile, for example, we give one of our own. When we pace another's intensity, we increase our level of response. Pacing is a tool that can create rapport, a relationship of harmony. When people are in rapport with each other, they are more forgiving and accepting.

Pacing is not aping or mimicking behavior. It's getting inside the model of the other person's world and then displaying the aspects of yourself that are similar to those of the other person. All of us have a strong tendency to like people who are most similar to us. When people naturally get along, they pace automatically. Psychologists have long noted that when two people don't get along, if one of them makes an effort to pace the other, this can create rapport where it hadn't previously existed.

Generally, it's easy to pace someone who is in a good mood. Yet it's amazing how many customers will not get a smile from service provid-ers but hear "Next!" as their greeting. It's more difficult to pace some-one's happiness when we are frustrated or overworked, so if a company's customer-facing staff aren't friendly to customers, management needs to consider easing heavy workloads and cumbersome systems that may be creating frustration.

If someone is crying, obviously you don't need to cry to pace that person. But you have to show sympathy. And be careful to help protect customers in such a situation by not drawing attention to their tears. Remember, customers want to retain their sense of dignity. If you can help customers through difficult situations like this, they'll likely become partners with you.

While it's easy to pace someone in a good mood, it takes skill and experience to effectively pace upset people and bring them back to a more pleasant frame of mind. When someone is angry, the appropri-ate initial pacing is not to get angry as well but to mirror the intensity and show increased concern. Smiling when someone is very upset will probably only make the angry person more upset. Sometimes pacing can be something as simple as saying, "Sir, you look very upset. How can I help you?" The words pace the emotional state.

Generally, a speeded-up response will also help with someone who is upset. If you have a standard procedure that requires you to ask for name, address, telephone number, and so on, skip it when customers are upset. You can always get this information later when they are calmer. They're thinking, "What the hell does my Social Security number and mother's maiden name have to do with anything? I want my problem solved! Now!" To pace these customers, do something quickly about their problem and ask other pertinent questions, such as what they need to take care of their problem.

Sometimes service providers are required to pace several people at once. For example, if you're helping people who are standing in a long line and they're all anxious for something to happen, don't talk only with the person standing immediately in front of you. Broaden your frame of reference and make contact with the entire line. You can do this by making eye contact with and nodding at those standing in the line. Such assuring nonverbal language can help calm a sizeable group of people. We have seen dozens of cases in which airline personnel, hotel check-out cashiers, and retail clerks pace the person in front of them beautifully and completely ignore a very nervous line forming right behind the satisfied customer. Quick eye contact tells people you know they're there, you haven't forgotten them, and you're going to help them. Our natural human tendency is not to look out at the larger audience, especially if we sense they're irritated about how slowly the line is moving. Customer-facing staff must learn that a too-narrow focus can create more upset customers.

Valuing Language and Timing

After working for over twenty years with thousands of managers, customers, and service providers, we believe that you can say just about anything to anybody if you choose the right words and the right time. This is a critical principle when dealing with upset customers.

For example, observe on-board airline personnel: rarely will you hear them order passengers around. They generally say, "I need . . ." or "We need . . ." and then state what they want, instead of saying, "You must . . ." or "You have to . . ." They don't want to create angry passengers who are confined in the small space of an airplane. Saying to customers, "Your willingness to sit still (or wait or . . .) is greatly appreciated," even when they aren't sitting still, is a nice turn of words and frequently gets the desired results.

Learn to feel comfortable with phrases such as "I can help you better if . . . (you would step over here, answer a few questions first)," "Could you please help me understand what happened step by step" and "Could you help me by slowing down just a little." These phrases are more capable of turning the volatile emotions of an upset customer in a positive direction than "Miss, if you don't do this, then . . .," "Sir, I can't help you if you don't . . . ," "Madam, you must . . . ," or "Sir, we have a procedure here, and it must be followed."

It's tempting to pull rank on customers, especially if their behavior is irritating. After all, you have what they want, at least for the moment. But remember, they also have what you want, namely, their continued patronage. We've heard customers being told, and have been told ourselves, "You're wrong." It doesn't matter at all if this is true. It is an insulting thing to say to a customer—or anybody for that matter.

Here are a few other ways you can alienate customers with your choice of words:

- *Attempting to read customers' minds:* "You didn't really want that color (or size or style) did you?"
- *Talking down to customers:* "You probably forgot to plug it in."
- *Playing "That's nothing" with the customer:* "You think you have it bad. The last customer . . ."
- *Blaming customers:* "You should know better than to have expected . . ."
- *Threatening customers:* "Your problems are going to get bigger if you don't . . ."

- *Giving unsolicited, undiplomatic advice:* "These pants wouldn't have split if you just lost a bit of weight (or bought the right size)."

Very rarely is using the word *no* going to get you very far with customers. "No, we can't get that for you today" sounds like the denial that it is. How about "We can have it for you tomorrow"? "No, that's impossible" is too stark. How about "Let's consider the possibilities"?

Also eliminate words such as *but* and *however* from your vocabulary when talking with customers. An upset person will hear only the words that follow *but* and *however* and not the ones before. For example, if you say to someone, "You look great, but you are overdressed for the occasion," all he or she will hear is the criticism. Similarly, when you say to customers, "I can do this for you, but it will take three days to arrive," they will focus on the delay and not what you are doing for them. Frame the sentence positively. "We can get it for you, and it shouldn't take any more than three days."

Another rarely satisfying phrase that many people use is "I'll try, but I can't promise." First of all, trying is not doing. To try is to attempt without any assurance that the action will be completed successfully. For example, try to pick up something. If you picked it up, you weren't trying; you were picking it up. Most of the time when service providers say, "Well, I tried," customers suspect that they didn't make a very big effort. Be more direct and customers will appreciate it. "Here's what I'll do." Generally, one clear, declarative statement is worth ten "I'll try's."

Saying No and Still Retaining Goodwill

It's actually fairly easy to say no to someone and keep that person as your friend. We do it all the time. Conversational analysis (CA) is the study of how people talk to each other. The field has identified some basic rules for how people make conversation work. One of them is taking turns. It's not a conversation if one person does all the talking. CA has also looked at the interaction that goes on between friends when they say no to each other.

Imagine that someone asks you to go to lunch but you can't because you have a report to complete. The first thing you do is to put an expression of regret on your face or make some type of noise that sounds like effort. (Actually, with these nonverbal signals, everyone gets it immediately that your answer is going to be no.) This is followed by a positive statement: "I'd love to be able to." Next comes the rejection, generally stated as an apology: "I'm so sorry, I just can't." This in turn is followed by an explanation: "Unfortunately, I've got a report I have to finish by the end of the day." Finally, another positive statement is made, generally with a follow-up offer: "I'd really like to. Do you think we could go to lunch later this week?" Friendship retained. According to students of CA, this pattern is universal throughout the world.

Instead of saying to our customers, "Sorry, it's not possible," why not go through the same type of rejection we use when saying no to a good friend we want to keep? Imagine that a customer asks for an order to be delivered tomorrow and that's not possible. First, put a look of regret on your face or make an "effort" sound. (Of course, the sound is what works when you're on the telephone.) Then make your positive statement: "I'd love to be able to get that delivery to you by tomorrow. I'm so sorry, that's not going to be possible." Then give an explanation: "This package has to be assembled and picked up, and it's already 6 p.m. on the East Coast, where it ships from. The warehouse is closed already." And make one final positive statement with a follow-up offer: "I'd really like to get this to you as soon as possible. I can arrange for it to be delivered the day after next. Will that work for you?" Relationship probably retained.

We do so much in conversations with our friends and family to preserve our close relationships. It makes a lot of sense to use the same approaches when attempting to retain customers.

Forming Partnerships

To reverse the hostility of upset customers, you must get them to work with you. A partnership will put you on the same side as your customers in your common attempt to overcome obstacles. Think of obstacles as whatever is stopping customers from being satisfied.

The language of partnership is used in these examples:

- "Let's see what we can do together."
- "I know you're upset, and I'm very happy to work with you to solve this problem."
- "Let's do this . . ."
- "If you do this . . . then I'll do this . . ."

In addition to using the right words, you can use various kinds of partnering behaviors. These include the following:

- *Investigatory:* "Let's get to the bottom of this." "We'll figure this out."
- *Advisory:* "Here's the best thing we can do." "We can approach this a couple of ways."
- *Counseling or listening:* "Tell me what happened. I want to know as well."
- *Analytical:* "Here's how we can proceed—step by step." "Let's go through it in order."
- *Reassuring:* "Did I understand that correctly? Did I get all of it?"

Forming a partnership requires that you don't hand customers off to someone else unless absolutely necessary. If you have to get someone else involved, assure customers you'll get back to them to check that everything was satisfactorily handled. Customers fear that they're going to get shuffled from person to person, each time having to explain their story. Most people have had that experience more than once. Give your name to upset customers so they know you're not trying to hide. If you're on the phone with a customer, use a "soft transfer"; stay on the line until the customer is talking to the next person. You can also ask for the customer's telephone number so you can call back if you get disconnected. It happens much more frequently than most companies realize.

Many customers' needs are so complex today that they are not easily met by simply purchasing something sitting on a shelf. These customers require tailored products and solutions. We can no longer just buy a screwdriver or batteries. We need to buy the right kind of screwdriver and the correct size batteries. The information that customers hold in their heads is an essential part of meeting their needs. If customers feel they are in partnership with a company representative, they are more likely to be forthcoming with essential information that will eventually lead to their satisfaction. This is a partnership that generally leads to positive feelings on both sides.

If your customers are unsure about what they know, then take responsibility and make certain they have the correct information. A friend told us that before her daughter was released from a hospital after childbirth, she was asked to view an hour-long video about the proper care of new infants. The advice included, "Don't feed them regular milk you get at a grocery story. And don't give them french fries or Chicken McNuggets." Our friend was aghast that such seemingly obvious information had to be taught to new mothers. The hospital staff assured her that several young mothers had said, "Well, my grandpa eats Chicken McNuggets and he doesn't have any teeth. So why can't the baby?"

Getting Personal

If your goal is just to settle complaints, then a detached approach might work. But if you are interested in converting upset customers into partners, then something more personal must be displayed. Let your customers know that a real live person is standing there trying to help them. Give your upset customers lots of personal attention. Many times attention alone is sufficient to calm someone. Customers' anger is in part motivated by their desire to capture attention, so if you give them yours, their extreme responses are less necessary.

An obvious but frequently overlooked technique is to use the person's name. The impersonal *Sir*, *Madam*, or *Miss* drives some people crazy. It's easy enough to ask customers their names. If they don't want to tell you, ask them what you should call them. Explain that you don't want to offend them by being impersonal.

Tell them your name. Once customers have your name, they'll feel you have nothing to hide. Give them your business card if you have one.

They'll feel more in control because they now have a name for future reference. Also, if they have your name and you have theirs, you're no longer complete strangers to each other. We don't form partnerships with organizations and machines; we form partnerships with people.

If customers say something demeaning to you and you feel hurt, it's okay to say so. If you don't know what to do next, admit it. "I'm confused myself. I don't know what to do, but I'm going to find out." At least customers have a chance to see that they are dealing with a live human rather than a machine that they can kick and abuse. Customers don't expect you to know everything, but they want to know your priority is to help them.

If you need to apologize to customers, do so with your entire being. Too many customer service people say "Sorry" in such a tone that customers know they don't mean it. This is a ritualized "sorry" action chain reflecting bare-minimum social formalities. Let customers know how personally bothered you are about the company having let them down and how perhaps you've lost a chance to serve them in the future. (By the way, it's okay to ask for their future business. "I know we failed you this time. I sincerely hope you'll give us a chance to serve you again in the future. It would mean a lot to me personally. I know this situation today is definitely not our normal style.")

To really serve customers well requires an attitude that says you want to help satisfy their needs, you want to demonstrate that your company is capable of doing this for them, and you're going to do as much as you can to help. This is a customer-focused attitude. It's not product or company focused. If you maintain contact with your own humanity, you have a better chance of remembering that these suffering, upset customers are also humans who are simultaneously frustrated and confused. Perhaps they're trying a technique of browbeating the person standing in front of them that worked for them in the past. In other circumstances, they're probably very nice people. You just caught them at a bad time.

Additional Advice to Managers

Some of the specific customer problems your company faces may be best handled by a group of specially trained service representatives. If your customer-facing staff need to pass customers along to others who are trained to handle certain problems, ensure that customers don't feel shuffled throughout the organization. Train your staff to pass customers along without further upsetting them. "I can understand why you're upset; I would be, too. Fortunately, we have a team of people who are equipped to handle this exact issue. I'm going to transfer you immediately. If for some reason you should get disconnected, then . . . [here suggest some alternative, such as 'I'll call you back' or 'Here's the direct-line number to reach the person who can help you']."

Sometimes customers increase their demands and insist on speaking with a manager because they're not satisfied with the answers they've received from the person who started to help them. If you ever find yourself in this position and decide to back the customer in opposition to what your staff member said, be very careful about how you phrase your words. Praise and support the staff member in front of the customer and explain that there must be a misunderstanding that you'll review with the staff member. As a manager, you are now dealing with both an internal customer and an external customer, and you have to satisfy both of them. You can anticipate and defuse this common problem by discussing with your staff how you will handle these situations in advance of their occurrence.

DISCUSSION QUESTIONS

- How often and under what circumstances do your customers go ballistic?

- What kind of education have you had to deal with visibly upset customers? How do you not take blaming customer behavior personally?

- How do you respond to anger action chains when confronting hostile customers? What questions do you have ready to ask upset customers?

- When helping customers at counters, how do you pace the entire line that is forming in front of you?

- What language do you use to partner with customers rather than alienate them?

- How do you use personal connectivity when dealing with upset customers?

~ 9 ~

It's All in the Words

Responding to Written Complaints

It's easy for customers to threaten that they'll write letters after receiving bad service. But writing is not without cost. In order to write complaint letters, customers have to gather paper, a pen, an envelope, a stamp—or a computer—and their wits. Depending on how rapidly they write, this could take somewhere between ten and thirty minutes. People who write with lots of details tell us they have on occasion spent hours composing their letters. They may have to go to a Web site and enter their comments according to the format required by the company. Both authors have complained on Web sites and have faced situations where an error message forced them to start over more than once. After you do that a couple of times, you're feeling a little like *Peanuts'* Charlie Brown waiting for the football to be pulled away—again—at the last minute by Lucy.

Contrast this with the kind of response you'd get from Mike Eskew, CEO of UPS. He says that it's easy for any CEO to seem remote to customers. So he personally handwrites a response to each letter addressed to him. He says, "If you don't take the time for such gestures, the company becomes a machine."[1] Imagine that!

Written Complaints: A Red Flag

Companies can be sure that by the time customers get around to writing a letter, at least one of the following things is going on:

- *Customers are upset.* It takes effort to write a letter. Many people will say they're going to write a letter of complaint, but in fact, most don't follow through.
- *Customers are dissatisfied with the outcome of their verbal complaints.* For many people, the written complaint comes after trying some other method to resolve a situation or deciding that the channels available to them to complain won't work.[2]
- *Customers are building a paper trail because they want to take legal action.* If something serious has happened and customers are contemplating legal action, then they may be seeking documented evidence that they gave the company a chance to fix their complaint.
- *Customers weren't able to find anyone to complain to in person.* Given a chance, most customers prefer to speak to someone directly. If customer service representatives aren't readily available or customers don't know how to complain or to whom, they may resort to letter writing.
- *Customers feel uncomfortable with face-to-face complaining.* Such customers may find letter writing to be a more comfortable way of lodging a complaint.
- *Customers have some personal reason why they couldn't or didn't want to complain earlier.* Perhaps customers were rushed or had tired children with them. Some customers might have speech defects or inadequate language skills. Sometimes a crowd of onlookers will create embarrassment for customers.
- *Finally, customers may have been encouraged to write a letter of complaint.* Sometimes customer service providers will ask for a letter, in some cases even telling the customers that this is the only way their complaint can get attention. Again, written complaints represent extra

effort on the part of the customers, and unless they have some emotional push to energize them to write, they probably won't bother.

It's clear that people who write complaint letters have a variety of reasons for doing so. Therefore, to reply with generic responses is a big mistake.

How Do Companies Respond to Written Complaints?

The considerable research on business responses to complaint letters consistently demonstrates a tremendous opportunity for improvement. Studies conducted in the 1970s on complaint letters about consumer products reveal that 21 to 45 percent of complaint letters never even got a response, let alone a poor one.[3] Forty to 72 percent of customers were dissatisfied with the responses they received! Furthermore, companies took between two weeks and a month to respond to the customers' letters.

Did the situation improve in the 1990s? In a 1994 survey of three hundred complaint and praise letters sent to a variety of service businesses (airlines, hotels, restaurants, banks, credit card companies, car dealers, and car rental agencies), just 41 percent of the letters even generated a response. Surprisingly, banks were nearly perfect in their response rate, followed by car rental agencies and hotels. Restaurants, credit card businesses, and auto dealers didn't respond to a single letter![4] The average time for a response was close to twenty days.[5] These numbers didn't change much in the late 1990s and the 2000s. A 1998 research study validated the notion that over 50 percent of the time, customers judged the "interactions, procedures and outcomes" of what was done for them as unfair.[6]

A 2004 study of responses to written complaints found a weak 50 percent response rate. The research also concluded that customers expect a response to their complaints. In fact, the survey, conducted by the Customer Connection, a division of the Better Business Bureau, found that the top-rated "most damaging complaint" was not getting a response.[7] This lack of communication generates stronger negative feelings on the part of customers: "I am more than negative . . . they have shed all responsibility in this situation . . . I'll never do business with them again and I will tell everyone I know not to, also."[8] Customers, by and large, really don't expect mountains to move for them. But they don't like being snubbed. They want a timely response, and they want someone to own up to the problem and not weasel out of his or her responsibility. Customer evaluations regarding the lack of response letters reveal feelings not too dissimilar from those of a lover being ignored by someone obviously not very interested in him or her. When you look at the research over the past thirty years, you have to wonder why most businesses don't make more of an effort to simply respond to written complaints.

Some businesses get more complaint letters than others. Hotels, for example, get a lot more letters than do retail shops. Hotels encourage written feedback on preprinted forms that can be easily turned in at the front desk, and customers typically have more time to write letters while sitting in their hotel rooms than after they return home. Companies that have developed more ongoing relationships with customers will tend to get more letters as well. But for most people, writing a letter takes a great deal more energy than complaining in person.

If a company merely returns a thank-you-for-the-complaint form letter, customers will be satisfied to a small degree—unless they had issues that needed to be resolved. Then, of course, customers expect a specific response to their complaint. But if the company takes the complaint letter seriously and reflects that earnestness in its response, customers will take the company seriously, too. One thing is for sure: customers are probably upset when they write their letters. If the response letter is not satisfactory, negative feelings (sadness and anger) will be reinforced. When company representatives respond to written complaints, they have time to think through the best service recovery approach.

By the time many companies get around to responding to written complaints, some customers have already forgotten about their letters. Whether or not the original complaint is foremost in a customer's mind, the company's response is an opportunity either to recover the customer's goodwill or to alienate that customer a second time.

Very often people who write are loyal customers inclined to give organizations an extra chance to improve matters. Based on its customer surveys, TARP reports that between 55 and 70 percent of people who write complaint letters will remain customers if they receive a rapid reply (within two weeks). If the reply they receive is both rapid and satisfactory, 90 percent will remain customers.[9] What about the other 10 percent? It's important to remember that no single strategy or technique will keep 100 percent of your customers.

Promptness Wins the Day

When an organization receives a complaint letter, it must get back to that customer rapidly. (If nothing else, your promptness will make you stand out as being responsive compared to your competitors.) If the complaint cannot be addressed immediately, we recommend that an initial reply acknowledging that the letter was received be sent within two days of receipt. If the complaint is faxed, the acknowledgment of receipt needs to be faxed back or a return telephone call made within two days. A speedy response sends a strong message of concern to the customer.[10]

The complaining (gift-giving) customer requires at least a kind of receipt saying, "Yes, we got your letter and something is going to happen." The company may not be able to handle the issue immediately, but it can get back to the customer right away. In this initial reply, customers need to be told that the issue will be resolved within two weeks. Two weeks is a reasonable period of time for the company to investigate the situation if necessary and for customers to feel they aren't being delayed. Response letters need to be personal and warm, and a named person should actually sign it.

The initial reply can also be handled by telephone. If you call the complaining letter writer, using the Gift Formula makes a huge impact. Identify yourself and say, "The first thing I want to say is 'Thank you.'" Emphasize why the letter is appreciated and apologize. If it turns out that the customer made a mistake, keep in mind that the company won't lose anything by apologizing. Empathy, which basically is good listening, costs nothing. Promise that something will happen within two weeks and then ask for whatever information you need to resolve the issue. Frequently, letters are incomplete or are unclear. Customers will be happy to provide extra information at this point; in fact, they'll feel flattered that someone took the time and trouble to call them.

John Goodman, vice chairman of TARP Worldwide, says that it's actually cheaper to handle incoming written complaints by responding via phone than by letter or by e-mail. It's also faster in many cases. Goodman says that "at one high-tech company that complex e-mail [for example, e-mail that discusses technical issues or deals with multiple accounts] was five times as expensive to handle as covering the same issue by phone."[11]

Feedback That Comes In Across the Web

The figures are rather overwhelming. As of 2006, 88 percent of Americans had e-mail accounts, and 147 million used e-mail every day.[12] There were 1.2 billion e-mail users in the world as of 2007, or approximately one in every six humans. About 183 billion e-mails are sent every day, and the authors, like many of our readers, receive 182 billion of them as spam— or at least it feels that way.

Customers like e-mail because it's easy to use and it gives them immediate access to organizations. Most of the time, customers receive an automated response indicating that their e-mail has been received and stating when they can expect to get a response. However, even automated responses need to be phrased appropriately. Some years ago, the Gap used to send out an automated reply that read, "While we cannot get back to you personally, we do appreciate your input."[13] That response didn't provide much satisfaction or a feeling of connectivity. Researchers Judy Strauss and Donna Hill, in one of the first major studies covering consumer complaints sent by e-mail, found that less than half (47 percent) of the firms studied created higher customer satisfaction with their in-kind e-mail responses. They found that simple things make a difference. This included a fast response, an e-mail that addressed the specific problem, and an e-mail that was signed with a real person's name.[14]

When complaints are made about Web sites or e-businesses, speed is even more critical. According to some strong research, providing a variety of ways for customers to communicate online is also very helpful in keeping customers coming back. Here's what one study concludes: "When approached as a defensive marketing strategy, complaint management is now considered an excellent competitive tool for e-businesses. Taking complaint management seriously affects product/service quality, website design, and operational policies [which in turn] facilitates repeat business and customer loyalty."[15]

Online customers frequently face challenges with technology to make their purchases, often with no help from the e-tailer. Many customers give up in frustration and simply click to another Web site.[16] Not only does the business lose the sale and possibly the customer, but it has no information as to what caused the loss. The reality is that e-businesses don't always know what engages their customers and what makes them leave their sites in frustration. For this reason, getting rapid feedback in the form of complaints is extremely valuable for them.

Without detailed and accurate information as to what is working and why it's working or, conversely, what isn't working and why, businesses are left without the type of feedback that will help them fix or redesign their Web sites.[17] It's possible to check how customers rate various online shopping sites on the web site BizRate.com. Users of the site can view consumer ratings on a smiley-face scale and also read customer comments. BizRate seems to attract exceptionally high consumer ratings, especially when academic researchers estimate that only 36 percent of customers are satisfied with their online shopping experiences.[18]

A 2003 study found that satisfaction and intention to repurchase in the hospitality industry were directly related to how quickly companies responded to complaint e-mails.[19] Ford Motor Company's webmaster, Thomas Weber, describes e-mail as a fast medium. Twelve years ago, Weber said, "Some of these people might well be sitting at their PC waiting for a return e-mail."[20] That expectation has only increased in the last decade with chat rooms creating a demand for immediacy. In the Strauss and Hill study, less than half of customers even received a response to their written e-mail complaint. Less than 30 percent received replies in twenty-four hours. If people are sitting by their PCs waiting for a response, we hope they have food and beverages with them.

Strauss and Hill found less personalization used in e-mail responses as compared to formal letters, with no more than 55 percent addressing the customer by name and about 57 percent providing an employee's name. Just a little over half offered an apology, and only 35 percent explained why the problem occurred.[21] The organizations didn't use the opportunity to reinforce product or service benefits. Just a little over one in four offered something to customers for their trouble. One member of the study received two identical e-mails from two different company representatives, one almost three weeks later than the other. Both gave the writer coupons but in different amounts. That can cause some head scratching.

Here's some good advice to companies that are willing to communicate with their customers via e-mail:

- Don't offer e-mail communication if you aren't going to respond.
- Make sure that any incoming e-mail is routed to the right department.
- Ask customers to choose the category of complaint they are sending, giving them a drop-down menu, so their e-mail can be forwarded to the correct department.
- Make sure you are appropriately staffed to respond in a timely fashion.
- Look carefully at your automated responses (perhaps sent out immediately after a customer's e-mail is received) and make sure you communicate a desire to get back to customers in a specified period of time. Personalize these responses to the degree you can—at least with the customer's name; get the gender right and if you're not sure, apologize and explain that you hope you got it right.
- Always mention the specific problem the customer faced.
- Demonstrate through language that you are grateful to be informed.
- Consider some type of redress for the customer, such as a coupon.
- Sell the quality of your brand or products.

- Create a signature line that includes your Web site address and your company's toll-free number.
- Finally, remember, any electronic response you send can easily be sent to hundreds or thousands of people around the world, so make sure you never respond in anger.

Sometimes taking a deep breath before responding is a good idea. Let's look at an example of e-mails that were ultimately published in the national New Zealand newspaper.[22] In less than twenty-four hours after the article hit the newsstand, more than fifty local Kiwis had decided to jump into the fray. The full series of exchanges has been posted in numerous blogs. The responder, a caterer, definitely has lost some business.

This shortened set of e-mails enables you to feel the level of acrimony in the exchange. Here's what happened. A staff member of a real estate company was asked to organize a company party. She wrote a series of e-mails to a catering company, the owner of which (perhaps overworked at this particular time of the year) got annoyed and blasted the customer for her stupid questions, complete with typographical errors and a threat not to use the real estate company to list her house that she said she planned to sell.

> I personally don't have the time or inclination to sit on the computer all day playing email ping pong. Please confirm your order by 9 am this morning otherwise I will take it that the order is no longer required the QUOTE IS $9.00 PER PERSON. (at this late stage chicken drumsticks will not be an option Thai chicken cakes or mini chicken satays, will be) AND MAY I SUGGEST YOU COLLECT YOUR OWN STRAWBERRIES.

The customer responded by saying that this was the rudest e-mail she had ever received and she would not use the company's services again. This was followed by a full-scale frontal assault by the caterer, again complete with misspellings.

> Get into the real world young lady... Re rudest e-mail tells me once again you are not in the real world and haven't fully matured but it

will happen. You were probably bottle feed till late teens . . . I will hopefully be calling your boss before Christmas re our not listing our property with [your agency]. I am sure they will be interested and could give you more to do. And you thought my first e-mail was rude. I expect you still believe in Santa Clause.

In retaliation, the never-to-be-again customer sent the e-mail thread to colleagues (remember, we told you how people love to share examples of bad customer service treatment, and reading an e-mail exchange of this type is like watching a television soap opera), who then forwarded it to other friends. Within hours, it had made it around New Zealand and to the United States. The caterer could possibly recover from this bad publicity by offering to host that agency's party for free and inviting newspaper and television reporters as well. Both the caterer and the staff member of the real estate agency could shake hands, laugh about the exchange on television, and get some positive press coverage out of this. And the whole city of Auckland could cheer.

It didn't happen.

The Gift Formula for Written Complaints

Organizations receiving many complaint letters may wish to experiment with the following suggestions to find out which work best. Do not assume that anyone can write effective response letters; writing them is an art. Here's an example. A blogger wrote a tongue-in-cheek complaint letter to Amazon.com about not winning the opportunity to purchase an HP notebook PC for the ridiculously low price of $299. As A. Hildebrandt wrote, "I had planned on using this laptop to write novels while sipping mochas at my local Starbucks." He promised to dedicate his first novel to Jeff Bezos, head of Amazon. A few days later, he received a response, similar in tone, playful, exaggerated, and very witty, from Autumn Walker of Amazon Executive Customer Relations.[23] Walker bantered, "Take heart; Norman Mailer wrote all of his novels by hand. And you've surely heard the phrase, 'the pen is mightier than the sword'? It would sound absurd to substitute 'laptop' for the word 'pen.'"

It's a wonderful exchange, and the blogger ends his column, "Amazon, I love you."

Can you do that for every letter that comes in? Obviously not. The time involved is simply too great. But occasionally, letters arrive that give people inside the organization an opportunity to strut their stuff. When this happens, your business is more than business.

Loyal customers may be positively amazed based on how rapidly and how well your response letters are written. On the other hand, a new generation of cynical customers can be birthed depending on how slow, inauthentic, and canned your approach is. As with the Gift Formula described in chapter 6, a progressive sequence of steps can work well for responding in writing to a written complaint. You need to do the following in your letter:

1. Thank the customer; explain why you appreciate the complaint and apologize.
2. Let the customer know what you have done.
3. Acknowledge the customer's point of view.
4. Personalize your reply.
5. Be simple but specific.
6. Exceed the customer's expectations (both with speed and what you are going to do).
7. Check customer satisfaction.

Thank the Customer

Starting with a thank-you is easily achieved in a letter. "Thank you for contacting us. We know that it took some effort on your part, and we truly appreciate your taking the time to let us know . . ." You can thank customers several times in a letter—for writing, for trying your products, and for continuing to use your products in the future. End your letter with another thank-you. Apparently, one thank-you in a letter goes unnoticed by the average reader.[24] Let customers know you appreciate their feedback and see it as a gift. Because they may have read this book also, it may be better not to use the word *gift*.

You don't have to call the complaint a *complaint*. In fact, avoid using the word *complaint*. Talk about the customer's feedback, information, comment, or evaluation. Apologize for what has happened.

Let the Customer Know What You Have Done

If your organization needs to do something specific, do it within two weeks as promised in the initial acknowledgment sent shortly after a customer's letter is received. Tell customers if something within the organization has changed as a result of their feedback, and thank them for that. When customers complain about situations that cannot be fixed for them, knowing that others won't have to go through a repeat of the trouble is frequently enough to satisfy them. Listen to customers. They will frequently say that the only reason they're complaining is so that they or others won't have to go through the same rigamarole.

Acknowledge the Customer's Point of View

It is hardly ever worthwhile to win arguments and lose customers. A company becomes a historical memory when its epitaph reads, "Here lies a company that won every argument with its customers—and went bankrupt!" Show empathy and caring for your customers. Apologize for the trouble they've endured; tell them you're upset they had to go through this experience. But don't tell them you are disappointed to learn about their problem. Tell them you are disappointed in your product or service performance but not in hearing from them. There's a difference.

You gain nothing by questioning customers' integrity. Give them the benefit of the doubt. Generally, there are two sides to any question, and from their point of view, their version is the truth. If some point must be questioned, phrase the question very, very softly. Use questions such as, "Could you help us to understand how this happened?" and "Is it possible . . . ?" Questions are always easier for people to accept without triggering their defensive reaction.

Your goal shouldn't be to defend policies (though that may be necessary), to expose customers as wrong (though that may be the case), or to cover corporate behinds (though this may be what you feel like doing). Your aim should be to respond to customers who are giving you gifts in such a way that they feel appreciated for the time and trouble they took to help you learn how to better satisfy them.

Personalize Your Reply

Avoid form letters. They stand out. The following phrases come from a letter written in response to a written complaint from us to the head of a Southern California hotel chain. It's so classic that we're repeating it from the first edition.

> I was disappointed to learn of the problems that you experienced. They exemplify a lack of attention to detail for which there can be no excuse.

This opening has two problems. First, we were told that we disappointed the head of this hotel chain because we spoke up. This is precisely the reason why some people never complain. It is easy to see the difficulty with "I was disappointed" if it is stated harshly. Whether intended in this way or not, this "statement" can be inferred by the customer to mean, "You ruined my day with your complaint letter." We've checked through the responses to complaint letters we've written and found that many people use this phrasing or something very close to it, which leads to the second problem.

This phrasing sounds canned, as though this hotel chain's CEO uses it in all his responses. He writes, "to learn of the problems that you experienced." What problems? He has the complaint letter in front of him. Why not personalize the letter by mentioning the specific feedback provided? In this case, the hotel told us we'd be picked up at Los Angeles International Airport (LAX) in the hotel's courtesy van within five minutes. This was reasonable, as the hotel is within five minutes of LAX. Nonetheless, it took the authors over an hour to reach the hotel. We would have gladly paid a taxi fee to save the time. While we were waiting for the van, airport personnel told us that this particular hotel always "lied" about pickup times. All these details were spelled out in our complaint letter, but the response we received failed to address any aspect of our complaint specifically.

Actually, the rest of the CEO's response reads as if it could have been sent out for dozens, if not hundreds, of different types of complaints.

> I have spoken with my Front Office Manager and Executive House-keeper in regard to this problem. Rest assured they understand in no uncertain terms that our success depends upon the skills of all our employees, and they have asked me to extend their apologies for the inconveniences.

The letter makes it sound as if the CEO ran over to this hotel, pointed his finger at the front office manager and executive housekeeper and scolded them ("they understand in no uncertain terms"). This is hardly a solution to the problem. Could the CEO have thought that the authors wanted to get hotel staff in trouble? This is another reason why people don't complain: they don't want to get someone in trouble. And does anyone seriously believe that this CEO actually talked with the front office manager and executive housekeeper of a branch hotel about not picking someone up on time at LAX? Furthermore, unless this hotel is organized in a unique manner, executive housekeepers have nothing to do with airport courtesy vans.

And to which inconveniences is he referring? Why not identify them specifically if, in fact, our letter has really been read? This entire letter suggests that the head of this hotel chain said to an assistant, "Crank out response letter number four, and put this person's name on it." We have shown this letter to various hotel managers, and several have told us—with embarrassment—that this is exactly what happens. They also say it would take too much time to respond personally to every letter they receive. If this is the case, then hotel executives need to teach people on their staff how to personalize form letters. After all, form letters such as the one we received can actually be more costly than business executives may imagine. Hotel executives also need to identify who can write quickly. Some people ponder over each word. Others whip out a perfectly formed letter virtually error free.

Personalization can be achieved by using the letter writer's name at some point beyond the salutation. If position titles are referred to, the names of the people in these positions also should be used. This particular CEO could have listed the names of the front office manager and executive housekeeper. A personalized letter would also have used the customer's own wording and phrases.

The last paragraph of this CEO's letter read:

> I certainly hope you will consider using us as the need arises on future visits to our area. If I can be of any assistance please call upon me personally.

What does this CEO mean? Does he want us to call him to make our reservations or to ring his cell phone if the bus is late picking us up at the airport? Here's how this last paragraph could have been personalized:

> We are changing our approach to handling airport pickups to be more accurate in our time estimates. So thank you for your suggestion. And we certainly do hope that you will stay with us again the next time you fly into Los Angeles so that we can show you how we've improved. In fact, I would much appreciate hearing from you again to see if we have improved! If you want to call me personally, I can be reached at extension 123. Again, thank you for taking the time to write to us. We really do value you as a customer, even though our behavior toward you the last time you were here sure didn't seem as if we did! Thank you again.

There would be a very good chance of a return visit to this hotel or others in the same chain if we had received that kind of letter. At a minimum, we'd be curious to see if the fabrications about van pickup times had stopped.

Be Simple but Specific

Avoid jargon, technical terms, or "internal" vocabulary such as acronyms that those inside the company understand but customers don't. Your response letter shouldn't confuse the customer. If the customer has questions about the product, send along another set of instructions, guarantees, or records. Don't assume customers keep theirs. Make sure you respond directly to what the letter writers are asking. Many response letters have nothing to do with what customers want. Let customers know what you're going to do, whether they will enjoy the tangible benefit from it or not.

Don't worry if your letter is somewhat long, especially if the customer has sent you a lengthy letter. Research demonstrates that recipients of response letters respond more favorably to longer letters, or at least letters that are close in length to the ones they wrote.[25] Customers see this as evidence of your concern. Research also suggests that letters signed by top-level executives are better received than those signed by customer service representatives.[26]

Exceed the Customer's Expectations

If appropriate, take an extra step with your customers. Some companies send along a small gift—something customers can use with the company's name printed on it, such as a pen, key chain, or notepad. Most letter writers report highly favorable responses to manufacturers who send along discount coupons or small refunds, though virtually none of the customers expected to receive anything.[27]

Approximately thirty years ago, United Airlines responded to a complaint letter written by Janelle that is described in the first edition of this book. UA responded in a way that inspired Janelle, who has accumulated over 3 million miles on United. An extremely loyal flier, indeed. Typically, a single response, regardless of how well crafted it is, won't buy thirty years of loyalty. Somehow, over these many years of flying, United has figured out when and how to respond to Janelle so she keeps coming back after experiencing problems, which she does. Recently, she faced a number of delayed luggage arrivals. On one trip that involved four stops, Janelle's luggage was delayed on all four stops. The "delayed-luggage gremlins" were attacking right and left, so staff in the TMI office began taking bets on whether her luggage would arrive with her or not. Janelle herself kiddingly asked United staff if she had done something to offend them.

Finally, Janelle wrote a letter. She got a telephone call and a letter in quick order. Then it happened again; no luggage. When Janelle arrived at the TMI office the next morning, a caller was holding for her. The voice at the other end of the line said, "We did it again, didn't we?" Perfect. A vice president from United was calling and obviously had been alerted to the delayed-luggage report that was filed the previous night. Again, we say that so much of effective complaint handling is in the way it is done. After all, the luggage still hadn't arrived.

Many company leaders assume a bookkeeper mentality when dealing with complaining customers. They become so frightened that someone will take advantage of them that they actually set up policies with the primary purpose of averting exploitation and end up not satisfying anyone. They may as well be saying, "We'll do everything we can to make sure no one cheats us, right down to alienating our honest customers." Normally it costs so little to surprise and delight customers that, unless you are selling jet planes, it doesn't matter if a few people try to cheat you.

Check Customer Satisfaction

If a specific action is taken by the company, follow up to make sure that the customer is satisfied with the way the complaint was handled. And also follow up internally to ensure the organization has learned from this complaint.

If you want a simple summary of a good response letter (or a good customer exchange in person), here's what it should deliver. It should

- Fix the problem
- Fix the relationship
- Fix the system[28]
- And above all, make sure something was learned from what happened

Don't Be Afraid to Use Your Personality

Dutch and Danish researchers suggest that identifying the emotions expressed in complaint letters can help organizations determine how to retain customer loyalty. Emotions are a prime motivator of loyalty; therefore, they argue, the emotional tone of a letter matters as much as the nature of the complaint itself.[29] For example, customers who express sadness in their letters are more likely to remain loyal if you handle them well. These customers are sad that the organization is not acting the way they want it to act, and they want to remain loyal. A letter conveying a sad tone needs to be met with a very strong apology and a clear statement that the service or product failure is not a normal occurrence and that the letter has been very helpful in identifying what needs to be done so the same situation doesn't happen again.

Customers who display anger, however, have a different reaction and are less easily won back. They can be recovered, but recovery needs to be done carefully and the customers' problems redressed quickly. These customers not only need to know that they are going to get a refund (or something else), they also need to know that they are right. These customers prefer a strong statement that reads something like, "We understand that we might lose you as a customer because of how you were treated. We sincerely hope that doesn't happen, if for no other reason than your feedback has been extremely useful to us. You were absolutely correct in your description of what happened, and there's no excuse for how you were treated. We'd like the opportunity to try to make it up to you, so we are offering you a significant discount on your next product/service—if you'd be willing to try us one more time." Strong anger needs to be met with strong words—not hostile words but words that match the intensity of the customer's letter. Then you have a chance. Unfortunately, some customers are so angry that they state they'll never return, and many of them mean it. Depending on the strength of the expressed anger, it may be a good idea to let those customers go. See what you can learn from their complaints, but realize that investing more time and energy into these people may not yield any benefits.

Finally, customers who write positively about the company while also complaining are a red flag. They're like very polite but disappointed guests; although they don't say anything negative, you can tell that they thought the food you served was below par and they're probably not coming back to your home. They probably have very high standards, and even though they don't express anger about the service error, they may switch providers because their high expectations were not met. When you perceive this tone in a letter, it's a good idea to emphasize your quality and share with the customer the quality changes you have planned for the future.

Software programs that print out nicely typed generic response letters will never address the kind of complexity to which these Dutch and Danish researchers refer.[30] With some software programs, all you have to do is to type in the person's name, the nature of the complaint, and what you are going to do. Click a button and, poof, a completed response letter prints out or is ready to be e-mailed. It's fast, so a single person can respond to dozens of complaint letters in a short period of time. There's a problem with these letters, however. First, they have almost no personality. Second, once an organization sets up the software, the letters all come out the same except for the customer's name, the nature of the complaint, and the solution. This can lead to all sorts of strange situations.

One customer we learned about took a trip to Alaska. His luggage didn't arrive with him, causing many problems with the sport activities he had planned while visiting Alaska. He got one of these software-generated letters, and it actually read pretty well. After traveling up and down the glaciers of Alaska, the customer ended up in Seattle in a nice hotel for a few days' rest before returning home. He dropped off his recovered luggage with the bellman, but it never made it to his room.

Some days later, he got an apology letter from the hotel—identical to the one the airline sent. This customer was dumbstruck and wanted to know how this could possibly happen. "What's going on here?" he challenged in a three-page handwritten letter to the airline. He was not to be mollified. He felt cheated and deceived because he accepted the first letter as genuine. One danger of using these complaint software programs is there will always be another company using the version you have.

We've had a chance to review a number of these off-the-shelf response letters. (Some even have grammatical errors in them.) Most, unfortunately, seem to be filled with inauthentic sentences, such as "We have every desire to address your needs and provide the best solution available to resolve your issue as soon as possible." A single letter has to cover a can of cola that exploded, a luggage claim that was handled poorly, food served at a restaurant that made someone sick, an incorrect invoice received for the second time, a rude staff person, an extreme delay in getting a response, misplaced documents, and many other situations. As a result, generic letters float above the real problem the customer faced, giving an impression of inauthentic "blah, blah, blah."

Because of our interest in complaints, we tend to complain a lot from our TMI offices. We want to see what kinds of responses we get and always give legitimate complaints, even if we are sometimes rather picky. We recently sent a complaint letter to Southwest Airlines, indicating that we hadn't gotten "luv" from one of the agents we spoke with while arranging for a ticket. Mitch, a service representative, sent back a six-verse rhyming response. The first three verses could have fit almost any type of complaint, but the last three verses hit a sweet spot with our complainer. This response is clever; it was customized, reflecting the content of the original complaint letter; and it emphasized the brand position Southwest has staked out.

> When you called last month, you heard only a frown.
> Just the facts and no heart; we so let you down.
> I am so sorry the Agent you spoke with that day,
> Wasn't acting with LUV in our usual way.

Because we hire for attitude and train for skill,
Perhaps that day, she was simply feeling ill.
We offer great Service, and just as you said,
Greatness includes both the heart and the head.

So thanks for your letter and for sharing your view,
Your letter is helpful, and we really thank you.
It's true the standards of our brand are set high,
And we'll work hard to meet them so you have the freedom to fly.

DISCUSSION QUESTIONS

- What is your average response time to complaint letters? Do you use form letters when responding? If your response takes more time than usual, do you let your customers know why you haven't gotten back to them yet?

- What are all the ways your customers can get back to you in written format?

- Under what circumstances do your customers write complaint letters?

- Who responds to your customers' complaint letters?

- Do your response letters specifically speak to the customers' needs, or are they generic?

- Do you do anything to exceed customers' expectations when they write?

- Does everyone in your organization know the address where complaint letters should be sent?

- Do you get regularly updated information about your written complaints?

~ 10 ~

From a Whisper to a Global Shout

Today we are in the unique position of having to deal with a louder, faster, and more prolific communication channel for consumers who feel they have been wronged: the Internet. John Prescott Ellis, former media columnist with the *Boston Globe*, wrote what has become the most compelling statement about the Internet in today's world: "The internet changes everything it touches, and it touches almost everything."[1] It certainly touches how people complain. Any complaint posted on the Web is accessible to anyone sitting in front of a computer that is connected to the Internet. If you haven't seen what is happening with complaints on the Web, we implore you to invest an hour of your time and get a little taste of what is there. Peter Blackshaw, CEO of Planetfeedback, says, "The Internet is one of the world's most powerful focus groups."[2] And it's there for you to sit in on.

The scope of the World Wide Web lets people communicate with each other in a way never before imaginable: prolifically, globally, and pretty much anonymously. A new software package on the market generates an automatic complaint letter that can be sent online or in hard copy. All a user has to do is enter his or her name and answer a few basic questions, and the program creates an angry, coherent complaint letter from an extensive database of words and phrases. Each time it is used, an entirely different letter is produced. The damage caused by talk among a few fellow commuters standing at a bus stop in no way compares to the damage that a single irate consumer can perpetuate on the Internet. In today's world of video cameras, information highways, and instantaneous communication, it really is impossible to hide bad service. Market researchers believe that the traditional methodologies used to gather customer opinions are changing. Surveys, focus groups, and one-on-one interviews are being replaced with chat rooms, blogs, message boards, and online forums.[3] The world has definitely changed.

We've organized this chapter to make the point that while you can't ignore the Internet and what is uploaded onto it, our focus needs to be about what can be done. We are convinced that you aren't entirely defenseless against this mountain of easily shared opinion.

Opinion Is Everywhere, and It's Very Creative and Engaging

Don't think it's all ranting on the Web. A lot of Web sites are working at being civil. MassLive.com hosts a number of forums. The "wine & dine" forum has a lot of activity on it: people living in Massachusetts post information, ask questions, and by and large keep each other informed about where to eat, where to get great beer, what's open, what's not.[4] Many U.S. states have lists of this type, as do several other countries. YellowPages .com also enables any visitor to its site to rate restaurants.

But even "civil" Web sites allow people to share their negative experiences. The outrageous examples are always entertaining to read, but entry after entry of just "ordinary" bad service comments can put a serious dent in business at a retail store, hotel, hospital, or restaurant.

While you are exploring the Web, enter a phrase such as "a terrible hotel" and see what comes up on the various search engines. Most of the comments are very interesting, and by reading less than one paragraph in many cases, you get to imagine someone's stay at a bad hotel, the disgust they experienced, and the wish that they had read reviews before showing up. More and more people are becoming savvy about going online and reading what others have said before making a reservation at a hotel they know nothing about. It's like one gigantic dinner-table conversation. It's hard to understand why smaller, less well-known hotels that are so thoroughly slammed don't make some changes to avoid this type of feedback. Equally hard to understand is why big international chains don't do something about the bad feedback received by hotels that carry their name.

Here's one comment about a British hotel: "This is a very terrible hotel. The rooms are ok but service is totally crap. We asked to pay a supplement for the traditional English breakfast. The Restaurant Manager came to say that if we were not satisfied with their breakfast, he would pay for our breakfast outside and asked us to get out. He said that in a very very rude manner and claimed that we were not his guest but the hotel's guest. He was also shouting that we should get out from his restaurant if we were not happy?!!!! Reported him to the Hotel's General Manager but got no decent apologies. We were treated with no respect. Please don't use this hotel."[5] If you saw this review before booking a room at this hotel, would you make a reservation? This type of review can have a huge impact on people's purchasing behavior.

It used to be that reviews about restaurants, movies, theatres, cars, car repair services, clothing—you name it—were done by professional reviewers.[6] The professionals still do that, but today you can read "real" people's comments about real experiences. (Many people wonder if, in fact, restaurant reviewers get special treatment.) Enter "a terrible restaurant" into Google and you'll get 1,920 hits as of early 2008; you'll get 8,180 for "a terrible hotel." Then enter the name of a restaurant or a hotel and see what kinds of reviews or other entries are available.

It used to be that when people traveled by car, they made sure they had a road map with them. Now people go to the Internet and print out a travel road map for themselves, or they use a GPS device in their car. It's getting to the point that most people who regularly spend time on computers instantly think of the Internet as a place to get information for everything, and we do mean everything. It has become a habit to go to one of the big search engines and type in various combinations of words to get an answer to a question from the billions and billions of pages of information available to us all. The Pew Internet and American

Life Project surveyed American use of the Internet and concludes that 78 percent of adults use the Internet to research products (February–March 2007 survey), with 88 percent from the eighteen to twenty-nine age group.[7]

Hila Etzion, professor at the University of Michigan, has looked at both positive and negative reviews of retail sites and concludes after a six-year study of online electronic product sites that negative ratings definitely impact sales.[8] Dr. Etzion points out that a certain volume needs to be reached for the public to take the complaints as valid. The message for organizations: read what is being said about you. Just because a complaint is not presented in writing on the form your business demands doesn't mean there's no complaint. In effect, all these Web sites give businesses an opportunity to sit in on semiprivate conversations about them. We've always said that one of the reasons why a complaint is a gift is that the customer is saying it to you so you can do something about it. All these conversations on the Net are giving you this opportunity as well.

A lot of these Web sites are very interesting. Tom Hespos, president of Underscore Marketing, indicates that most comments on the Web are not off-the-wall statements. He says that there are definitely some "drive-by shootings" revealed by phrases such as "this company sucks." But most people of this type, he argues, "who leave valueless comments are quickly ostracized by online communities . . . the people who get value [from your Web site] will shout down the haters quickly. More often than you'll hear from the haters, you'll get people posting details of interactions they've had with your company. You will hear from people about why they had a bad experience."[9] You can even find Web sites where job interviewees post their comments about the experience of being interviewed at a particular company. Some of these comments are not pretty, and names of the interviewers are listed.[10]

There is no question that some people will go way out of their way to create a message that is so compelling, it's guaranteed to be passed around the world and read with a great deal of interest. Years ago, a customer created a slide show about a very terrible hotel experience. The customer has since asked that it not be passed around any longer. However, it can still be found on the Internet.[11] It's generated such intense interest that a formal academic study was conducted on the four thousand unsolicited e-mails that the slide show creator received.[12] One consequence of putting something up on the Internet is that it's very difficult to get it completely out of circulation later. The original customer feels that the hotel has suffered enough, especially since the general manager put a lot of focus on customer service after the bad service had been exposed.[13]

The slide show on the very terrible hotel inspired someone to create a similar slide show about American Airlines called "Yours Is a Very Terrible Airline." It's extremely well done and no doubt will enjoy as long a shelf life as the "original." The creator writes in a comment to remarks about the show, "American Airlines finally contacted me (after I e-mailed the presentation and sent a CD labeled "FOR TRAINING PURPOSES") to apologize profusely and provide round trip airline tickets. Nevertheless—traveler be warned!"[14]

The Better Business Bureau receives 1.7 million requests annually for information about companies. Consumers check on the reliability of specific businesses before they make a purchase. (The industry that gets the most requests for information is the insurance industry.)[15] To a certain degree, a Web site like the Better Business Bureau's is similar to eBay, which has a remarkable ability to control quality for both buyers and sellers. Each time a purchase is made on eBay, the buyer and the seller have the opportunity to rate each other. This is important because you have almost zero recourse if you think you are buying a Prada bag on eBay and end up getting a fake made in China. If the seller wants to continue selling on eBay, complaints of fakes will dry up business immediately.

The BBB threatened to expel Kodak from membership for refusing to respond to customer complaints in 2007. As a result, Kodak discontinued its membership. Bloggers have taken up the story and have invited comments. As the bloggers say, "This is not a Kodak moment."[16] We would add, it's definitely not seeing complaints as gifts.

The important takeaway from examples of this type is that everyone in a company needs to be aware of the power of the Internet. Service providers may think they are invisible to the rest of the world as they stand behind their check-in counters or talk with someone on the telephone, but in fact the Internet can easily expose anyone. It might be a good idea for organizations to show the two slide shows mentioned as examples of what can happen when customers are treated poorly. In both cases, the customers were, without question, wronged.

Many product problems are first identified on the Internet. Intel Corporation's chip problem in the mid-1990s was, in fact, first discussed on the Internet before it created a media splash. The unfavorable publicity forced Intel to backtrack on its initial position of ignoring a small computing problem caused by the Pentium chip. *PC Week*, the widely read weekly computer magazine, posed a question at the time of Intel's notoriety: "While we engage in a lot of discussion over whether the Internet is ready for business, maybe we should be asking if business is ready for the Internet."[17] Customers used to complain in a somewhat orderly, private manner. Not anymore.

We know some organizations that are so befuddled by what is happening on the Internet that they choose to ignore any comments written there. It's definitely an option. But if something splashes big in the media, the impact can be considerable. No one is defenseless—individuals or corporations. Let us remind you again that if you start with the philosophy that complaints are gifts, you'll have more bravery to check what's actually being written about you. In our humble opinion, the Internet is simply too big to ignore. We offer three suggestions that can be easily remembered if you don't mind using the common acronym MPG (miles per gallon). In this case M stands for *monitor*, P is *pretense*, and G is *guidance*. It's yes to monitoring and guidance and a definite no to pretense.

M: Say Yes to Monitoring

Any large corporation should have someone who regularly monitors what is being written about it. Intuit ran into a problem with one of its software programs, TurboTax. Certain features annoyed users, and they wrote to online forums threatening a boycott. Intuit was able to quickly integrate the feedback, make changes, and solve the problem by making changes in TurboTax.[18] Since then, Intuit has been regularly monitoring the Internet, believing it's well worth the effort. Scott Gulbransen, a spokesperson for Intuit, acknowledges, "Many people don't like to call and complain." And if you see one entry about a product, it's very tempting to add your own comment that agrees with the writer's.[19]

With a little sleuthing you can find all the Web sites that mention your company name. You can set up a Google alert so that every time a certain phrase is found on the Internet, Google will forward it to you. If you are part of a well-known brand, you want to be careful about how you ask for information because you can be inundated if your brand name is frequently mentioned. Several software programs can help. One scans 1 million blogs, one hundred thousand message boards, and six thousand traditional media sources. If a company releases a new product, any of these programs can track immediately what is being said online.

Apple Computer was getting trashed in blogs about its iPod batteries in late 2004. Apple quickly made some changes to save the brand—though still not quickly enough to avoid massive Internet conversations and a class-action suit.[20] Blogs are extremely important to monitor because they are opinionated conversations being conducted in cyberspace. The people who get to hear these conversations aren't just those who were invited to sit at a dinner table. Anyone who comes across them on the Web gets a seat, can link the conversation to his or her own Web site, and can e-mail a copy of the blog to many people. It's almost overwhelming, but monitoring helps.

A few years ago, Janelle met a man in the United Kingdom who had developed a very nifty device to let companies see how customers reacted to service while talking with someone in a call center. Customers could at any point push a telephone number (from one to ten) indicating how they felt about how the conversation was going. This is real-time evaluation—incredibly valuable for any company if you adopt the philosophy that a complaint is a gift. Janelle was excited and asked how sales were going. The man told her that he couldn't sell any of them. When companies watched how customers evaluated them in demonstrations, they said there was no way that the ratings were legitimate. They were simply too low. This is probably the feeling that many organizations have when they read all the negative comments about them, their service, and their products. "It can't be!" But it is. And to deny it would be the equivalent of early Americans' refusal to place their ears to the ground to hear distant hoofbeats. The sounds or silence provided valuable clues as to what to do next, and no one would ever have thought about cutting off this source of information.

Many Web sites attempt to keep communication within a specific group of people, but anyone with a computer and an electronic communication connection can read what has been written. It's very easy to become a member of most Web sites. At the Web site for members of the Starbucks Workers Union, many comments are about bad working conditions. People make both positive and negative statements about the union, the host of the site. Customer complaints are discussed, and the range of opinion is diverse. Certainly someone at the corporate offices of Starbucks is avidly reading this Web site.

We know of one financial information company that has taken monitoring perhaps a step too far. Whenever this organization finds anything negative about it on the Web, it threatens legal action. When word gets out about this behavior, the company won't look honest; it'll appear to be stifling independent evaluation. Clearly, the goal here isn't to eliminate negative feedback; it's to be aware of it. Shutting it down on the Internet with legal threats doesn't stop the discussion.

It definitely is possible to learn from complaints on the Web. Jeff Jarvis, whose blog is called BuzzMachine, has had an enormous impact on Dell Computers. *BusinessWeek*'s lead story in August 2005 was about Dell and Jarvis.[21] Jarvis wrote an open letter to Dell's CEO Michael Dell, "The bottom line is that a low-price coupon may have gotten me to buy a Dell, but your product was a lemon, and your customer service was appalling." Dell got some moments of fame after customers started putting photos and videos on the Web of their laptops exploding when batteries malfunctioned. After a second *BusinessWeek* lead story, Jarvis is now singing Dell's praises, saying that the company has seen the value in listening and ceding control to customers. Jarvis writes, "In the age of customers empowered by blogs and social media, Dell has leapt from worst to first."[22] As a result of the Jarvis impact, Dell committed $100 million to improving its sales and support activity.[23]

The airlines appear to have decided to ignore Web sites where customers pour out their souls about the way they have been treated. Almost everyone seems to agree that complaining on airline-related Web sites does little for the complainers except perhaps to enable them to vent. Several complaints about U.S.-based airlines (for example, at Untied.com for United Airlines, and at NorthworstAir.org for Northwest) are painful to read, though we suspect that most people don't believe that the airlines do awful things to everyone and that they all hope to escape the same horrid treatment. A spokesman for Northwest Airlines, Jon Austin, admits, "We don't monitor those sites. If someone has a legitimate gripe with us, the best thing to do is to come to us directly."[24]

For companies that do monitor such sites, if they see an aired complaint that somehow never made it to someone who would do something about it (this happens all too frequently in large corporations, where the customer is sent a scripted, generic apology, and that's it), they can contact the customer and minimize the damage. Companies that monitor the Web may find a large number of customers who are so introverted that complaining online is the easiest way for them to complain. Companies may find a whole group of customers talking that would never talk to them in the past.[25] These customers can be brought into direct communication with the organization.

P: Say No to Pretense

While you may be tempted to go online anonymously and defend your organization or in some way try to influence the market, it's a definite no. The problem is in getting caught. In this sense, it's no different from the temptation to cook your books when your numbers look bad. Let's look at one example that is not too extreme but very embarrassing for a top-notch company that had no need to engage in this type of behavior.

John Mackey, CEO of Whole Foods Market, posted statements between 1999 and 2006 under the name Rahodeb (an anagram of his wife's name, Deborah). He went a long time without getting caught, but most would argue that it was inevitable he would. Mostly he praised Whole Foods and attacked rivals, including Wild Oats, which Whole Foods was in the process of buying. Because of the company's acquisition intentions, many wonder whether the postings were illegal, if not unethical. Apparently, other senior executives within the company knew what Mackey was doing. The *Wall Street Journal* finally outed Mackey's activities, and the Whole Foods Market board reacted by barring any postings made anonymously by employees on behalf of the company.[26]

When you read a collection of Mackey's comments, you have to wonder whether his purpose was to influence the market (he posted messages in Yahoo Finance stock forums) and that in the process he violated rules by sharing information that would be considered insider information. Here are a couple of his comments:

- *On a new Whole Foods line:* "Their new 365 Organic label has great packaging and great products in my personal experience. Their salad dressings which you criticize I particularly like. Have you had the 365 Organic Miso dressing? It's my personal favorite."
- *On the possibility of a buyout in March 2002:* "Would Whole Foods ever sell out to another company? Probably not as long as Mackey is running the company. The company seems pretty committed to being independent."[27]

At one point he claims to be George W. Bush and finishes his posting by saying it doesn't really matter who he is. When someone states that he is really John Mackey, he denies it by saying that the idea seems pretty far-fetched. There's something glaringly dishonest in these postings, especially referring to himself in the third person while writing under a pseudonym. As a result of this activity, Mackey was named a loser CEO by the *Wall Street Journal.* On this news, one reader commented: "If assuming a pseudonym that you use to trumpet your own praises, defend your haircut, and call yourself cute on a Yahoo business messageboard are not all clear signs of being a loser, I do not know what is."[28]

This story will play itself out in the months to come, but damage has been done to the organic grocer's reputation. The Federal Trade Commission is attempting to block Whole Foods' acquisition of Wild Oats, claiming it would eliminate competition in the organic food market. The FTC is using these blogs as evidence that the merger shouldn't be allowed to go through. The Whole Foods Declaration of Interdependence states,

"Our ability to instill a clear sense of interdependence among our various stakeholders is contingent upon our efforts to communicate more often, more openly, and more compassionately. Better communication equals better understanding and more trust." For six years, "better communication" was not happening, and now Whole Foods is going to have to deal with this whopper from their CEO. At a minimum, it's going to make customers wonder if the company is gouging customers and if its so-called organic vegetables and fruits really are organic after all.

It's too dangerous to do anything that could ruin the reputation of a well-established and well-loved organization. Specifically, it's not a good idea to assign staff the responsibility of finding negative comments about your organization on the Web and then have them write something positive without indicating they are from your organization. At some point, one of these people might become disgruntled and reveal that he or she was forced to write positive statements about the company. Remember that the Web is a place for conversation, and if someone were lying to your face, you wouldn't appreciate it. Any hint of pretence or fabrication is not good on the Web, where conversations can stay posted for years.

G: Say Yes to Guidance

One of the most effective ways to take the Complaint Is a Gift philosophy and apply it to the Internet is to engage in real conversations with customers. These can be guided to your own Web site. A number of major companies have set up blog councils, including Microsoft, Dell, Cisco, Coca-Cola, Nokia, Wells Fargo, and General Motors. Jeff Jarvis in his BuzzMachine blog is clear that if these giant corporations treat their blogs as public relations devices, they will probably fail. Jarvis sees a blog as a conversation. Alec Saunders, former Microsoft manager, gives this advice: "Good heavens, people! Get a grip! You don't need a cozy little exclusive club to figure out what to do with blogs. Just get on the net, start talking to your customers and advocates, and start interacting with people outside the strictures of twentieth century command and control marketing. Council, Shmouncil."[29]

People who are communicating on the Net subscribe to the manifestos outlined in *The Cluetrain Manifesto*, a book that was a call to action for modern businesses operating in an electronically connected marketplace.[30] However you might feel about that book, the first three manifestos are relevant to how organizations might best converse with customers on the Internet.

1. Markets are conversations.
2. Markets consist of human beings, not demographic sectors.
3. Conversations among human beings sound human. They are conducted in a human voice.

This means that you can't guide your customers to a Web site that is anything less than a real conversation. Customers in their blogs, in comments to blogs, or on Web sites designed to create an electronic conversation can alert companies to problems in the same way they can do this with verbal complaints. Just as customers in person ask companies, "Why don't you . . . ?" they now do it on the Internet—except their conversations are being listened in on by thousands of people. Seventy-eight percent of bloggers say they read blogs, and 31 percent consider them to be credible sources.[31]

Organizations can help guide this traffic to a few locations instead of being spread all across the Net, where admittedly it is difficult to monitor. One way to do this is through a blog on your own Web site. What the bloggers above seem to be saying is that you can't treat this like a public relations or marketing exercise. You have to carry on a conversation as if you were there—live—with that person, not so different from a live complaint coming at you fast and furious.

Here's how Lionel Menchaca, a Dell blogger, describes what happened at Dell: "Probably the best time to launch a blog is when things aren't going so well. We started monitoring the blogosphere [in 2006]. At our worst point, almost 50% of the commentary was negative. That made it easy for us to decide to jump in. These negative conversations were happening with or without us, and it was pretty clear we had a better chance if we entered those negative discussions. Today, we're seeing about 23% negative. While that's moving in the right direction, there's plenty of progress to be made."[32] Dell bloggers aren't the only ones who think the company has turned the corner on this. General agreement in the press is that Dell's uncharacteristic swiftness in its admitting missteps has resulted in its ability to address complaints.[33]

Organizations can guide communication to their own Web sites in several ways. These include writing blogs, providing information that is available only on your Web site, and setting up conversations or live chats with members of your staff. Organizations can provide incentives to get consumers to provide reviews (hopefully good ones), as it seems that having numerous favorable reviews of a company and the quality of its products impacts sales positively.[34]

Once customers are at your Web site, make it easy for them to navigate. Ask every single employee to spend time at the company's Web site and then take all their feedback and improve what customers are experiencing. Make sure your toll-free number (if you want people to call you) is on every single page of your site. Don't hide it several clicks away from your home page. Take a look at www.Zappos.com and you'll see one of the rare Web sites where the 800 number is prominently displayed on every page.

Make it easy for customers to find out where to provide feedback. Some companies hide their feedback pages, perhaps because they are afraid of a storm of complaints. They also may avoid using the word *complaint*. Other labels commonly used for feedback pages include "customer service management," "accounts reconciliation," or even "information hotline." Jagdip Singh, at Case Western Reserve University, believes that it should be obvious to consumers where to go when they have complaints.[35] Someone who is already alienated from the marketplace is not likely to recognize that "customer service management" is the place to lodge a complaint. Some Web sites use a combination of words for their feedback pages, such as "Complaints, Compliments, and Complications" (or "Challenges" or "Confusion"). Such a phrase enables customers to complain but to categorize their problems as complications. Remember, customers don't like to see themselves as complainers.

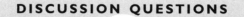

DISCUSSION QUESTIONS

- How carefully are you monitoring discussion about your company on the Internet? What is being said about the company?

- How can you drive more traffic to your Web site or to your communication channels?

- How can everyone in your company get more involved in learning from the Internet?

PART THREE

Dishing It Out
and Taking It In
The Personal Side of Complaints

Although you may have some difficulty keeping your wits about you when a customer complains, the situation becomes much more complex when the feedback is aimed directly and specifically at you or is offered by someone close to you. A lot of people dish out attacks very well. In fact, they dish out even more whenever anyone comes close to criticizing them. Others don't know how to protect themselves from such attacks.

It's a delicate act to find the right balance between learning from feedback and protecting yourself from some people's need to attack. Without awareness of our own behaviors, however, it's very difficult to change, so well-founded criticism can help us to improve.

If all of us could commit to giving "well-wrapped" gifts when we complain, we would make the jobs of customer-facing staff a lot more pleasant. We also would make it possible for them to help us get our own needs met. In addition, well-delivered complaints to our friends, family, and colleagues would make it possible for us to stay connected to them. Everyone would win!

~ 11 ~

When Feedback Gets Personal

Most of us would rather not be told that our behavior is inappropriate, that we smell funny, that we got someone's name wrong, or that we were late. In most cases, we also do not like to tell someone else such bad news—even if it's true. Advertisers are aware of this human inclination, so when producing commercials for mouthwash products, they help buyers devise clever, indirect ways to tell offenders their breath is bad.

The alternatives to receiving personal feedback are either to be perfect, which is a little difficult, or to remain unaware of defects, limitations, or inappropriate behavior. The key to learning from personal complaints and criticism—just like customer complaints—is not to get defensive but to view them as gifts. Many years ago, Janelle had a boss with a memorable temper. He would scream at his staff—in public and at the top of his lungs. One evening he broke his foot kicking down a door in a fit of anger. Everyone cheered. "This is who I am," he would shout. "And if you don't like it, then just leave." His employees did, in droves, as did his wife and children. He paid a big price for being who he was.

Personal feedback can save us from future embarrassment. For example, if part of your underwear is exposed when you are about to speak before three hundred people, you'll gladly thank whoever points this out. The same is true if you have a big glob of spinach stuck to your front teeth just as you're about to take your wedding vows. In fact, if your friends don't alert you to these social faux pas, you'd probably get angry with them. "How could you not tell me? I made a complete fool of myself and you didn't say a word!"

We need input if we are to develop personally. Our self-awareness is woefully inadequate, even if we become hyperaware. Frankly, most of the time we're utterly subjective. Objective feedback is more likely to be provided by others. Our spouses or partners are generally reliable sources of information. Warren Bennis, leadership author, freely admits that he depends on his psychiatrist wife to provide him with input. Many heads of companies seek out colleagues, actively solicit input from their peers, and hire coaches to get feedback. Today, people also use electronic cybernetic feedback (for example, voice analysis, body movement, or muscle contractions), tape recordings, and videotaping to get objective feedback. Virtually none of this feedback is comfortable.

If nothing else, you may just get away with a lot more by being receptive to feedback. That's what one reader of the first edition told us: "You wouldn't believe how much stuff I get away with [with] my wife by thanking her for her criticism!" Who knows, maybe that's enough!

Growing from Personal Criticism

The criticism we receive probably has some truth in it, even if it feels unfair or attacking. In fact, the more upset we are about criticism ("How dare they say that!"), the more likely we are to be guilty of what we're being criticized for, in at least some small way. Most of us are in denial about at least some, if not many, aspects of our behavior. But individuals can grow and improve from discovering their weaknesses just as entire organizations do.

When we were children, we constantly heard critical feedback from our parents, siblings, friends, and teachers. Children consistently get into trouble trying to figure out how the world works. Indeed, an infant who never gets in trouble is probably not very exploratory. How can children know that pulling on a piece of cloth will cause everything on top of it to fall, unless they experiment? How can children know in advance that rolling off the bed may cause a bone to break when they land? How can children know that screaming is inappropriate in a restaurant if no one ever says anything? Fortunately, most children don't take personally the comments of caution or correction they receive from adults. Youngsters seem to understand that they don't know how the world operates and that the "big people" will tell them. The point is that children constantly work at improving themselves. Adults have a more difficult time accepting feedback.

For children or adults, of course, how the feedback is delivered matters. It can be a lot easier to respond openly when the environment and tone of criticism or complaint are warm and supportive. If the atmosphere is chronically critical or abusive or nagging, children may stop listening, just as many married couples tune their spouses out, denying the truth of what the other person is saying. On the other hand, some people do not know how to set limits on the criticism they receive; they accommodate everything anybody says to them, constantly checking to make sure they are in line. They forget what they themselves want as they strive to please the outside world, and they adjust their individual personalities to the needs of the environment. For adults or children, reactions at either end of this scale, from total denial to total accommodation, are undesirable.

Some readers may be thinking, "Why should I change? This is who I am, and if the world doesn't like me, then that's just the way it is. I'm not going to change." That's fine. Everyone gets to choose how much information to take in from the outside world. At some point, however, we have to decide what price we are willing to pay for being just as we are without consideration of others' thoughts or feelings. And by making some changes in response to feedback we receive, we may actually find it more pleasant or effective for us to be who we are.

Janelle belongs to the National Speakers Association. She's had lengthy discussions with fellow speakers, some of whom have very strong opinions about audience feedback. Some refuse to accept it. If someone comes up to them after their presentation and says, "Do you want some feedback?" they will say no because they know that something negative is going to be said based on how the person started. It's true that audience members will sometimes deliver very strange feedback—strange in that the speaker can't do anything about the "problem." For example, Janelle has been told she is too tall. That's a hard one to fix, but "You need a manicure" is about something that can be fixed. It's tempting to respond with an in-kind attack: "Yeah, and you look like you could lose twenty pounds." But that doesn't move the relationship in a positive direction. Janelle has found that it's best to simply say, "Thank you. You're right. I do need a manicure."

We can't control how others deliver their criticism or complaints. But we can control how we respond to the feedback we get. Sometimes that one-on-one feedback is the most difficult to hear with objectivity. As Joan Baez, the folk singer, put it, "The easiest kind of relationship for me is with 10,000 people. The hardest is with one."[1] This chapter includes a few steps you can take to make criticism a little easier to handle.

Here's what we've learned from listening to hundreds of people. Treating complaints about your behavior as gifts within your family unit will significantly reduce the number of spats you have. A lot of people in long-term relationships tend to have fights over events that would embarrass them if they had to stand up in front of a group and acknowledge what they fight about. We've heard from multitudes of people who report that just saying "Thank you" to someone typically takes the wind out of an argument that previously might have ended up with the parties having an uncomfortable evening or, in some cases, not talking with each other for days.

Avoid Taking Criticism Personally

When someone points out our mistakes, it can feel as if our skin has been punctured with a sharp instrument. It seems to physically hurt. When this happens, it's best to acknowledge the pain and then quickly move to a less personal assessment of the complaint or criticism. Heads of government undoubtedly experience the personal frustration that results from devoting their lives to public service, working hard to be responsible for community interests, and then finding themselves at the center of daily attacks. Ed Koch, former mayor of New York City, used to regularly ask residents, "How am I doing?" He would shout the question across the street when he was recognized in public. You can bet that New Yorkers didn't always give him positive feedback. Contrast this with public officials who have called complaining members of their audience rabble-rousers or troublemakers. Indeed, in some countries, criticism of public officials can result in fines, prison sentences, or even death.

Many times the criticism we receive as service providers isn't personal, insofar as the person who is criticizing you would likely criticize anyone in your position. In close relationships, however, criticism about behavior is difficult to take as anything but personal—even when it's offered kindly. For example, if married people tell their partners that they're putting on more than a little weight, they shouldn't have raised a certain topic at the dinner table, they're late again, their snoring keeps them awake at night, they once again forgot to run an errand they promised to do, they were too harsh with the children, they were warned about that near-empty gas tank, they say yes to too many social invitations, they overspent the budget, they left their clothes lying around again, they tracked mud onto the new carpet, or they don't even know how to change a lightbulb, it's very difficult for the partners not to take these complaints personally. We rather expect our partners to love everything about us.

An effective personal-complaint policy would enable you to acknowledge the discomfort that comes from the criticism and then quickly shift your attention to see what can be learned. "Ouch! That hurts"—say it aloud if you like, and let the other person know how you feel. Many times the other person has no idea of the impact of his or her words, and one of the biggest myths is that humans don't get hurt from emotional slights. That old childhood expression "Sticks and stones may break my bones, but words will never hurt me" is patently untrue. The alternative to acknowledging hurt feelings is to nurse them and then either eventually blow up and attack the other person or wait for an opportunity to get back at the person indirectly. We do this by using passive-aggressive strategies, such as withholding information or talking behind the other person's back.

Distinguish Between Helpful Criticism and Intentional Attacks

Some people aren't interested in helping you to grow when they criticize. Their aim is to make you feel bad. If you're committed to using criticism as a part of your personal development, you'll find it easier to distinguish between attacks and helpful criticism. People are sometimes motivated to attack for reasons that may have nothing to do with you, including the following:

- They are overtired and will attack anyone.
- You just happened to be there. Perhaps they had a bad day or are having a bad life. Anybody would be an appropriate target, and you got in the way.
- You remind them of someone they do not or did not like. It could be their first boss, mother, father, brothers, or sisters. Since these others are not around, they will take their dislike out on you.
- They were ordered to show up at some event or to do something they didn't want to do. If the person who commanded them to do something isn't there, they'll take it out on whoever is in charge.

Seminar leaders frequently are subjected to this last kind of attack from participants who have been ordered to attend an event. Such participants will pick holes in everything they can. Their evaluation may read, "This seminar was a complete waste of time." They are really trying to let their boss know that they shouldn't have been sent to the program, but they don't want to say this directly.

Unfortunately, it's difficult not to take these frontal assaults somewhat personally. At times service providers are subjected to resentments that should be leveled at someone else. For example, a person may have been ordered to go to the grocery store when he or she didn't want to, and the check-out clerk gets attacked for a wide range of things that ordinarily would not bother that shopper. If your customers haven't been expressing their concerns as they happened, you may find yourself on the receiving end of a cumulative attack.

Transactional psychology refers to this behavior as "cashing in green stamps." Stores used to give people trading stamps as a reward for money spent. People would take these green stamps home and place them in savings books. When the books were full, the shoppers could trade them in for merchandise. People do this with feelings as well. They don't deal with situations as they occur but save the unresolved situations in stamp books with someone's name on them. When a book is full, the owner says, "I can't take this anymore. This is the last straw. I've had it!" The stamp book is about to get cashed in, and someone is going to be attacked in a major way, probably over a minor issue.[2]

Some people take pleasure in making others feel bad because of their own hurt feelings. Perhaps they did something on a previous occasion and were unfairly attacked for doing it, and it feels only fair that someone else get attacked for doing the same thing. Their mission in life has become to shoot someone else down. Children very quickly learn to say no to their younger siblings, reprimanding them and even slapping them—if this is what's been done to them by their parents. If we don't resolve our hurt feelings about being attacked unfairly, we can relish taking them out on someone else.

Attacks of this type aren't personal. They just feel that way. If we are clear about accepting criticism as a means to grow, develop, and improve, then when we face an attack that is being directed at us just because we happen to be there or because the person got upset with us by not resolving old issues, we're less likely to take the attack personally. We can first ask ourselves, "Can I learn anything from this situation, or was I merely in the path of someone's unexpressed anger?" If we do this, we'll more quickly be able to sort out genuine criticism from impersonal attacks.

The Difference Between Nagging and Complaining

It is useful to distinguish between nagging (continually referring to the same issue over and over again for annoyance value) and complaining (an expression of pain or dissatisfaction). People nag for two reasons. The first is that they don't feel listened to. They want to be heard, but they don't know how to express their complaint other than to repeat it.

It might also be that they want to punish someone by being annoying, so they get into a habit of repeating the same criticism over and over again, even though they know it won't do any good. They may not even be aware of this complaint pattern. Couples who have been married for a long time sometimes get into this habit. They may actually get along well together, but anyone watching from the outside sees a lot of bickering.

Nagging is a strategy that rarely works. By the time children have heard their parents say a thousand times that they should keep their rooms cleaner, they're no longer listening. French audiologist Dr. Alfred E. Tomatis, in a fascinating and controversial body of work, has discovered that children become "tone deaf" to the sound pitch of their parents when they nag at them. This deafness even lasts into adulthood.[3] Many children dig their heels in when they hear a repeated complaint. They won't give their parents the "I told you so" satisfaction. Some children so rarely listen to their mothers and fathers that the parents are forced to resort to the reverse psychology of never asking their children to do what they want them to but instead forbidding it.

The second reason why people nag is a more subtle one. Their specific, repeated complaint may be part of a metamessage. Their deeper needs aren't being met and they're reluctant to discuss those needs, or they may not be fully aware of what is truly bothering them. So they choose some unattractive or annoying observable trait, characteristic, or behavior of their partner and bring it up over and over again. When two people meet and fall in love, they have all kinds of small quirks that neither will notice, let alone mention as problems. In fact, they may like these peculiar patterns, thinking of them as endearing. After years of not getting their needs met satisfactorily, individuals focus on their partner's annoying behaviors that have been there all along. They fail to acknowledge and admit that perhaps financial problems, parenting styles, power sharing, sexual frustration, or lack of social stimulation is what really bothers them and focus instead on table manners or toothbrushing habits or dressing patterns. Perhaps they fear that the basic problems of their relationship are unsolvable. To admit that something as basic as sex is wrong with their relationship might be too threatening, so the couple focuses on smaller, more manageable, and less important issues. However, even if the criticized person changes, the underlying frustration will still be there, and the nagger will find something else to complain about.

Gift Formula for Personal Complaints

With minor adaptations, the eight-step Gift Formula for handling customer complaints can be used for handling personal criticism.

1. Thank the person for the feedback.
2. If you made a mistake, admit it.
3. Apologize—maybe even beg for forgiveness.
4. Promise to do something about it, and then do it.
5. Take steps to improve.
6. Enlist the other person's help to monitor your progress.

Thank the Person for the Feedback

Express your gratitude to this person for saying something in the same way we have suggested that you thank customers who give you a complaint. Keep in mind that it's difficult to change if you're not aware of your mistakes, and someone just offered you an external glimpse at your behavior. It may sometimes be more appropriate to start with an apology rather than a thank-you or to apologize without any thanks. For instance, if you spill red wine on a white carpet and the owner screeches, "You just spilled your wine!" don't go into a thank-you routine; it makes no sense in such a situation. Start off with an apology (and immediately pour a lot of salt on the wine to draw it out of the carpet).

A few years before his death, Buckminster Fuller, noted inventor and popular lecturer, told a large group how planet centered we are. He said we use the words *up* and *down* because we assume everything is centered on planet earth. He suggested we use *in* and *out*—in toward the planet and out toward the rest of the universe. He told the group that he was trying to change his own vocabulary and stop saying *up* and *down*. At the next break, a young man came up to Fuller and told him that he counted the number of times that Fuller had used *up* and *down* in the hour and a half after Fuller had made his point. Fuller immediately wanted to know how many times. "One hundred and twenty-three," announced the counter. Fuller was aghast. "Thank you for telling me," he told the young man. "Obviously, I have a long way to go myself," he said. It would have been easy for Fuller to get defensive. He could have said, "Well, obviously, if you were counting my words, you weren't listening. What a waste of your time." But he didn't. He took it as a gift.

You can express your thanks in a variety of ways: "Thanks for letting me know you are bothered" or "Thanks for telling me. I know that can't have been easy." Keep any cynicism out of your voice or you might as well not thank the person. You will make the situation worse. If you can do this, and it's possible with practice, you will create a little space between your personal feelings and the situation. You will be less likely to lash out and defend yourself. Remind yourself that you're interested in continuous personal improvement and even if it hurts a little, hearing criticism is one of the more direct and immediate ways to grow.

If You Made a Mistake, Admit It

It also may be helpful to begin by admitting that you've made a mistake. Tell the other person, "You're right." You lose nothing by doing this, just as a company loses nothing by agreeing that the customer is right. Admitting your mistakes helps to avoid fights as well. If people are out to attack and you simply agree with them, you take away their steam. In fact, if they've been harsh in their criticism of you and you agree, they'll probably backtrack. "Well, actually, I didn't mean to be so blunt. It isn't all that bad. Maybe I'm a little tired."

If, on the other hand, the criticism is unjustified, let it go. Use mental images to avoid taking the attack personally. Visualize yourself as a duck with the criticism running off your back like rainwater. Or see the critique coming toward you as a sharp arrow and then merely step out of the way. You don't have to be an easy target. You can also remind yourself that with time (and probably less than you think) you'll forget the attack. Criticism is a small thing in the totality of your life. Regard mistakes as unavoidable and as part of your own learning process. The biggest obstacle to your development is believing that you already know everything. You don't, and you never will.

If, in the heat of the moment, you are so distracted by the criticism just leveled at you that you forget that you've been given a gift, you can always come back later and do some "service recovery" at a personal level. "You remember this afternoon when you criticized me? Well, I didn't react very positively, and I want to thank you now for taking a risk and telling me how you felt. I know that can't have been an easy thing to do. And then I blew it by getting angry at you." It's never too late to accept a gift.

Apologize

Say you're sorry. If necessary, even ask for forgiveness. Many of us think that apologizing is easy to do. Actually, it may be one of the more difficult tasks required of any of us. Watch how people struggle to get those words "I'm sorry" out of their mouths. Many people think they give away something if they apologize. Actually, we have a chance of receiving forgiveness if we apologize well. Apologies are one of the most powerful social exchanges between people. Genuine apologies can repair suffering and injured relationships—if delivered from the heart. At the same time, if expressed poorly, apologies can further damage a relationship.

To be effective, an apology must first be specific. When we apologize in response to a criticism, it's fairly easy to be specific if the person has provided details. If necessary, explain why you behaved in the manner you did. Perhaps you were tired or rushed or overwhelmed. Explain that you did not mean to hurt the person, if appropriate.

Dr. Aaron Lazare, chancellor of the University of Massachusetts Medical Center and an expert on conflict resolution, wrote some ten years ago, "A good apology . . . has to make you suffer. You have to express genuine, soul-searching regret for your apology to be taken as sincere."[4] Your remorse should communicate that you're distressed over hurting the other person, that the relationship means a lot to you, and that you're disappointed in yourself for your behavior. Lazare advises that you don't have to wait for criticism to apologize. Remember, dissatisfied customers don't always complain; many just walk away. In our personal relationships, we don't have to wait for someone else to say something critical to extend the olive branch, but Lazare emphasizes that every apology needs to be customized to the individual receiving it. That's why simply saying "Sorry" will rarely work.

More recently, Lazare writes about political apologies that are, in his estimation, meaningless: "But I hope the public won't be deceived into thinking that these politically motivated demands for apology and their responses are in any way representative of the true process of apology. A successful apology—a real apology—results in the dissolution of grudges and reconciliation between two parties. The offended parties feel like they have received 'gifts' and usually attempt to offer 'gifts' in return. People are brought together, not pushed apart. The thirst for 'apologizing' in Washington these days, though, is all about pushing apart. If you ask me, it's a sorry spectacle, indeed."[5]

An article in *Yale Law Journal* talks about apologies as "powerful forces in everyday life."[6] The authors argue that in criminal law cases, apologies are not a substitute for punishment, but they do enable the victims to begin the healing process. Some attorneys have made the point that apologies are virtually absent in American law. This may account for the huge amount of lawsuits that are filed. People fear that they're admitting liability if they apologize.[7]

Some CEOs are getting the message that apologizing to stakeholders has advantages. The means that some are using is the annual report, in which they openly discuss their mistakes. David Stewart, chairman of Addison Corporate Annual Reports and producer of annual reports for several major corporations, says, "The business environment is going to dictate more CEO candor. If you don't analyze your mistakes first, there is sure as hell somebody today who will."[8] William Dunk, a New York–based management consultant, thinks that the "CEO mea culpa" is a very healthy sign "because until you own up to your problems you don't have a chance of solving them."[9] Ben & Jerry's, the very successful and slightly offbeat premium ice cream company, apologized about and explained its number one customer complaint in its annual report—inadequate amounts of "chunky goodies" in its pints of ice cream. Apparently, the mixing process makes it difficult to evenly distribute all the goodies, and while some customers hit the jackpot with lots of Heath Bar chunks in their containers, some customers get anemic ice cream. Ben & Jerry's quality control efforts don't always cull all the less chunky pints. "We're sorry" the company said in an appealing Ben & Jerry's way, and probably anyone who reads this statement won't feel so bad the next time he or she happens to get one of the cartons that's a little stingy on chunky goodies.

Sometimes a kind of symbolic atonement is necessary to truly demonstrate that you're sorry. In business, this can mean giving the customer something—reduced prices, coupons for future work, or small gifts. In our personal lives, it may mean giving a gift, though you must be careful not to expect that the gift buys forgiveness. The authors have seen couples abuse each other, send flowers in atonement, and then get upset when the flowers don't generate absolution. The follow-up gifts, which are tokens, mean something only if the apology was sincere in the first place.

In business, an apology can regain business you may have lost in the past—perhaps when you weren't even around. Such an apology is particularly powerful because the person will know you didn't cause the original problem. "I'm so sorry that happened. I realize I wasn't here at the time, but nonetheless our reputation was on the line. I hope you will give me a chance to make it up to you. I will personally do everything I can so this doesn't happen again."

Obviously, a strong apology will mean a lot to someone who is close to you. It also communicates a strong message in the more impersonal relationships between buyers and sellers or customers and service providers. With a little practice, we can all become better at expressing our regret over mistakes that happen. This, in turn, enables us all to let go of problems faster, heal past wounds, and move on in our behaviors and relationships. Sometimes people say, "I will never, ever forgive you for that." This is a shame, as holding on to anger and blame is a heavy burden. Apologies are a major impetus to forgiveness. If we apologize well, the other person can more easily forgive us. But the phrase "I'm sorry" isn't enough by itself. The person saying it must demonstrate that he or she means it and is willing to do something about it.

Promise to Do Something About It, and Then Do It

Just as we need to fix grievances for a dissatisfied customer, so too must we act to fix personal mistakes. For example, if someone calls you on the telephone and lets you know that you were late in picking him or her up as you promised, think how the following words could smooth hurt feelings: "Thanks for calling me right away. My behavior was thoughtless. I got so involved with my work, I didn't even notice what time it was. I'm so sorry. You must be really annoyed with me [or worried sick that something happened to me]. Can you ever forgive me? I'll leave the house right away." And then go pick the person up! And don't be late the next time, either.

Take Steps to Improve

You may need to be reminded more than once to make improvements. It's possible you'll have to analyze your pattern to find out if some fundamental conflict rests underneath it. Many of us get side benefits from behaviors that are useless and annoying to others. Perhaps we get attention, or perhaps if we don't do something and hold out long enough, someone else will take care of a problem for us. Maybe we have some deep-seated fear that if we do something, something bad will happen. For example, we knew a young couple who eventually broke up. The woman refused to take any criticism because of her lack of self-confidence and a tremendous fear that dealing with criticism would bring up emotions that she couldn't handle. The issues that her boyfriend wanted to address were not insolvable issues. But her fear was a major issue.

Enlist the Other Person's Help to Monitor Your Progress

You may need to ask the person criticizing you to help you make long-term changes. Encourage him or her to remind you whenever you engage in this particular behavior. Share the fact that you want to change but that without feedback, it's difficult to do so. There is a good chance that the way you hear about this behavior in the future will be considerably different from how you were told the first time. You are now in partnership with the other person. And whenever you repeat this behavior, you can use a slightly modified Ronald Reagan line, "There I go again. Thanks for reminding me." Humor always helps.

Check Your Level of Reaction to Criticism

Below are five different reactions to personal criticism. You can think about them as levels of ability to learn from other people.

1. You don't openly admit that you made a mistake. In fact, you reject the criticism outright and go on the attack. You remind the other person of mistakes he or she has made. "Look who's talking," you may say. You point out that when someone else did the same thing, nothing was said.

2. You reluctantly admit your mistake, spending time and energy explaining why you did what you did and emphasizing that you aren't the only one to do this.

3. You openly admit that you made a mistake and apologize, but secretly you feel unjustly attacked. If you do change, it takes you awhile to overcome your negative feelings.

4. You choose to take the criticism positively and thank the person for pointing this out to you. You thank him or her for taking an interest in you, apologize if necessary, and correct the mistake immediately.

5. You take the criticism as an opportunity to improve. Not only do you correct the mistake immediately, but you thoroughly investigate the reason for it. You find ways to avoid making the same mistake again. Perhaps you even get back to the person who criticized you and let him or her know what you have done as a result of the feedback.

To check how you react to personal feedback, picture the following situations and mark, from 1 to 5 as described above, what your likely reaction would be. In each of these situations, imagine that you know deep down that these people are right in what they say about you, even though they may not be perfect themselves.

- A close friend complains that you are never available to spend time with him or her anymore.
- A work colleague criticizes you for your sloppy follow-through: you promised to do something and you didn't.
- Your boss lets you know that you keep arriving late to staff meetings, and this creates problems for everyone in attendance.
- Your children tell you that you are always criticizing them. "Don't you love us anymore?" they ask.
- Someone in your household complains that you always leave a mess in the bathroom that he or she has to clean up.
- You show up late for an appointment with a colleague. Your co-worker says something negative about this to you, even though he or she frequently keeps you waiting.
- A friend tells you that you talk too much and are always trying to dominate the conversation, especially at parties.
- Your staff lets you know through an anonymous feedback survey that they think your managerial style leaves something to be desired.

DISCUSSION QUESTIONS

- How can people in your organization use feedback from each other as the basis for personal growth and development?

- How much energy is consumed by staff conflicts because people don't feel comfortable handling personal criticism? What can be done to change this pattern?

- What needs to happen to make your organization's culture one in which people are willing to apologize?

~ 12 ~

When You Complain, Make Sure You Are Giving a Gift

 If everyone gets into the habit of demanding quality service and quality products, we're more likely to receive higher quality. Why should a business improve its service offerings if it gets no feedback that something is wrong? You may say, "But what if I'm just picky? Maybe it's just my peculiar tastes" or "What right do I have to complain when they're trying so hard?" or "I'm sure they are people, just like me, and I occasionally make mistakes." Maybe all this is true. But that still doesn't mean you shouldn't give feedback to help organizations get better at serving you.

We are aware of a relatively strong movement about creating a complaint-free world led by Will Bowen, an American evangelist. His thesis is that if we all stopped moaning, the world would be a better place. He urges people to purchase one of his purple bracelets. Every time you complain about something (out loud), you switch the bracelet to your opposite wrist. The goal is to wear it for twenty-one consecutive days without having to switch it. At the time of the rewriting of this book, almost 5 million people had purchased bracelets from Bowen's Web site. Part of Bowen's philosophy is that complaining rarely does anything good. Perhaps that's what needs to change. No doubt a lot of the complaining that most of us do in our personal lives really does little. But we're talking about something different here. We're discussing making this a better world to live in because we speak up.

If you're dissatisfied because some service or product didn't meet your needs, you can say nothing, leave, and go to a competitor. After all, that's what most customers do. We would argue that when you do that, you're being unfair to the first company. How can a business know how to satisfy you if you don't let them know what happened? Isn't it a good idea to give people who frequently work long hours a second chance to make it right for us? Would you personally like this opportunity if you were in their position? If your feedback enables an organization you regularly buy from to improve its service, then you make it a stronger company. It's then able to serve you better over the course of your relationship.

Think of complaining as proactive constructive feedback. Just as companies must switch their attitudes about complaints, so too must consumers change how they think about complaints. Think of them as gifts—and wrap them beautifully.

Complaining Helps Make the World a Better Place for All of Us

Most service providers appreciate a professional, nonattacking tone of voice when handling complaints from customers. If they don't react positively to you while you are doing everything possible to stay polite and they still aren't helping you, then take your business elsewhere. Be sure to tell them you aren't coming back. Every time we see bad service and say nothing about it, we subtly encourage the company to continue with that same level of service. Here are some examples:

- Every time we go into a department store and no clerks are available to help us because they're having private chats in groups, ignoring customers, and we don't say anything, we encourage this behavior. If they go to work somewhere else, these clerks will no doubt continue the same behavior, which is a common problem in the retail environment. A survey conducted by Yankelovich Partners revealed that 65 percent of shoppers say that in the previous six months they had tried to buy a product in a retail shop but gave up and left because clerks weren't available to serve them.[1]

- Every time we stand in a long line in the grocery store because additional cash registers aren't being staffed and we don't point this out, we enable managers to believe that they can get away with inadequate service.
- Every time we get passed from one department to another without being helped and we don't speak up, we allow the company to not improve its internal communications.
- Every time we go to a restaurant that is overbooked and we have to wait thirty minutes for our reserved table and we don't speak up, diners let the owners believe this is an acceptable practice. Some restaurants do this intentionally so the waiting diners will run up a bar tab.
- Every time we receive shoddy luggage service at a hotel and the bellhop sticks a hand out for a tip and we give the bellhop money, we're telling the bellhop that tips aren't connected to the service behavior but are a requirement.
- Every time we're served restaurant food that is too salty, overcooked, too tough, or whatever, and we don't say anything, the restaurant has no way of knowing its food is substandard or that the new chef isn't working out.
- Every time a credit card company sends our bill late with barely enough time for us to make our payment without incurring late charges and we don't threaten to cut up our card if the practice continues, we allow the company to believe that this devious policy is okay.
- Every time we allow the post office to deliver packages late and we just grumble to ourselves and say nothing to our postal carriers, we enable mail delivery services around the world to continue at minimal levels. And with the competition they face, this is no gift to them.

So, don't get embarrassed. But do speak up. Or write a letter if saying something is too difficult for you. If you use the following suggestions, you can complain with a minimum of personal discomfort and maximize the chances to get what you want—or at least to help improve service for someone who follows you.

Seven Steps to Becoming an Effective Complainer

The following seven steps don't have to be followed in this order. However you use them, they'll help you get what you want without becoming a ballistic customer, when the techniques discussed in this book will be used on you!

1. Be clear what you're dissatisfied about.
2. Be polite.
3. Be specific and realistic.
4. Describe the cost to you and what you expect.
5. Make constructive suggestions.
6. Thank the person for his or her help.
7. Give the organization another chance.

Be Clear What You're Dissatisfied About

Giving a gift to someone almost always takes some effort. You have to get the present, wrap it, and finally deliver it. The same is true with feedback. You have to find the right person to complain to, you have to be willing to retell an event that perhaps was unpleasant, and generally you have to do it in front of a live person—if you decide not to write a complaint letter. As a result, it's a good idea to have clarity about your complaint. Ask yourself, "Why am I complaining? Why am I giving these people a gift? Is it to vent? Is it to get something repaired? Is it for a product exchange or to get my money back? Is it to make sure that this never happens again? Is it to show them how clever I am?"

Most of the time we're upset about the product or service or the way it's been delivered. We're not upset with the service provider. Therefore, keep your remarks directed to the product or service—don't get personal. The moment you attack the people trying to help you, they're much more likely to become defensive. Even if they don't show it, they're less likely to cut you any slack or offer you something extra. That's not in your best interest.

If it helps to remind yourself, you can say, "It's not you I'm upset with" or "I know it's not your fault, but I am upset that I have been kept waiting for an hour and nothing has been said." Most service providers will have a more open ear to hear what you have to say if you let them know you're not angry with them. In order to avoid getting personal, it always helps to maintain a crystal-clear picture of what you want. When you do this, you keep your rational brain focused on your goal, and you'll be less likely to get sucked into the morass of your emotions. Express your complaint immediately. Many times people tell themselves that they'll complain when they get home by calling or writing a letter. Most of us won't.

You don't have to say, "I have a complaint." If you were on the receiving end of such a statement, some little part of you would probably internally groan and wonder what kind of trouble just walked up to you. You can begin your complaint by asking a question: "Excuse me, is there possibly a better way to do this?" The moment we ask questions like that, we start building partnerships. Bernard Hale, vice president of human resources and logistics at McGaw Labs, reminds us, "Feedback is especially important in building partnerships. You have to trust each other enough to tell about the warts—'what's happening here is not good.'"[2]

Give the person you're talking with a chance to fix the complaint, unless you know from past experience that the only way to get help is to ask for a supervisor or manager. Most customer-facing staff have been empowered these days to handle simple recurring complaints. If you immediately ask for a manager, you may end up alienating the manager and the person you started talking with, who now feels slighted that you didn't think he or she was capable of helping you.

Think through what your rights are in this situation. You may have none except the power you possess as a customer to leave. In many situations, however, consumers do have rights. Airlines, for example, are forced to compensate you in some way if they bump you to a later flight because of an oversold situation. If you have a confirmed reservation at a hotel, the hotel has some obligation to make sure you at least get a comparable room at a nearby hotel. If you think you may have to negotiate with the company, set a minimum that you are willing to accept.

Be Polite

It helps if you bring your gift to the company in a friendly and calm manner. Some people find it useful to start by saying something positive, which may also help you settle down and bring a note of reality about your dealings with this organization. "I've always had such good service from your company, and now this has happened" or "I've been a loyal, faithful, and satisfied customer of yours for ten years, but today I have a problem" or "Normally, I receive such good service at your company. Today has been different."

Janelle once had a major problem with an Apple laptop computer. It caused her intense grief on a major international trip and involved attempting to get the computer fixed while she was in Ireland. She spent hours on the phone with Apple, calling from abroad. Nothing worked. When she returned to the United States, she sent the computer in to be repaired. It came back still not working. Unfortunately, the problem was an intermittent one. And Janelle was preparing to leave for another long trip with just a few days to spare. She had no opportunity to take it to an Apple Shop or to send it in for repairs. It's helpful to understand that Janelle is a major fan of Apple Computers: she's an early adopter of everything the company sells, she tells magnificent stories about the company, and she always proudly displays her Apple computer wherever she is.

Finally, Janelle was bumped to a product specialist who heard Janelle tell the same tale she had by this time told a dozen times before to Apple call center staff, who would only recommend either reinstalling everything again (this had been tried three times to no avail) or sending in the computer. No one seemed interested that she needed a computer for her speaking tour. This product specialist once again offered nothing but the same tired solutions, and since the problem was an intermittent one, the chances of the repair team finding it were minimal.

At that point, Janelle became very quiet. Then she said with a deep sense of sadness in her voice, "I'm very disappointed in Apple. I've been one of your biggest fans. I've probably sold more Apples for you than either of us can even imagine. I've used only Apples. I have had my entire office on Apples, through your strong times and your very weak times. And now I desperately need something from you, and you're not willing to help." She finished by saying, "I feel a huge crack in the foundation of my loyalty to Apple. I don't know if I can continue with you if you're not willing to help me."

This statement was followed by a long silence on the part of the product specialist. Finally, he said, "You're right. I'm going to arrange to have a new computer sent to you overnight. Keep the one you have until the new one arrives so you can transfer all your documents on to this one, and then send it back." Yes, Apple Computers! And yes, complaints!

It's best to avoid cynical remarks. They just increase defensiveness, and that's not the attitude you want people to have while you are trying to get them to help you. For example, "Do you always treat your guests like dogs?" will probably induce a blank stare from the service provider. What the service provider would really like to say is, "Only when they are dogs, and you seem to be one, sir," but he or she has been counseled not to do that. You may get your problem solved, but that person isn't going to do anything extra for you. Remember, you want service, not revenge.

Sometimes humor helps when you need something. For example, with a big smile, we have asked service providers who have denied a request what they would do if the Queen of England asked for the same thing. Generally, they smile and say, "Well, yes, for the Queen we might grant the request." We respond with another big smile and say, "The Queen isn't here, so how about if I take her place?" We get a lot of requests met this way.

Help service providers help you. Point out reasons why it's in their best interests to help you. In most cases, they want to help. At a minimum, you can get them into a frame of mind where they're willing to do something extra for you. If you clearly see that nothing will be done and you have divorced yourself from their company, then tell them that you won't be coming back. If you intend to write a letter to the head of the company, tell them that as well. Sometimes a statement of this type will open up some room for negotiation. It's not a good idea, however, to make empty threats. Writing that letter may provide closure for you with that organization.

Many customers have become very sophisticated in their letter writing. A recent book, *101+ Complaint Letters That Get Results,*[3] with many sample letters included, outlines a step-by step procedure to get results from writing complaint letters. The authors tell their readers whom to write (the head of the company), how to get the CEO's name and address (using sneaky techniques), how to put pressure on the company by threatening to send copies to public agencies or newspapers, and how to pace your letter writing so you don't shoot all your bullets in the first round.

Be Specific and Realistic

Don't exaggerate. If you start your complaint with "The most unbelievable thing has just happened to me," it's difficult for the service provider not to think you're a bit hysterical. State as precisely as you can exactly what happened. Keep your facts straight and in order. If you tend to jump around a lot in your storytelling, take notes in advance and then follow them.

Describe the Cost to You and What You Expect

The cost may be in monetary terms, emotional terms, or time lost. You aren't necessarily asking that you be compensated, but it is important to let people know how you've been affected. Let service providers know what it will take to satisfy you. You won't necessarily get exactly what you want. If you overstate your case, though, the organization is likely to just write you off. So be realistic in what you expect. Put yourself in the service provider's shoes and imagine what you would be willing to do for someone like you. If you expect something to be done in a certain time frame, then state your deadline. If you have to go back for resolution of your complaint, make sure you get the names of the people with whom you have talked. Most people will show more care in their treatment of you if they know you're writing their name down.

Make Constructive Suggestions

You've probably got a few good ideas that this company can try so your situation doesn't happen again. Ask the person you're talking with to be sure to pass this information on to his or her manager or to an in-house committee that addresses quality issues.

Thank the Person for His or Her Help

You are serving each other, so thanks are in order. Tell the service provider how much you appreciate what he or she did for you. It helps reinforce the person's helping behavior. If you're going to come back and give the company additional business, tell the person about that as well. All these statements reinforce that a complaint is a gift.

Give the Organization Another Chance

As businesspeople ourselves, we probably speak for most businesses when we say that our intention is to meet our customers' needs. Sometimes we miss the mark. When this happens, we surely hope our customers will give us the opportunity to fix the problem and give us another chance. Write a letter to the organization if it fixed some problem exceptionally well for you. This helps reinforce the notion that successful resolution of complaints is a good way to cement relationships with customers.

If You Choose to Become an Activist

Activist behavior involves reaching out to a third party to get help with your complaint. Here are some ideas that can help:

- If you worked with an intermediary person, go to him or her. For example, contact your travel agent if you had a travel-related problem.

Sometimes your travel agent will carry more clout than you. If you bought an airline ticket on Expedia, for example, Expedia may be better at solving your travel problem than the airlines themselves.

- Contact your local Better Business Bureau. It may not be able to help you directly, but it does keep track of trends and can warn other people.
- Get on your computer and google the names and addresses of government regulatory agencies that can help you. For example, states in the United States all have insurance regulatory commissions. They can and will help. The U.S. Department of Transportation can help with airline travel complaints.
- Contact your state attorney general's office if you think some laws may have been violated.
- Get on the Web and post messages at some of the complaint Web sites to alert other people to the problems you've had. You may receive advice from a reader who had a similar problem and got it resolved.
- Write a letter to your local newspaper or related industry magazine.

Hopefully, if you complain effectively, there won't be a need for Activist behavior. When that happens, you've gained something—and so has the organization. It's something we can all work at to accomplish.

DISCUSSION QUESTIONS

- How can you give feedback to your colleagues in such a way that you maintain strong, effective working relationships?

- What are all the ways you currently use to give each other feedback inside the organization? How can you improve these ways?

CONCLUSION

Looking to the Future

The history of complaint handling over the last twenty years paints its own compelling story about the future. The vast amount of research conducted points to basic truths about complaints that haven't changed much in the past two decades and probably will not change much unless a fundamental shift occurs in the prevailing mind-set about complaints. As a clear-cut example, the limited response to written complaints (about 50 percent) hasn't budged in two decades. Yet this is something that could be easily changed.

We have to ask ourselves why behavior patterns on the part of both consumers and organizations continue to remain the same. There's no reason for customers to not complain at a greater frequency than they do. And there's no reason for organizations to not be better at responding to complaints. Everyone would gain if that happened. Organizations would improve their quality and retain their loyal customers in greater numbers. And customers could purchase with greater assurance that, in fact, what they are promised is what they will receive.

Clearly, the answer has to do with the fact that people simply don't like negative feedback. And that's our destined future until this basic mind-set about complaints shifts. We see some softening of attitudes toward complaints. In fact, a lot of people are using the title of this book to describe their approach to complaint handling. That's a good start.

But to make substantial changes in the total marketplace, it's going to take more than changes in some companies and some industries. Effective complaint handling starts with appreciating that organizations don't exist without customers. This statement is extremely easy to make, and most companies would be horrified to be labeled as a company that believes otherwise. But when you look at how they handle complaining customers, it's clear from their behavior that they do believe otherwise. It doesn't have to be this way—as witnessed by the fact that a number of organizations are definitely getting better at responding to customer feedback. Some entire industries are even better than others. It's possible that we will see a divide in the future between a select group of powerfully branded companies that have real conversations with their customers and those companies that don't.

Change starts with the belief that feedback is nothing to be frightened of. In fact, it's the biggest gift we can get from the marketplace, whether the feedback is good or bad. Once that mind-set is firmly in place and staff know that their leaders operate from that position, it is relatively easy to get them to respond appropriately to customers. That's an excellent beginning point.

From this foundation, staff can begin to learn the complexities surrounding complaint handling. And it is a complex subject. In fact, the more we learn about it, the more complexity is revealed. We predict that the future of complaint handling is going to be about customized responses to customers. This means that those companies that already see complaints as gifts have a huge head start on those organizations that still place their focus on getting new customers rather than working to keep the ones they already have.

We predict that in the next ten years, we'll learn how to identify and then deliver the "best" solutions to recover each customer's goodwill, just as many manufacturers have gotten very good at so-called mass customization or as relationship marketers have learned how to position offers precisely to a customer's needs or preferences. The same progress is likely to happen with complaint handling. Indeed, one research group concludes, "Customers may not be homogeneous in their response tendencies toward service failure/recovery encounters . . . [We need to] enable organizations to design service recoveries in a way traditionally reserved for the design of products, that is, by bundling attributes and exploring various combinations to find the 'best' (i.e., most satisfying) solutions for customers."[1]

One thing we definitely know: the better you get at meeting individual needs in the solutions you craft for your complaining customers, the more likely you are to retain those customers and hear from them when things aren't right. They'll trust you more to deliver on your promises and you'll get more gifts—not from whining customers but from customers who want you to do better because they'd like to maintain a relationship with you![2]

NOTES

Introduction

1. Jeane Bliss, "Connecting with Customers," *Chief Executive*, July–August 2006, http://www.chiefexecutive.net/ME2/Segments/Publications/Print.asp?Module=Publica tions::Article&id=BB98F27ABCF04699A83BB7A6BFA2D671 (accessed December 28, 2007).

2. *Customer Experience Impact Report*, RightNow Technologies, August 2007, http://www.rightnow.com/pdf/whitepapers/CEI-2007.pdf (accessed December 28, 2007).

3. "BBB Reports Nearly One in Five Adult Americans' Trust in Business Decreased in Past Year," Better Business Bureau, 2007; detailed survey results are available at http://www.bbb.org/trustindex (accessed January 11, 2008).

4. For a complete discussion, see Stephen L. Vargo et al., "Satisfiers, Dissatisfiers, Criticals, and Neutrals: A Review of Their Relative Effects on Customer (Dis) Satisfaction," *Academy of Marketing Science Review* 11, no. 2 (2007), http://www.ams review.org/articles/vargo2-2007.pdf (accessed January 8, 2008).

5. For example, see one such study covering different complaining behaviors of hotel customers from Turkey, the Netherlands, Britain, and Israel: Atila Yuksel, Ugur Kilinc, and Fisun Yuksel, "Cross-National Analysis of Hotel Customers' Attitudes Toward Complaining and Their Complaining Behaviors," *Tourism Management* 27, no. 1 (February 2006): 11–24. For a comparison between Danes and Spaniards, see P. Shaw, "The Intercultural Validity of Customer-Complaint Handling Routines," *Document Design* 2, no. 2 (2001): 180–193; for a comparison between Canadian customers and customers from the People's Republic of China, see Michael K. Hui and Kevin Aul, "Justice Perceptions of Complaint-Handling: A Cross-Cultural Comparison between PRC and Canadian Customers," *Journal of Business Research* 52, no. 2 (May 2001): 161–173; and for a comparison between UK and U.S. customers, see Christopher A. Voss et al., "A Tale of Two Countries' Conservatism, Service Quality, and Feedback on Customer Satisfaction," *Journal of Service Research* 6, no. 3 (2004): 212–230.

6. One such example is research conducted at the Norwegian School of Management, which concludes that when looking at the initial service failure, satisfaction with

complaint resolution had the strongest impact on customer loyalty. Tor Wallin Andreassen, "What Drives Customer Loyalty with Complaint Resolution," *Journal of Service Research* 1, no. 4 (1999).

7. Janelle Barlow and Paul Stewart, *Branded Customer Service* (San Francisco: Berrett-Koehler, 2004).

8. This topic is discussed and available in downloadable documents at http://www .tmius.com.

9. Janelle Barlow and Dianna Maul, *Emotional Value* (San Francisco: Berrett-Koehler, 2000).

10. Patrick Barwise and Sean Meehan, *Simply Better: Winning and Keeping Customers by Delivering What Matters Most* (Boston: Harvard Business School Press, 2004).

11. The data were accessed by entering "customer complaints" in quotation marks and then looking at each year for this period.

12. K. Sheram and T. P. Soubbotina, *Beyond Economic Growth: Meeting the Challenges of Global Development* (Washington DC: The World Bank, 2000).

13. Gordon Bethune, as quoted in J. P. Donlon, "Learning from the Customer," *Chief Executive* (March 1, 1996), http://www.chiefexecutive.net/ME2/Segments/Publi cations/Print.asp?Module-Publications::Article&id=057CA5453F10402A91F04753 5D4205DC (accessed January 12, 2008).

14. E. de Coverly et al., "Service Recovery in the Airline Industry: Is It as Simple as Failed, Recovered, Satisfied?" *Marketing Review* 3, no. 1 (September 1, 2002): 21–37.

15. Wally Bock, "Getting Ideas Is the Easy Part: Here's What You Need for Innovation," Three Star Leadership Blog, June 8 2007, http://blog.threestarleadership.com/2007/ 06/08/getting-ideas-is-the-easy-part-heres-what-you-need-for-innovation.aspx (accessed December 28, 2007).

Chapter 1

1. These last three questions were asked of Janelle Barlow by Apple (plus, "What is your Apple customer number?") when she called to ask a question about an e-mail that said the company was cancelling her order. Then she was asked to verify her name and billing address. Finally, the Apple representative told her to ignore the e-mail. It was incorrect. All this took three and a half hours on the phone and being transferred to three offices staffed by very nice people, but people, nonetheless, suffering under some type of out-of-control system. And this is Apple, the company that is trying to make it possible for Janelle to be creative. Janelle was offered $100 off her order for her "inconvenience." The following week the scenario was repeated, though this service representative told Janelle she should never ignore any e-mail from Apple and asked her to send in all her information again. It ultimately took one month for Janelle to get the software she wanted.

2. A. Banu Elmadag and Mert Tokman, "Understanding the Effects of Self-Service Technologies on Service Performance: An Exploratory Study of Service Employees," The University of Alabama, Culverhouse College of Commerce and Business Administration, June 22, 2004, www.cba.ua.edu/~sbeatty/Readings/SST_employee _final.doc (accessed December 28, 2007).

3. European Branch Manager Survey (conducted September 2006 to November 2006) of eighteen European countries, as reported in "Learn About the Role of Complaints

Management in Improving Customer Service in European Retail Banks," *Business Wire*, March 21, 2007.

4. Andre Andersson and Fredrik Karlsson, "Kundtillfredsstallelse bland smaforetagare," (bachelor's thesis, Lulea University of Technology, 2007).

5. Chad Autry, Donna J. Hill, and Matthew O'Brien, "Attitude Toward the Customer: A Study of Product Returns Episodes," *Journal of Managerial Issues* (Fall 2007).

6. To read more about customer attribution, see Bernard Weiner, "'Spontaneous' Causal Thinking," *Psychological Bulletin* 97 (1985): 74–84; Valerie S. Folkes, "Consumer Reactions to Product Failure: An Attributional Approach," *Journal of Consumer Research* 10 (March 1984): 398–409; Valerie S. Folkes, "Recent Attribution Research in Consumer Behavior: A Review and New Directions," *Journal of Consumer Research* 14 (March 1988): 548–565; S. Krishnan and Valerie A. Valle, "Dissatisfaction Attributions and Consumer Complaint Behavior," in *Advances in Consumer Research*, ed. William L. Wilkie (Miami: Association for Consumer Research, 1979), 445–449.

7. Emerson Center for Business Ethics, "Customer Complaints: Closing the Gap," St. Louis University (April 1999): 1–6.

8. "And the Winner Is Wegmans," press release, Wegmans, April 16, 2007, http://www.wegmans.com/about/pressRoom/pressReleases/foodNetwork.asp (accessed December 28, 2007).

9. "100 Best Companies to Work For 2007," *Fortune*, January 22, 2007, http://money.cnn.com/magazines/fortune/bestcompanies/2007/full_list/ (accessed December 28, 2007).

10. "Record Low Temperatures, High Energy Costs Putting the Big Chill on Home and Business Owners," press release, Dryvit, January 19, 2004, http://www.dryvit.com/fileshare/doc/in_the_news/pr_ornl_rvalue.htm (accessed December 28, 2007).

11. The Marvin Windows, Dryvit, and Louisiana-Pacific examples are all cited in Daniel Walker Guido, "Above and Beyond: If All Manufacturers Handled Product Defects the Way These Three Companies Did, Builders Would Find Protecting Their Reputations a Whole Lot Easier," *Builder Magazine*, January 22, 2002. Details about the three companies were captured from their Web sites. This article is also available at http://www.builderonline.com/Industrynews.asp?channelID=59&sectionID=62&articletype=1&articleID=10000 20157 (accessed December 28, 2007).

12. Ted Garrison, "The New Equation: Customer Loyalty Equals Profitability," *G.I.A.: The Official Newsletter of the Georgia Irrigation Association, Inc.* (Summer 2005): 4, http://www.tedgarrison.com/articles2.cfm?itemid=2 (accessed December 28, 2007).

13. Bill Clinton (speech delivered in Las Vegas, Nevada, January 21, 2008).

14. Guy Kawasaki is the author of *Selling the Dream, Rules for Revolutionaries, The Art of the Start, Word of Mouth Marketing* and *How to Drive Your Competition Crazy*. Kawasaki, "How to Change the World," December 27, 2007, http://blog.guykawasaki.com/ (accessed December 28, 2007).

15. See Neil Ross, "Marina Profits: Use Your 'Head,'" *Boating Industry* 57, no. 7 (June 1994): 30–32; Ralph L. Day et al., "The Hidden Agenda of Consumer Complaining," *Journal of Retailing* 57, no. 3 (Fall 1981): 86–106; John Goodman at TARP says that he thinks the number is around 2 percent and that most of his business clients would support this number.

16. The Fish Market, http://www.birminghammenus.com/thefishmarket (accessed December 28, 2007).
17. Gwen Moran, "Green Eggs and Scam," *Entrepreneur*, January 1, 2002.
18. Tom Weir, "In-Store Counterattack," *Grocery Headquarters*, September 1, 2005.

Chapter 2
1. Fred Wiersema, as quoted in "Are You Ready for a Relationship?" *Chief Executive Magazine*, November 1999, http://www.chiefexecutive.net /ME2/Segments/Publi cations/Print.asp?Module=Publications:: Article&id=2C77123B33984A84A6C1FD D8719A4C11 (accessed December 28, 2007).
2. Jeffrey Pfeffer, *What Were They Thinking? Unconventional Wisdom About Management* (Boston: Harvard Business School Press, 2007).
3. As cited in Stacey L. Bell, "Launching Profits with Customer Loyalty," *CRM Magazine*, April 2000, http://www.destinationcrm.com/articles/default.asp?articleid=582 (accessed December 28, 2007).
4. Justin Martin, "6 Companies Where Customers Come First," *Fortune Small Business*, http://money.cnn.com/galleries/2007/fsb/0709/gallery.where_customers_come _first.fsb/index.html.
5. Claes Fornell and Birger Wernerfelt, "Defensive Marketing Strategy by Customer Complaint Management: A Theoretical Analysis," *Journal of Marketing Research* 24, No. 4 (November 1987): 337–346.
6. Janelle Barlow, e-mail to author, April 2001.
7. Diva, "I Heart Zappos," http://www.zazlamarr.com/blog/?p=240 (accessed on December 28, 2007).
8. Connie Koenenn, "Pleasing the Customer Should Be Job One," *Los Angeles Times*, March 6, 1997, E-5, Orange County edition.
9. John Davis, as quoted in "Get the Dope from the Customer," *American Salesman* (August 1990): 22.
10. Eileen McDargh, e-mail to Janelle Barlow.
11. Fred Wiersema, as quoted in "Are You Ready for a Relationship?"
12. Rod Wilkerson, "Comment," May 4, 2007, Matt Woodward's blog, http://www .mattwoodward.com/blog/index.cfm?event=showEntry&entryId=583895D2-B6 D1-7932-1ECA2FA194068CA4 (accessed December 28, 2007).
13. Jim Norton, "Customer Complaints Are Golden," *Small Business Boomers*, December 1, 2006, http://www.smallbusinessboomers.com/customer-complaints-are-golden/ (accessed December 28, 2007).
14. As reported in Tibbett L. Speer, "They Complain Because They Care," *American Demographics*, May, 1, 1996. This magazine ceased publication in November 2004 and is now part of *Advertising Age* magazine.
15. Richard Branson, as quoted in Rebecca Fannin, "Brand Leaders 2005," *Chief Executive*, October 2005, http://www.chiefexecutive.net/ME2/Segments/Publications/Print .asp?Module=Publications::Article&id=D9E488C3C6BF4D5FBACC56B88901 B31A (accessed December 28, 2007).
16. Tom Krazit, "Dell Shifts Support Calls After Customer Complaints," *IDG News Service*, November 25, 2003, http://www.microscope.co.uk/articles/article.asp?li

ArticleID=126822&liArticleTypeID=1&liCategoryID=2&liChannelID=16&li
FlavourID=1&sSearch=&nPage =1 (accessed December 28, 2007).

17. Gabriela Rico, "Will Customer Complaints Bring Call Centers Back to the US?"
Arizona Daily Star, November 27, 2007.

18. Andrew Lockwood and Ni Deng, "Can Service Recovery Help When Service Failures
Occur?" *Journal of Hospitality and Tourism Management* 11, no. 2 (August 1, 2004):
149–157.

19. Ibid.

20. Priscilla A. LaBarbera and David Mazursky, "A Longitudinal Assessment of Consumer
Satisfaction/Dissatisfaction: The Dynamic Aspect of the Cognitive Process," *Journal
of Marketing Research* 20 (November 1983): 393-404.

21. Steve Coomes, "Turning Newcomers into Lifetime Customers," Pizza Marketplace,
June 15, 2006, http://www.pizzamarketplace.com/article.php?id=5228 (accessed
December 28, 2007).

22. According to an American Institute of Economic Research study and cited in "Average
Lifetime Spending on Cars," PF Blog, January 29, 2005, http://www.pfblog.com/
archives/1513_average_lifetime_spending_on_cars_240000_or_more.shtml
(accessed on December 28, 2007).

23. Corbett L. Ourso, "Keep Customers Coming Back," *Drug Topics* 138, no. 21
(November 7, 1994): 14–16.

24. John Tschohl, "Do Yourself a Favor: Gripe About Bad Service!" *American Salesman*
39, no. 6 (June 1994): 4.

25. Glenn Rifkin, "New Economy: The Staples Merger of Its Web site and Catalog
Business," *New York Times*, June 25, 2001.

26. In fact, the National Retail Federation has found that multichannel shoppers buy
more and buy more frequently than single-channel shoppers. This all makes sense
when you consider that a single retail store such as Staples may carry eight thousand
items, but Staples.com is able to offer two hundred thousand items. Ibid.

27. IBM reports 95 percent will give the company another chance if problems have
been satisfactorily resolved. As reported in Christopher W. L. Hart, *Extraordinary
Guarantees* (New York: Amacom, 1993), 21.

28. Joseph P. Cavaness and G. H. Manoochehri, "Building Quality into Services," *SAM
Advanced Management Journal* 58, no. 1 (Winter 1993): 4-10.

29. Jaclyn Fierman, "The Death and Rebirth of the Salesman," *Fortune*, July 25, 1994:
82. The figure "5 times as much to sell to new customers" is cited in Frank Uller,
"Follow-Up Surveys Assess Customer Satisfaction," *Marketing News* 23, no. 14
(January 1, 1989): 16.

30. Eric Frenchman, "What the Vonage," *Pardon My French*, May 18, 2006, http://
pardon myfrench.typepad.com/pardonmyfrench/2006/05/what_the_vonage.html
(accessed December 28, 2007).

31. LaBarbera and Mazursky, "A Longitudinal Assessment," 393–404.

32. David Powley, "We Have Not Had Any Customer Complaints," SaferPak, 2006,
http://www.saferpak.com/csm_art9.htm (accessed December 28, 2007).

33. Bernice Kanner, "Seams Like Old Times; A Clothier Brings Back Quality," *New Yorker*
27, no. 1 (January 3, 1994): 14.

34. Mavis Scanlon, "Meet the System—Southern California: Adelphia Runs Up the Numbers Before the Deal Goes Down," *Cable World,* June 6, 2005, http://findarticles .com/p/articles/mi_m0DIZ /is _2005_June_6/ai_n13823647.

35. Linda Deckard, "IAAPA Panel: The Pros and Cons of Franchises at Amusement Parks," *Amusement Business* 105, no. 50 (December 13, 1993): 15.

36. Sometimes these attributes change based on how the research is conducted, but basically, people who complain feel more entitled and think there's a good chance that their needs will be met. See Jagdip Singh, "A Typology of Consumer Dissatisfaction Response Styles," *Journal of Retailing* 66 (1990): 57–99; J. Dart and K. Freeman, "Dissatisfaction: Response Styles Among Clients of Professional Accounting Firms," *Journal of Business Research* 29 (1994): 75–81; and Tom Hayes, "Using Customer Satisfaction Research to Get Closer to the Customers," *Marketing News* 27, no. 1 (January 4, 1993): 22–24.

37. Ron Zemke and Chip Bell, "Information Access," *Training: The Magazine of Human Resources Development,* July 1990, 42.

38. Justin Martin, "6 Companies Where Customers Come First," *Fortune Small Business,* http://money.cnn.com/galleries/2007/fsb/0709/gallery.where_customers_come _first.fsb/index.html (accessed January 7, 2008).

39. Gerald D. Stephens, "Please, No More Complaints," *Best's Review, Property-Casualty Insurance Edition,* January 1991, 61.

40. Robert Hunter, as quoted in Becky Yerak, "Insurers Say 95% of Katrina Claims Met: Critics Contend 'A Lot Still Unhappy,'" *Chicago Tribune,* August 23, 2006.

41. Go to http://www.sixapart.com/vox/tour/?s=house&loc=tour340 (accessed December 29, 2007).

42. Saska, "About Me," http://fiendishgleeclub.vox.com/profile/ (accessed December 29, 2007).

43. Saska, "Customer Service Gone Shockingly Right," http://fiendishgleeclub.vox.com/ library/post/customer-service-gone-shockingly-right.html (accessed December 29, 2007).

44. For a specific study of this type, see Marsha L. Richins, "Negative Word-of-Mouth by Dissatisfied Customers: A Pilot Study," *Journal of Marketing* 47 (Winter 1983): 68–78.

45. See Jerry R. Wilson, *Word-of-Mouth Marketing* (New York: John Wiley & Sons, 1994), section 1.

46. Michael A. Lapre and Gary D. Scudder, "Performance Improvement Paths in the U.S. Airline Industry: Linking Trade-offs to Asset Frontiers," *Production and Operations Management* 13, no. 2 (Summer 2004): 123–134.

47. "Survival Rates of Companies with Dissatisfied Customers," A Study by the Better Business Bureau serving Eastern Missouri & Southern Illinois, August 2007, http:// 209.85.173.104search?q=cache:UfqSinqtygkJ: www.stlouis.bbb.org/InternalStudy .pdf+BBB,+Eastern+Missouri,+Southern+Illinois,+August+2007&hl=en&ct=clnk &cd=1&gl=us (accessed January 11, 2008).

Chapter 3

1. David Thurston, "Moan Sharks," *Sunday Morning Post Magazine,* May 15, 1994, 30.

2. Bonnie J. Knutson, "Validating a Typology of the Customer from Hell," *Journal of Hospitality and Leisure Marketing* 6, no. 3 (September 1, 1999): 5–22.

3. Allan Wysocki, Karl W. Kepner, and Michelle W. Glasser, "Customer Complaints and Types of Customers," University of Florida, 2001, http://edis.ifas.ufl.edu/HR005 (accessed January 8, 2008).

4. Alan R. Andressen and Arthur Best, "Consumers Complain, Does Business Respond?" *Harvard Business Review*, July–August 1977, 98.

5. Argued by Donald Hughes, manager of the Consumer Research Division of Sears, Roebuck & Company in 1977, in Andreasen and Best, "Consumers Complain," 96.

6. Reuters, "Lonely Guy Shocked to Get $83,000 Phone Bill," December 14, 2007, http://www.reuters.com/article/newsOne/idUSN1322682220071214 (accessed March 13, 2008).

7. Jagdip Singh and P. E. Wilkes, "When Consumers Complain: A Path Analysis of the Key Antecedents of Consumer Complaint Response Estimates," *Journal of the Academy of Marketing Science* 24 (1996): 360–365.

8. Martha Rogers, as quoted in Stacey L. Bell, "Launching Profits with Customer Loyalty."

9. John W. Huppertz, "Firms' Complaint Handling Policies and Consumer Complaint Voicing," *Journal of Consumer Marketing* 24, no. 7 (2007): 428–437.

10. Daryl Travis, as quoted in "Are You Ready for a Relationship?"

11. Gary Kelly, as quoted in Fannin, "Brand Leaders 2005."

12. Edward F. McQuarrie, "Taking a Road Trip: Customer Visits Help Companies Recharge Relationships and Pass Competitors," *Marketing Management*, April 1995. This paper is available at http://lsb.scu.edu/~emcquarrie/research.htm (accessed December 29, 2007).

13. Roberta Maynard, "Warming to the Idea of Customer Feedback," *Nation's Business* 86 (February 1, 1998): 11.

14. SST technology is blooming, and since typically no personnel are around to get feedback from customers, alternative ways to get feedback will have to be implemented. People are beginning to look at this issue. See Nichola Robertson and Robin N. Shaw, "Conceptualizing the Influence of the Self-Service Technology Context on Consumer Voice," *Services Marketing Quarterly* 27, no. 2 (January 2006): 33–50.

15. Theresa D. Williams, Mary Drake,and James Moran, "Complaint Behavior, Price Paid and the Store Patronized," *Internal Journal of Retail and Distribution Management* 21, no. 5 (September–October 1993): 9.

16. These statements are a summary of research by Stephanie Kendall, a survey research specialist with Questar Data Systems, who surveyed ten thousand managers and customer-contact employees in seventy-five organizations. Quoted in Zemke and Bell, "Information Access."

17. Murray Raphael, "Bring Them Back Alive," *Direct Marketing* 53, no. 1 (May 1990): 50.

18. "Retailing Today," *Shopping Centers Today*, International Council of Shopping Centers, June 2006, http://www.icsc.org/srch/sct/sct0606/retail_in_brief.php (accessed December 28, 2007).

19. "Return to Spender," Snopes.com, http://www.snopes.com/business/consumer/nordstrom.asp (accessed December 28, 2007).

20. Susan Greco, "Real World Customer Service," *Inc.* 16, no. 10 (October 1994): 36–43.

21. "Toll Free Business Statistics," TollfreeNumber.org, 2007, http://www.tollfreenumber.org/toll-free-services/ (accessed January 8, 2008).

22. Daniel M. Rosen, "Expanding Your Sales Operation? Just Dial 1-800 . . . ," *Sales and Marketing Management* 142 (July 1990): 82.

23. Jeanne Luckas, as quoted in Carl Quintanilla and Richard Gibson, "'Do Call Us': More Companies Install 1-800 Phone Lines," *Wall Street Journal*, April 20, 1994, B1.

24. TARP, as quoted in Daniel S. Levine, "Companies Getting Message About Voice Mail Complaints," *Telecommunications*, January 20–26, 1995, 3–4A.

25. John Goodman, as quoted in Levine, "Companies Getting Message About Voice Mail Complaints."

26. Rosen, "Expanding Your Sales Operation?" 84.

27. Quintanilla and Gibson, "Do Call Us."

28. Bob Filipczak, "Customer Education," *Training* 28, no. 12 (December 1991): 31–36.

29. William H. LaMaire, "A New Trend: On Pack 800 Numbers," *Food Engineering* 62, no. 4 (April 1990): 60.

30. For a complete discussion, see M. Davidow and P.A. Dacin, "Understanding and Influencing Consumer Complaint Behavior: Improving Organizational Complaint Management," in *Advances in Consumer Research*, ed. M. Brucks and D. MacInnis (Provo, UT: Association for Consumer Research, 1997), 2:450–456.

31. Glenn F. Ross, "Tourist Dissatisfaction with Foodservice," *Foodservice Research International* 8, no. 4 (1995): 291–309.

32. You can visit Darty's Web site. It's very interesting, but you'll need to know some French, Italian, German, or Turkish to get through it. Isabelle Prim and Bernard Pras, " 'Friendly' Complaining Behaviors: Towards a Relational Approach," Centre de Recherche DMSP, June 1998.

33. Frederick Reichheld, "Transforming the Value Proposition: The Life Insurance Industry," eCustomerServiceWorld.com, http://www.ecustomerservice world.com/earticlesstore_articlesasp?type=article&id=1083 (accessed December 28, 2007).

34. See Alan J. Resnik and Robert R. Harmon, "Consumer Complaints and Managerial Response: A Holistic Approach," *Journal of Marketing* 47 (Winter 1983): 86–97.

35. Valerie S. Folkes and Barbara Kotsos, "Buyers' and Sellers' Explanations for Product Failure: Who Done It?" *Journal of Marketing* 50 (April 1986): 74–80.

36. "Haier Rises Through Reform and Opening Up," *People's Daily Online*, http://english.peopledaily.com.cn/200108/06/eng2001 0806_76638.html (accessed December 28, 2007).

37. "China's Power Brands," *BusinessWeek*, November 8, 2004, http://www.business week.com/magazine/content/04_45/b3907003.htm (accessed December 28, 2007).

38. "Six Chinese Brands Make Global Top 500 List," *China Economic Net*, May 19, 2006, http://en.ce.cn/Industries/Consumen-Industries /200605/19/t20060519_7026724 .shtml (accessed December 28, 2007).

39. Customer loyalty is probably easier to generate in professional relationships when expectations are exceeded than in any other kind of business relationship. It is also easier to destroy. For a complete discussion, see Stephen W. Brown and Teresa A. Swartz, "A Gap Analysis of Professional Service Quality," *Journal of Marketing* 53 (April 1989): 92–98.

40. E-mail to Janelle Barlow, March 2003.

41. Sleep Country USA, "About Us," http://www.sleepcountry.com/Page.aspx?nid=7 (accessed March 14, 2008).

42. Mary Jo Bitner, Bernard H. Booms, and Mary Tetreault, "The Service Encounter: Diagnosing Favorable and Unfavorable Incidents," *Journal of Marketing* 54, no. 1 (January 1990): 71.

43. W. Edwards Deming, as quoted in Mary Walton, *The Deming Management Method* (London: Mercury Books, 1989), 66.

44. Philip B. Crosby, *Let's Talk Quality: 96 Questions You Always Wanted to Ask Phil Crosby* (New York: Penguin Books, 1990), 104; and Philip B. Crosby, *Quality Is Free* (London: Penguin Books, 1980).

Chapter 4

1. John Goodman and Cindy Grimm, "Beware of Trained Hopelessness," *ICCM Weekly*, May 2007.

2. *Customer Experience Impact Report*, RightNow Technologies.

3. Charles I. Underhill, "Dispute Resolution at the Earliest Stages: Internal Complaint Handling and Customer Refunds," OECD, HCOPIL, ICC Conference on ADR, The Hague, December 11–12, 2000.

4. Mitchell can be reached at http://www.customermfg.com.

5. Summarized in Alan R. Andreasen, "Consumer Complaints and Redress: What We Know and What We Don't Know," in *The Frontier of Research in the Consumer Interest*, ed. E. Scot Maynes et al. (Columbia, MO: American Council on Consumer Interests, 1988), 708.

6. Ibid.

7. Andreasen and Best, "Consumers Complain," 98–100.

8. E. Schuman, "The War Against Retail Return Abuses," *eWeek*, December 17, 2004.

9. Lisa McQuilken and Robin N. Shaw, "Service Failure and Recovery in the Presence of Service Guarantees," ANZMAC 2005 Conference: Services Marketing, http://smib .vuw.ac.nz:8081/www/anzmac2005/cd-site/pdfs/16-Services/16-McQuilken.pdf (accessed December 28, 2007).

10. See research by Jochen Wirtz, Doreen Kum, and Khai Sheang Lee, "Should a Firm with a Reputation for Outstanding Service Quality Offer a Service Guarantee?" *Journal of Services Marketing* 14, no. 1 (2000): 502–512.

11. Jochen Wirtz and Doreen Kum, "Designing Service Guarantees: Is Full Satisfaction the Best You Can Guarantee?" *Journal of Services Marketing* 15, no. 4 (2001): 282–299.

12. It's interesting to read customer feedback on the Web about Sewell Cadillac. It's not all positive. In fact, some of it is harsh, and there's no way to know the truth about a dissatisfied customer. But it would appear that Sewell Cadillac is very good at taking care of high-end customers who buy new automobiles and ones who have been with the company for some time. Customers who buy Sewell's used cars or bring in their cars purchased elsewhere for service don't always have the most positive experience.

13. Carl Sewell and Paul B. Brown, *Customers for Life* (New York: Pocket Books, 1990), 59.

14. Grace Wagner, "Satisfaction Guaranteed," *Lodging Hospitality* 50, no. 6 (June 1994): 46–48.

15. Jeff Wenstein, "Delivering What You Promise," *Restaurants and Institutions* 103, no. 2 (January 15, 1993): 113–115.

16. Ibid.

17. Christopher W. Hart, "Guarantees Deliver Customers," *Chief Executive*, March 20, 2007, http://findarticles.com/p/articles/mi_m4070/is_224/ai_n21067756 (accessed December 28, 2007).

18. Christopher Hart, *Extraordinary Guarantees* (New York: Amacom, 1993), 3–4.

19. Ibid.

20. Tom Jones, as quoted in Hart, "Guarantees Deliver Customers."

21. Rajiv Kashyap, "The Effects of Service Guarantees on External and Internal Markets," *Academy of Marketing Science Review*, no. 10 (2002), http://www.amsreview.org/articles/kashyap10-2001.pdf (accessed January 8, 2008).

22. Hart, *Extraordinary Guarantees*.

23. Statistics reported at http://nyjobsource.com/dominos.html, updated as of August 7, 2007 (accessed December 28, 2007).

24. Hart, *Extraordinary Guarantees*, 22.

25. Jochen Wirtz and Doreen Kum, "Consumer Cheating on Service Guarantees," *Journal of the Academy of Marketing Science* 32, no. 2 (2004): 159–175.

26. Ibid., 170.

27. These include Canada, Australia, New Zealand, South Africa, the UK, and signatories to the African Union Convention on Preventing Corruption, which includes Libya.

28. Some argue that this legislation is pretty useless. "Not only are whistleblower laws flawed through exemptions and inbuilt weaknesses, but in their implementation they are rarely helpful. Indeed, it might be said that whistleblower laws give only the appearance of protection, creating an illusion that is dangerous for whistleblowers who put their trust in law rather than develop skills to achieve their goals more directly." Brian Martin, "Illusions of Whistleblower Protections," *UTS Law Review*, no. 5 (2003): 119–130.

29. See Carl W. Nelson and Jane Niederberger, "Patient Satisfaction Surveys: An Opportunity for Total Quality Improvement," *Hospital and Health Services Administration*, Fall 1990: 409; Kjell Gronhaug and Johan Arndt, "Consumer Dissatisfaction and Complaint Behavior as Feedback: A Comparative Analysis of Public and Private Delivery Systems," in *Advances in Consumer Research*, ed. Jerry C. Olson (Ann Arbor, MI: Association for Consumer Research, 1980), 7:324–328; and John A. Quelch and Stephen B. Ash, "Consumer Satisfaction with Professional Services," in *Marketing of Services*, ed. James H. Donnelly and William George (Chicago: American Marketing Association, 1981), 82–85.

30. Laura Landro, "Some Hospitals Offer New Service: Helping Patients Complain," *Wall Street Journal*, June 19, 2003, D1.

31. Philip Greeland, "What if the Patient Were Your Mother?" *Archives of Internal Medicine* 165 (2005): 607–608.

32. A. J. Kellett, "Healing Angry Wounds: The Role of Apology and Mediation in Disputes Between Physicians and Patients," *Journal of Dispute Resolution* 111 (1987): 122.

Chapter 5

1. John Goodman, "The Truth According to TARP," *Competitive Advantage*, June 1999, revised September 2006.

2. Ibid.

3. Summarized in Andreasen, "Consumer Complaints and Redress," 708.

4. Ibid.

5. Andreasen and Best, "Consumers Complain," 98–100.

6. See http://www.dps.state.ny.us/ocs_stats.html (accessed January 2, 2008).

7. Chris Lee, "1-800 Training," *Training*, August 1990, 39.

8. Goodman and Grimm, "Beware of Trained Hopelessness."

9. Alex Taylor III, "It's Time for Ford to Give Up and Sell Jaguar," *Fortune*, August 21, 2006, http://money.cnn.com/2006/08/18/news /companies/pluggedin_taylor .fortune/ (accessed January 2, 2008).

10. Joe Sherlock, "Jaguar Woes," The View Through the Windshield, 2005–2006, http:// www.joesherlock.com/Jaguar.html (accessed January 2, 2008).

11. Chris Lee, "1-800 Training," *Training*, August 1990, 39.

12. It's important to note that the great deal of research conducted on this question is mixed, and this is why we say, "actually has a chance." The best way to look at this is to understand that creating a stronger relationship after service failure is a good goal, but it's not going to happen all the time. It's possible that the degree of loyalty customers feel when the service failure occurs influences how likely you are to get them back. Highly loyal customers may passionately want to come back to you, so positive handling of a complaint may make them more loyal. We do know it's a numbers game, and increased loyalty is not going to happen 100 percent of the time because a complaint has been handled well. To read further on this subject, see Tor Wallin Andreassen, "From Disgust to Delight: Do Customers Hold a Grudge?" *Journal of Service Research* 4, no. 1 (2001): 39–49; and Amy Smith and Ruth Bolton, "An Experimental Investigation of Customer Reactions to Service Failure and Recovery Encounters," *Journal of Service Research* 1, no. 1 (1998): 65–81.

13. Survey conducted by Forrester and reported by Don Peppers and Martha Rogers, "How Can Customer Service and Sales Departments Work Together to Create Trust?" *Ask the CRM Expert*, June 29, 2007, http://searchcrm.techtarget.com/expert/Knowl edgebaseAnswer/0,289625,sid11_gci1262759,00.html (accessed January 2, 2008).

14. John W. O'Neill and Anna S. Mattila, "Towards the Develoment of a Lodging Service Recovery Strategy," *Journal of Hospitality and Leisure Marketing* 11, no. 1 (2004): 51–64.

15. Singh, "A Typology of Consumer Dissatisfaction Response Styles."

16. Beth Kobliner, "How to Complain on the Road," *Money* 21, no. 12 (December 1992): 169–170.

17. Michael A Jones, David L. Mothersbaugh, and Sharon E. Beatty, "Switching Barriers and Repurchase Intentions in Services," *Journal of Retailing* 76, no. 2 (Summer 2000).

18. Ana B. Casado, Ricardo Sellers, and Francisco J. Mas, "Third-Party Complaints and Firm Performance: An Application in Spanish Banking," Departamento de Economia Financiera, Contabilidad y Marketing, University of Alicanta, 2004, http://econpapers .repec.org /paper/iviwpasec/2004-01.htm (accessed January 8, 2008).

19. For example, see Andreason and Best, "Consumers Complain," 96.

20. Suzanne Hamlin, "In the End, the Customer Is Always Right, Right?" *New York Times*, June 14, 1995, B1, B2; and John Filnn, "Customer Steams at Starbucks Chain," *San Francisco Examiner*, May 31, 1995, Bl–B2.

21. Seth Godin, *All Marketers Are Liars* (London: Penguin, 2005).
22. As reported on Marketplace, American Public Media, October 30, 2007, http://mar ketplace.publicradio.org/display/web/2007/10/30/java_jitter/ (accessed January 2, 2008).
23. "Death of Some Salesmen: British Financial Regulation," *Economist* 326, no. 7800 (February 17, 1993): 82.
24. R. L. Day et al., "The Hidden Agenda of Consumer Complaining," *Journal of Retailing* 57 (1981): 86–104.
25. Singh, "A Typology of Consumer Dissatisfaction," 93.
26. Mary C. Gilly, "Postcomplaint Processes: From Organizational Response to Repur- chase Behavior," *Journal of Consumer Affairs* 21, no. 2 (Winter 1987): 293–313.
27. Steven Austin Stovall, "Customer Service Doesn't Necessitate a Free Lunch," *Nation's Restaurant News* 28, no. 21 (May 23, 1994): 22.
28. While this study was conducted in the Netherlands, it seems on par with research conducted in the United States. Roland D. Friele and Emmy M Sluijs, "Patient Expectations of Fair Complaint Handling in Hospitals: Empirical Data," *BMC Health Services Research* (2006): 106, http://www.biomedcentral.com/1472-6963/6/106 (accessed January 8, 2008).
29. See Mary Jo Bitner, "Evaluating Service Encounters: The Effects of Physical Surroundings and Employee Responses" *Journal of Marketing* 54 (April 1990): 69–82.
30. Nancy Friedman, *Customer Service Nightmares* (Menlo Park, CA: Crisp Publications, 1998).
31. Christopher W. Hart, "Beating the Market with Customer Satisfaction," *Harvard Business Review* (March 2007), 30–31.
32. Mary C. Gilly, William B. Stevenson, and Laura J. Yale, "Dynamics of Complaint Management in the Service Organization," *Journal of Consumer Affairs* 25, no. 2 (Winter 1991): 295–323.
33. As a side note, these same researchers discovered that quality-of-care complaints were generally resolved (handled) quickly by the primary caregivers. In these cases, however, no recommendations for changes in policies or systems were made because the complaint never got to the "complaint managers." Whether managed or handled, complaints were not fully utilized to the hospital's benefit. Richard E. Walton and John M. Dutton, "The Management of Interdepartmental Conflict: A Model and Review," *Administrative Science Quarterly* 14 (1969): 73–84.
34. Jinkook Lee, "An Empirical Analysis of Elderly Consumers' Complaining Behavior," *Family and Consumer Sciences Research Journal* 27, no. 3 (1999): 341–371.

Chapter 6
1. http://www.reference.com/browse/wiki/Regifting (accessed January 2, 2008).
2. Blanchard recommends that whatever you give them as a small compensation, make sure it has value so they can associate that gift with the repair of their situation. Olivier Blanchard, "Customer Complaints Are Great," The Brandbuilder Blog, 2005, http://thebrandbuilder.blogspot.com/2005/10/customer-complaints-are-great.html (accessed January 8, 2008).

3. Steve Trollinger, "Offer Development and Marketing Strategies: Training Customers Not to Expect Promotions," *Target Marketing*, January 1, 2001.

4. Among others, Ron Zemke and Chip Bell found that on average, companies apologize for only 48 percent of their errors. See Ron Zemke and Chip Bell, "Service Recovery: Doing Right the Second Time," *Training*, June 1990, 42–48.

5. For example, Motorola has a five-step program to recover from bad situations. The first step is the apology. "Recovery absolutely demands some acknowledgment of error immediately following a breakdown in service," is how Motorola expresses it. Joan Koob Cannie advises readers to apologize as soon as possible. Apologies are her first step in a five-step approach to service recovery. Joan Koob Cannie, *Turning Lost Customers into Gold* (New York: Amacom, 1994), 100.

6. Employment relations experts also counsel that keeping open communication between opposing parties and apologizing to the offended party, without admitting guilt, can work wonders to prevent litigation. Lee Minkel, "How to Avoid Employment Litigation," *Employment Relations Today* 19, no. 4 (Winter 1992): 405–411.

7. Mahesh Bhandari and Michael Polonsky, "An Empirical Investigation of the Effect of Interaction Justice Perception on Consumer Intentions After Complaining," *Journal of Business Systems, Governance and Ethics* 2, no. 1 (2007): 11–20.

8. Stephen W. Clopton, James E. Stoddard, and Jennifer W. Clay, "Salesperson Characteristics Affecting Consumer Complaint Responses," *Journal of Consumer Behavior* 1, no. 2 (2001): 124–139.

9. Carol Hymowitz, "Everyone Likes to Laud Serving the Customer; Doing It Is the Problem," *Wall Street Journal* (February 27, 2006), B1.

10. Oren Harari, "The Lab Test: AT&T of Quality," *Management Review* 82, no. 3 (February 1993): 55–59.

11. This expression, "Punish your processes, not your people," is from Kent V. Rondeau, "Getting a Second Chance to Make a First Impression," *Medical Laboratory Observer* 26, no. 1 (January 1994): 22–26.

12. Norma Gutierrez, as quoted in Charlotte Klopp and John Sterlicchi, "Customer Satisfaction Just Catching on in Europe," *Marketing News* 24, no. 11 (May 28, 1990): 5.

13. Marcia MacLeod, "Never Say Sorry," *Airline Business*, April 1994, 50.

Chapter 7

1. Smith and Bolton, "An Experimental Investigation of Customer Reactions."

2. Amy K. Smith, Ruth N. Bolton, and Janet Wagner, "A Model of Customer Satisfaction with Service Encounters Involving Failure and Recovery," *Journal of Marketing Research* 36, no. 3 (August 1999): 356–372.

3. R. Folger and R. Cropanzano, *Organizational Justice and Human Resources Management* (Thousand Oaks, CA: Sage, 1998).

4. N. Roese, "Counterfactual Thinking, *Psychological Bulletin* 121, no. 1 (1997): 133–148.

5. Four strong articles include J. G. Blodgett, D. J. Hill, and Stephen S. Tax, "The Effects of Distributive, Procedural, and International Justice on Postcomplaint Behavior," *Journal of Retailing* 2 (1997): 185–210; Stephen Tax et al., "Customer Evaluations of Service Complaint Experiences," *Journal of Marketing* 62 (April 1998): 60–76;

D. Nel et al., "Customer Evaluations of Service Complaint Experiences in the Public Sector," *Journal of Public Policy and Marketing* 3 (2000): 67–84; James G. Maxham and Richard G. Netemeyer, "Firms Reap What They Sow: The Effects of Shared Values and Perceived Organizational Justice on Customers' Evaluations of Complaint Handling," *Journal of Marketing* 67, no. 1 (January 2003): 46–62.

6. Lisa McQuilken, Andrea Vocino, and David Bednall, "The Influence of Procedural and Interactional Justice, and Disconfirmation on Customers' Postrecovery Satisfaction Evaluations," *Proceedings*, ANZMAC Conference, 2007, 2759–2766.

7. Tax et al., "Customer Evaluations of Service Complaint Experiences," 62.

8. See R. M. Morgan and S. D. Hunt, "The Commitment-Trust Theory of Relationship Marketing," *Journal of Marketing* 58 (1994): 20–38.

9. For one of the better articles on consumer reactions to fairness, see R. L. Oliver and J. E. Swan, "Consumer Perception of Interpersonal Equity and Satisfaction in Transactions: A Field Survey Approach," *Journal of Marketing* 53 (1989): 21–35.

10. "United Lost His Baggage but Will Only Pay Half," Untied, http://www.untied.com/refundproblems/archive.html#half (accessed January 6, 2008).

11. C. Boshoff, "An Experimental Study of Service Recovery Options," *International Journal of Service Industry Management* 8, no. 3 (1997): 110–130.

12. The following examples are taken from Janelle Barlow, *Loyalty: Creating Emotional Partnerships with Customers*, The Emotional Value Series (Las Vegas: TMI US, 2000), 31.

13. Reprinted from Barlow and Maul, *Emotional Value*, 241.

14. Syed Saad Andaleeb and Amiya K. Basu, "Technical Complexity and Consumer Knowledge as Moderators of Service Quality Evaluation in the Automobile Service Industry," *Journal of Retailing* 70, no. 4 (Winter 1994): 367–382. Andaleeb and Basu considered automobile service and repair exclusively in their research.

15. Eric Hofer, *Working and Thinking on the Waterfront* (New York: Harper and Row, 1969).

16. Beverley Sparks, "Providing an Explanation for Service Failure: Context, Content, and Customer Responses," *Journal of Hospitality and Tourism Research* 31, no. 2 (2007): 241–260.

17. Beverley Sparks and Janet R. McColl-Kennedy, "Justice Strategy Options for Increased Customer Satisfaction in a Services Recovery Setting," *Journal of Business Research* 54, no. 3 (December 2001): 209–218.

18. Explored in Barlow and Maul, *Emotional Value*, 203–205.

19. Stephen Tax, Stephen Brown, and Murali Chandrashekaran, "Customer Evaluations of Service Complaint Experiences: Implications for Relationship Marketing," *Journal of Marketing* 62, no. 2 (April 1998). This article examines how prior positive experiences mitigate the effects of poor complaint handling.

20. Rick Garlick, "The Myth of Service Recovery," *Lodging Hospitality*, July 15, 2006.

21. Tom DeWitt and Michael Brady conducted four tests to find that when customers and service providers are in rapport, customers walk away feeling more satisfaction, a stronger desire to return, and less of an urge to make negative comments about their experience. DeWitt and Brady, "Rethinking Service Recovery Strategies: The Effect of Rapport on Consumer Responses to Service Failure," *Journal of Service Research* 6, no. 2 (2003): 193–207.

22. Bruce Nussbaum, "Delta's CEO Sends Me a Personal Letter Apologizing for Bad Service—That's Actually Pretty Good Service," Naussbaum on Design, May 30, 2007, http://blogs.businessweek.com/innovate/NussbaumOnDesign/archives/2007/05/deltas_ceo_apol.html (accessed January 10, 2008).

23. P. U. Nyer, "An Investigation into Whether Complaining Can Cause Increased Consumer Satisfaction," *Journal of Consumer Marketing* 17, no. 2 (2000): 9–19.

24. Amy Ostrom and Dawn Iacobucci, "Customer Trade-Offs and the Evaluations of Services," *Journal of Marketing* 59, no. 1 (January 1995): 17–28.

25. In a study of the optical industry, researchers found that the difference between customers who were "delighted" and those who were not had to do with reliability, timeliness, courtesy, friendliness, and perceived fairness. The researchers concluded, "It is interesting to note that dimensions differentiating customer delight are related to how the client or customer is treated, and these are just as important as those related to expertise." Delight was inferred when customers selected "very satisfied" on a five-point survey scale. Paula Saunders, Robert Scherer, and Herbert Brown, "Delighting Customers by Managing Expectations for Service Quality," *Journal of Applied Business Research* 11, no. 2 (Spring 1995): 101–109.

26. Passenger quoted in Scott McCartney, "To a United Pilot, The Friendly Skies are a Point of Pride," *Wall Street Journal Online*, August 28, 2007.

27. Ronald Zebeck, as quoted in "Are You Ready for a Relationship?"

Chapter 8

1. As reported by Jane Spencer, "Cases of Customer Rage Mount as Bad Service Prompts Venting," *Wall Street Journal*, September 17, 2003, D4.

2. Marcel Zeelenberg and Rik Pieters, "Beyond Valence in Customer Dissatisfaction," *Journal of Business Research* 57, no. 4 (April 2004): 445–455.

3. B. Stauss and W. Seidel, *Complaint Management: The Heart of CRM* (Mason, Ohio: Thomson Business and Professional Publishing, 2004): 107.

4. Misuigi Saotome, *The Principles of Aikido* (Boston: Shambhala, 1989), 222.

5. Morihei Ueshiba, *The Art of Peace*. trans. John Stevens (Boston: Shambhala, 1992).

6. The 2003 report concludes that U.S. companies are driving their customers crazy. Jane Spencer, "Cases of Customer Rage Mount."

7. Simon Kemp and K. T. Strongman, "Anger Theory and Management: A Historical Analysis," *American Journal of Psychology* 108, no. 3 (Autumn 1995): 397–417.

8. Anna S. Mattila and Heejung Ro, "Discrete Negative Emotions and Customer Dissatisfaction Responses in a Casual Restaurant Setting, *Journal of Hospitality and Tourism Research* 32, no. 1 (2007), 89–107, http://jht.sagepub.com/cgi/content/abstract/1096348007309570v1 (accessed December 31, 2007).

9. Edward T. Hall, *Beyond Culture* (New York: Anchor Books, 1977), 141.

10. For a complete discussion of how questions appeal to the adult side of our personalities, consult one of the classic transactional analysis books, such as Muriel James and Dorothy Jongeward, *Born to Win* (New York: Addison-Wesley, 1971): 243–244. Also consider articles that discuss the use of questions in interviews, such as Janet Treasure and Anne Ward, "A Practical Guide to the Use of Motivational Interviewing

in Anorexia Nervosa," *European Eating Disorders Review* 5, no. 2 (December 4, 1998): 102–114.

11. Oren Harari, "To Hell and Back: Learn to Discriminate Between Customers from Hell and Customers Who Have Gone through Hell," *Management Review* 85, no. 7 (July 1996): 55–58.

12. Chip Bell and Ron Zemke, as cited ibid.

Chapter 9

1. Mike Eskew, as quoted in Fannin, "Brand Leaders 2005."

2. See the Susskind paper cited for an interesting discussion of why fast-casual diners choose to complain to a manager or write a letter. In either case, the customer chooses these channels to complain because the complaint has risen beyond what customer-facing staff can handle. For this reason, Susskind recommmends that managers pay particular attention to escalated complaints and/or written complaints. Alex M. Susskind, "An Examination of Guest Complaints and Complaint Communication Channels: The Medium Does Matter!" *Cornell Hospitality Report* 6, no. 14 (November 2006): 1–12.

3. This is an enormous range of response rates and is based on data gathered in the 1970s. As far as the authors could discover, no wide-ranging systematic studies of response rates have been conducted since these early U.S. studies. In the 1970s, researchers tended to send out actual letters of complaint (real or made up) to see what kinds of response their letters received. Today, researchers are more concerned about ethical considerations; that is, they are reluctant to make companies think they have a problem when a research study is being conducted. To get around this, they either survey people who have written actual letters of complaint or they role-play situations. For a summary of this research, see Mary C. Gilly, "Postcomplaint Processes: From Organizational Response to Repurchase Behavior," *Journal of Consumer Affairs* 21, no. 2 (Winter 1987): 295.

4. William E. Fulmer and Jack S. Goodwin, "So You Want to Be a Superior Service Provider? Start by Answering Your Mail," *Business Horizons* 37, no. 6 (November–December 1994): 23–27.

5. In a similar study of complaint letters sent to manufacturers of consumer products, researchers found an 82 percent response rate to praise letters, and an 86 percent response rate to complaints. The average response time was seventeen days. About 7 percent of the letter writers reported that they felt the manufacturers valued getting their complaint letters, though they did feel the praise letters were more appreciated by the manufacturers. See Denise T. Smart and Charles Martin, "Manufacturer Responsiveness to Consumer Correspondence: An Empirical Investigation of Consumer Perceptions," *Journal of Consumer Affairs* 26, no. 1 (Summer 1992): 104–129.

6. Tax, Brown, and Chandrashekaran, "Customer Evaluations of Service Complaint Experiences," 60–76.

7. Emerson Center for Business Ethics, "Customer Complaints," 1–6.

8. Timothy C. Johnston, "Customer Satisfaction with Provider Response to Service Failure," Advances in Marketing: Proceedings of the Association of Collegiate Market-

ing Educators Annual Conference 2004, http://www.utm.edu/~johnston/papers/
AAIC04Johnston-T.pdf (accessed January 3, 2008).

9. Ibid.

10. We must note that this is not the case in all cultures. A study conducted in Chile
stands out for us. Researchers at the University of Talca found that promptness has
no effect on repurchase behavior and even less effect on service recovery evaluation.
Compensation came out as the strongest variable to affect repurchase behavior.
Perhaps the Chilean focus on the present in contrast to the U.S. focus on the future
accounts for this difference. Let us emphasize once more that consumer expectations
are not universal and that probably even within Chile, customers demand a quick
response in some circumstances. Fredy Valenzuela et al., "Assessing the Antecedents
of Service Recovery Evaluation and Their Impact on Repurchase Behavior," Working
Paper Series 3, no. 6 (2005), http://dspace.utalca.cl/retrieve/8245/SWP_3_6_2005
.pdf (accessed January 8, 2008). Sometimes the similarities among cultures is
striking. As more and more research is completed, we should be able to begin to more
effectively determine how universal these findings are. Dong-Geun Oh, concerned
with the complaining behaviors of academic library users in South Korea, found
that the basic complaining behavior model applies within South Korea as well as
other parts of the world and that the for-profit sector model applies equally well to
the nonprofit sector, such as libraries. Dong-Geun Oh, "Complaining Behavior of
Academic Library Users in South Korea," *Journal of Academic Librarianship* 30, no. 2
(March 2004): 136–144; and Dong-Geun Oh, "Complaining Intentions and Their
Relationships to Complaining Behavior of Academic Library Users in South Korea,"
Library Management 27, no. 3 (2006): 168–189.

11. Goodman, e-mail to Janelle Barlow, December 21, 2007.

12. Statistics are from http://www.e-maillabs.com/tools/e-mail-marketing-statistics.html
(accessed January 3, 2008).

13. As referenced in Judy Strauss and Donna J. Hill (1998), "Consumer Complaints by
Exploratory Investigation of Corporate Responses and Customer Reactions" *Journal
of Interactive Marketing* 15, no. 1 (February 13, 2001): 63–73.

14. Ibid.

15. Yooncheong Cho et al., "An Analysis of Online Customer Complaints: Implications
for Web Complaint Management," *Proceedings of the 35th Hawaii International
Conference on System Sciences,* 2002.

16. Lynn Goetzinger, Jungkun Park, and Rick Widdows, "Understanding Online Service
Failure: A Critical Incident Analysis from Consumer Complaints," SERVSIG Research
Conference, 2005, http://www.servsig2005.org/downloads/ServsigTechnicalProg.pdf.

17. For anyone interested in online customer satisfaction and its impact on the desire to
continue shopping, see Pingjun Jiang and Bert Rosenbloom, "Customer Intention
to Return Online: Price Percpetion, Attribute-Level Performance, and Satisfaction
Unfolding over Time," *European Journal of Marketing* 39, no. 1/2 (2005): 150–174.

18. To consult a major benchmarking study of electronic customer service, see
International Customer Service Association, http://www.supplyht.com/CDA/
Archives/0259acc0eb278010VgnVCM100000f932a8c0 (accessed January 7, 2008).

19. Anna S. Mattila and Daniel J. Jount, "The Impact of Selected Customer Characteristics and Response Time on E-Complaint Satisfaction and Return Intent," *International Journal of Hospitality Management* 22, no. 2 (June 2003): 135–145.

20. Thomas Weber, "Simplest Email Queries Confound Companies," *Wall Street Journal*, October 21, 1996, B1.

21. Strauss and Hill, "Consumer Complaints by Exploratory Investigation of Corporate Responses and Customer Reactions", 63–73.

22. Alanah May Eriksen, "Angry E-mail Exchange Goes Viral," *New Zealand Herald*, December 19, 2007.

23. Posted on the Consumerist, http://consumerist.com/consumer/good/amazon-sends-best-customer-service-e+mail-ive-ever-received-332639.php (accessed January 3, 2008).

24. Denise T. Smart and Charles Martin, "Manufacturer Responsiveness to Consumer Correspondence: An Empirical Investigation of Consumer Perceptions," *Journal of Consumer Affairs* 26, no. 1 (Summer 1992): 104–129.

25. Ibid.

26. Ibid.

27. Ibid., 120. Smart and Martin report that only 2 percent of their study cohort said that the manufacturer should have included refunds or discount coupons.

28. The first three phrases are based on comments in Julie M. Hays and Arthur V. Hill, "The Market Share Impact of Service Failures," *Production and Operations Management* 8, no. 3 (1999): 208–220; article available at Curtis Carlson School of Management, University of Minnesota, http://www.csom.umn.edu/assets/2746.pdf (accessed January 3, 2008).

29. Jan Mattson, Jos Lemmink, and Rod McColl, "The Effect of Verbalized Emotions on Loyalty in Written Complaints," *Total Quality Management* 15, no. 7 (September 2004): 941–958.

30. Ibid.

Chapter 10

1. John Ellis, as quoted in John Butler, ed., *E-Commerce and Entrepreneurship,* Research in Entrepreneurship and Management (Charlotte, NC: Information Age Publishing, 2001), 106.

2. Betsy Spethmann, "Brand Marketers Eavesdrop on the Internet to Track Consumer Trends," What's the Buzz? *Promo*, February 1, 2001, http://promomagazine.com/mag/marketing_whats_buzz/ (accessed January 5, 2008).

3. Ted Morris, "Listening to the Blogosphere: How Blogging Can Impact Your Brand," ESOMAR, Brandmatters Conference, New York, February 2006.

4. Search on Google or Yahoo for "wine and dine." MassLive.com is at http://www.masslive.com/forums/wineanddine/ (accessed January 4, 2008).

5. This review was found buried within the Web site http://www.webtourist.net/england/london/ (accessed January 5, 2008).

6. An interesting Web site is CarTalk, set up by National Public Radio's most-listened-to program, *Car Talk*, hosted by Tom and Ray Magliozzi. This Web site encourages people to send in evaluations of auto repair shops. With some of the positive

statements written about certain repair shops, those shops must be doing extraordinary business. All the news put up on the Internet is definitely not bad. Check out Autoworks, Ithaca, New York, http://www.cartalk.com/ct/mechx/shop.jsp?id=23780 (accessed January 5, 2008).

7. Pew Internet and American Life Project, April 26, 2006, http://www.pewinternet .org/trends.asp (accessed January 5, 2008).

8. "Customers Read Reviews (Companies Should, Too)," Word of Mouth Marketing Association, November 1, 2007, http://www.womma.org/blog/2007/08/customers-read-reviews-companies-should-too/ (accessed January 5, 2008).

9. Tom Hespos, "Negative Feedback Is an Opportunity," iMedia Connection, http:// www.imediaconnection.com/content/12351.asp (accessed January 5, 2008).

10. See http://www.vault.com.

11. See http://www.hyperorg.com/misc/DoubleTreeShow_files/frame.html.

12. Linda Shea, "Internet Diffusion of an E-Complaint: A Content Analysis of Unsolicited Responses," *Journal of Travel and Tourism Marketing* 17, no. 2/3 (February 15, 2005): 144–165.

13. Laura Bly, "Online Complaint about Hotel Service Scores," *USA Today*, January 4, 2002, Tech.

14. See http://www.slideshare.net/modadimagno/yours-is-a-very-bad-airline/.

15. "BBB Service Demand Reaches All Time High," January 27, 2006, http://www.site mason.com/newspub/hWgqiY?id=27189 (accessed January 5, 2008).

16. Dennis Rockstroh, "Kodak Ignoring Customer Complaints Through BBB," March 28, 2007, http://blogs.mercurynews.com/consumeractionline/2007/03/kodak _ignoring_customer_complaints_through_bbb.html (accessed January 5, 2008). Also see "Kodak Quits Better Business Council," MSNBC News, March 26, 2007, http://www.msnbc.msn.com/id/17803883/ (accessed January 5, 2008).

17. Eric Lundquist, "Take a Lesson from Intel: Listen to Internet Gripes," *PC Week* 11, no. 50 (December 19, 1994): 55.

18. "The Complaints You Never Hear," *CFO: The Magazine for Senior Financial Executives*, March 2004, http://goliath.ecnext.com/coms2/summary_0198-3131_ITM (accessed January 5, 2008).

19. Ibid.

20. "How to Track and Disarm Corporate Assassins," *1to1 Magazine* (January–February 2006).

21. Louise Lee, "Dell: In the Bloghouse," *BusinessWeek*, August 25, 2005.

22. Jeff Jarvis, "Dell Learns to Listen," *BusinessWeek*, October 17, 2007, http://www .businessweek.com/bwdaily/dnflash/content/oct2007/db20071017_277576.htm ?chan=top+news_top+news+index_top+story (accessed January 5, 2008).

23. Yuri Radzievsky, "Technology's Impact on Branding," *Chief Executive*, September 1, 2006, http://www.chiefexecutive.net/ME2/Segments/Publications/Print.asp?Mod ule=Publications::Article&id=4B21A524F1BB48BD83B21B39F378AFFS (accessed January 6, 2008).

24. Christoper Elliott, "Airlines Ignore Web Whines," July 5, 1999, http://www.elliott.org/ the-travel-critic/airlines-ignore-web-whines/ (accessed January 5, 2008).

25. See V. P. Goby, "Personality and Online/Offline Choices: MBTI Profiles and Favored Communication Modes in a Singapore Study," *Cyber Psychology & Behavior* 9 (2006): 1–13.

26. David Kesmodel, "Whole Foods Bars Executives from Web Forums," *Wall Street Journal*, November 7, 2007.

27. Josh Fineman and Danny King, "Whole Foods Chief John Mackey Says He Bashed Rival on Web," *Bloomberg News*, July 12, 2007, Mindfully.org, http://www.mindfully .org/Industry/2007/Whole-Foods-Mackey12jul07.htm (accessed April 9, 2008).

28. Commenter to article by Stephen Grocer, "The Losers in the Biggest M&A Year," *Wall Street Journal*, December 31, 2007.

29. Alec Saunders, as quoted in Jeff Jarvis, "It's Not the Blog," BuzzMachine, October 18, 2007, http://www.buzzmachine.com /2007/12/09/its-not-the-blog/ (accessed January 4, 2008).

30. Rick Levine et al., *The Cluetrain Manifesto* (New York: Perseus Books, 2000).

31. "Blogs Make Tech Impact: 78% of Tech Journalists Read Them," *Word of Mouth Marketing Association*, November 1, 2007, http://www.womma.org/research/010223 .php (accessed January 5, 2008).

32. Lionel Menchaca, as quoted in Jeff Jarvis, "Happy Birthday–to Dell," *BuzzMachine*, July 15, 2007, http://www.buzzmachine.com/?tag=dell (accessed January 5, 2008).

33. "Dell Still No. 1, But Blogger, Battery Recall Dent Image," *Advertising Age*, August 21, 2006.

34. Hila Etzion and Neveen Award, "Pump Up the Volume? Examining the Relationship Between Number of Online Reviews and Sales: Is More Necessarily Better?" International Conference on Information Systems, Montreal, Quebec, December 9–12, 2007.

35. Singh and Wilkes, "When Consumers Complain."

Chapter 11

1. Joan Baez, as quoted in Polly Drew, "Apology Comes with Risk, Reward," *Milwaukee Journal Sentinel*, February 6, 2005.

2. See Muriel James and Dorothy Jongeward, *Born to Win* (New York: Addison-Wesley, 1971), 189–195.

3. For a summary of Tomatis's work , see http://www.vanderbilt.edu/AnS/psychology/ health_psychology/TOMATIS.html (accessed January 15, 2008).

4. Aaron Lazare, "Go Ahead, Say You're Sorry," *Psychology Today*, January–February 1995, 43.

5. Aaron Lazare, "You Call That an Apology?" *Washington Post*, July 3, 2005.

6. Stephanos Bibas and Richard Bierschbach, "Integrating Remorse and Apology into Criminal Procedure," *Yale Law Journal* (October 1, 2004).

7. Alfred Allan, "Apology in Civil Law: A Psycho-legal Perspective," *Psychiatry, Psychology and Law* 14, no. 1 (April 1, 2007).

8. Randall Poe, "Can We Talk?" *Across the Board* 31, no. 5 (May 1994): 16–23.

9. Ibid.

Chapter 12

1. Melissa George, "Retailers Hit by Complaints of Poor Customer Relations," *Weekly Wall Street*, January 17, 1994.
2. Bernard Hale, as quoted in Helen L. Richardson, "I Don't Hear Your Complaining . . ." *Transportation and Distribution* 33, no. 10 (October 1992): 47.
3. Janet Rubel, *101+ Complaint Letters That Get Results*, 2nd ed. (Naperville, IL: Sphinx Publishing, 2006).

Looking to the Future

1. Smith, Bolton and Wagner, "A Model of Customer Satisfaction," 360, 370. Regarding financial institutions, see Ana B. Casado-Diaz, Francisco J. Mas Ruiz, and Hans Kasper, "Explaining Satisfaction in Double Deviation Scenarios: The Effects of Anger and Distributive Justice," Working Papers, Serie EC, Instituto Valenciano de Investigaciones Economics, S.A., September 2006, http://ideas.repec.org/p/ivi/wpasec/2006-09.html#provider (accessed December 31, 2007).
2. See Clay M. Voorhees, "A Service Perspective on the Drivers of Complaint Intentions," *Journal of Service Research* 8, no. 2 (2005): 192–204.

ACKNOWLEDGMENTS

Saying "thank you" is an effective way to acknowledge that a complaint is a gift. It's also a great way to publicly acknowledge everyone who helped us get a completed manuscript into the hands of the Berrett-Koehler staff. Our TMI colleagues around the globe are and always have been generous with their time and help. Thank you, Kostas Hatzigeorgiou, Leah Fisher, Sumit Sahni, Ralph Simpfendorfer, and Nadzeda Bogdanova. Thank you as well to our U.S.-based colleagues: Lewis Barlow, Jeffrey Mishlove, Beverly Lee, Dianne Kenny, Paul Holden, and Bob Branson. Thank you to our agent, Rita Rosenkranz, and to the team at Berrett-Koehler who have made this book possible from its first edition twelve years ago: Steven Piersanti, Jeevan Sivasubramaniam, Michael Crowley, Maria Jesus Aguilo, Kristen Frantz, Catherine Lengronne, Marina Cook, Peter Cavagnaro, and Tiffany Lee. And a special thank-you to John Goodman at TARP and Lee Barnes at Family Fare.

Perhaps, most importantly, we thank all the many people who sent us e-mails, talked to us in person, or spoke to us on the phone in the last dozen years either asking questions that helped us refine our thinking or shared examples about their implementation of these ideas. They amazed us over and over again with how powerful it is to thank customers for their feedback.

INDEX

275

ABOUT THE AUTHORS

JANELLE BARLOW, PhD, knows a lot about feedback, having spent more than thirty years receiving critiques about her speeches and seminars to management groups, her writing, and even her management style. And that's not counting all the feedback she gets from her family. Her keen sense for diverse ideas and approaches to management was shaped in part by living in Asia for three years. Even today she spends a great deal of her time traveling the world, speaking to audiences on the topics of complaint handling and branded service. She works with clients to help them handle complaints, brand their service cultures, and create genuine organizational change. Janelle became president of TMI US in 1996. A member of the National Speakers Association, she has earned the designation of Certified Speaking Professional. She currently sits on the Council of the International Federation for Professional Speakers.

She is the author or coauthor of several books, including *Emotional Value, Smart Videoconferencing,* and *Branded Customer Service,* all published by Berrett-Koehler. She also wrote *The Stress Manager* and *Unbind Your Mind: The Freedom to Be Creative.* She sits on the faculty of the University of Philosophical Research. Her doctorate is from the University of California, Berkeley, where she studied both political science and education. She also has a master's degree in international relations from the University of Pittsburgh and a master's in psychology from Sonoma State University.

CLAUS MØLLER is a leading management consultant and keynote speaker. Prior to setting up Claus Møller Consulting, he was the founder of Time Manager International. He sold TMI in 2003 and continues his pioneering work in the areas of leadership, time management, quality management, service management, and emotional intelligence. During a consultancy career spanning more than three decades, Claus has coined the following concepts: *Putting People First, A Complaint Is a Gift, The Human Side of Quality,* and *Employeeship.* He is the author of several best-selling management books and has won numerous awards for innovative thinking and project delivery. He also developed the world-famous Time Manager® planning and results tool and has worked extensively for a wide range of blue-chip clients, from IBM to American Express. Today, Claus Møller Consulting offers its clients executive coaching, leadership education, tailored seminars, keynote addresses, books, and diagnostic tools. The *Sunday Times* of London called Claus "the Victor Borge of Management," and he remains one of the world's most inspiring business and management speakers. Claus holds a master of science in marketing from Copenhagen Business School and is an Honorary Fellow of the All India Management Association.

Janelle Barlow can be reached at
    JaBarlow@tmius.com
    TMI US
    8270 West Charleston Boulevard
    Las Vegas, NV 89117 USA
    Tel. (702) 939-1800
    www.tmius.com

Claus Møller can be reached at
    CM@ClausMoller.com
    Claus Møller Consulting
    Batzkes Bakke 3
    DK-3400 Hillerød, Denmark
    Tel. + 45 48 22 51 00
    www.clausmoller.com

About TMI

As a part of the Athens PRC Group, the Management House, TMI has grown into one of the world's largest management training and consulting companies, with representatives in forty-three countries. More than 150 expert trainers and consultants present TMI concepts in twenty-four different languages. Each year, large and small organizations all over the world work with TMI consultants to focus their organizations on building stronger relationships with customers and to learn how to better manage time, people, and performance; to deliver exceptional service and quality; to manage culture change; and to treat complaints as gifts.

ABOUT BERRETT-KOEHLER PUBLISHERS

Berrett-Koehler is an independent publisher dedicated to an ambitious mission: **Creating a World That Works for All.**

We believe that to truly create a better world, action is needed at all levels—individual, organizational, and societal. At the individual level, our publications help people align their lives with their values and with their aspirations for a better world. At the organizational level, our publications promote progressive leadership and management practices, socially responsible approaches to business, and humane and effective organizations. At the societal level, our publications advance social and economic justice, shared prosperity, sustainability, and new solutions to national and global issues.

A major theme of our publications is "Opening Up New Space." They challenge conventional thinking, introduce new ideas, and foster positive change. Their common quest is changing the underlying beliefs, mindsets, institutions, and structures that keep generating the same cycles of problems, no matter who our leaders are or what improvement programs we adopt.

We strive to practice what we preach—to operate our publishing company in line with the ideas in our books. At the core of our approach is stewardship, which we define as a deep sense of responsibility to administer the company for the benefit of all of our "stakeholder" groups: authors, customers, employees, investors, service providers, and the communities and environment around us.

We are grateful to the thousands of readers, authors, and other friends of the company who consider themselves to be part of the "BK Community." We hope that you, too, will join us in our mission.

BE CONNECTED

Visit Our Website

Go to www.bkconnection.com to read exclusive previews and excerpts of new books, find detailed information on all Berrett-Koehler titles and authors, browse subject-area libraries of books, and get special discounts.

Subscribe to Our Free E-Newsletter

Be the first to hear about new publications, special discount offers, exclusive articles, news about bestsellers, and more! Get on the list for our free e-newsletter by going to www.bkconnection.com.

Get Quantity Discounts

Berrett-Koehler books are available at quantity discounts for orders of ten or more copies. Please call us toll-free at (800) 929-2929 or email us at bkp.orders@aidcvt.com.

Host a Reading Group

For tips on how to form and carry on a book reading group in your workplace or community, see our website at www.bkconnection.com.

Join the BK Community

Thousands of readers of our books have become part of the "BK Community" by participating in events featuring our authors, reviewing draft manuscripts of forthcoming books, spreading the word about their favorite books, and supporting our publishing program in other ways. If you would like to join the BK Community, please contact us at bkcommunity@bkpub.com.